performance in
postmodern culture

Theories of Contemporary Culture, Volume 1

Michel Benamou, *General Editor*

performance in
postmodern culture

edited by **Michel Benamou**
Charles Caramello

essays by **Cheryl Bernstein**
Herbert Blau
Daniel Charles
Régis Durand
Edmond Jabès
Raymond Federman
Ihab Hassan
Jean-François Lyotard
Richard Palmer
Jerome Rothenberg
Campbell Tatham
Victor Turner

center for twentieth century studies
university of wisconsin—milwaukee
coda press, inc
madison, wisconsin

Library of Congress Cataloging in Publication Data
Main entry under title:

Performance in Postmodern Culture.

(Theories of Contemporary Culture ; 1)
Includes bibliographical references.
1.   Performance—Addresses, essays, lectures.
2.   Art—Philosophy—Addresses, essays, lectures.
I.   Benamou, Michel.   II.   Caramello, Charles.
III.   Series.
NX212.P47   700'.1   77-25405
International Standard Book Number 0-930956-00-1

CONTENTS

PREFACE

This volume on postmodern performance, the first of a series of publications by which the Center for Twentieth Century Studies proposes to sift theories of contemporary culture, is a selection from papers written for scholarly events sponsored by the Center during 1976-77. My first thanks I address to the authors and to my co-editor, Charles Caramello. I also wish to thank Carl Lovitt and Sandra Visco of Coda Press who, contacted at the end of the summer, responded audaciously to our desire to appear in print within the year. Too many research projects languish long after completion. Let us hope this new series with Coda Press will continue to make available almost immediately the results of our inquiries.

The larger context of our work depends on the generous support of the College of Letters and Science at the University of Wisconsin-Milwaukee. To its Dean, William F. Halloran, and to George Keulks, Dean of the Graduate School, I express my deepest gratitude for fostering our activities, as I do to Robert Corrigan, Dean of the School of Fine Arts. The occasion for Victor Turner's essay was co-sponsored by Professors Victor Barnouw and Walter Neevel, who chair, respectively, the Department of Anthropology and the Program in the Comparative Study of Religion. To all many, many thanks.

The Center's program coordinator, Carol Tennessen, not only gracefully managed some forty art and scholarly events in one year but joined in the processing of manuscripts, as did my serendipitous Administrative Assistant Jean Lile. To the rest of the Center staff and the 1976-77 Fellows—Teresa de Lauretis, Campbell Tatham, David Allen and Dick Higgins, I also feel an enduring sense of obligation for their part in the research connected with this volume. Their help was invaluable in formulating theories and suggesting contacts with the performance arts. They provided the mindscape for a series of five open seminars on theories of performance conducted in Milwaukee by Umberto Eco, Allan Kaprow, Jean-François Lyotard, Herbert Blau, and Stephen Heath. Through Dick Higgins we received the visits of many performers, not only for two large colloquia, but also for a series supported by the National Endowment for the Arts which brought to Milwaukee John Cage, Allan Kaprow, Laurie Anderson, Helen and Newton Harrison, and Meredith Monk. Out of the interviews by Higgins with these and other artists we expect another publication.

The International Symposium on Post-Modern Performance, held November 17-20, 1976, was the occasion for which most of the essays in this collection were written. Circuslike only in the great vitality provided by poets, artists, novelists, dramatists, the symposium was strong in analytical soundings. Its goal was to explore as many currents of postmodern performance as possible. Five major addresses were delivered by Ihab Hassan (the keynote speaker), Dick Higgins, Herbert Blau, Jean-François Lyotard, and Carol Duncan. A panel on *Marcel Duchamp the performer*, moderated by Kathleen Woodward, included John Cage, Allan Kaprow, J-F. Lyotard, and Hubert Damisch. A second panel on *Happenings, Events, Activities* featured Dick Higgins, Jackson Mac Low, Jerome Rothenberg, and Carolee Schneemann. Ten workshops were held in the areas of semiotics, theatre, literature and interarts. Evenings of poetry (Rothenberg, Mac Low, and the Four Horsemen from Toronto), a multi-media performance by Raymond Federman, a reading of *Finnegans Wake* mesostics by Cage, and the American Premiere of Eugène Ionesco's *Man with Bags* (in the presence of the author and his translator Israel Horowitz) completed the three-day event. Obviously, *Performance in Postmodern Culture* could only be a distillation of those heady activities, but all the other scholars in attendance—especially Robert Corrigan, Richard Hughes, Wladimir Krysinski, David Cole, Erving Goffman, Walter Rewar and Jack Zipes—contributed to the effervescence of the symposium.

This book is, in a way, a Franco-American production since six of the fourteen principals are French, and four of them came to Milwaukee thanks in part to the support given by the *Paris Direction des Affaires Etrangères*, and the French Cultural Services of New York and Chicago. I also take pleasure in acknowledging a matching grant to the Center from the National Endowment for the Arts for the *Theatre/Film/Video* Conference held at the University of Wisconsin in Milwaukee, February 16-19, 1977, which included the essay by Régis Durand appearing in this collection. And finally, let me mention that a fine paper by Stephen Heath on film as performance can be read in *Ciné-Tracts*, No. 2 (Summer 1977), a special issue devoted to the results of that conference, which complements the interdisciplinary approach we have attempted to sustain throughout our investigation of performance as the unifying mode of the arts in our time.

Michel Benamou
Director, Center for Twentieth Century Studies
Milwaukee, 1 November 1977

Introduction

Presence and Play

MICHEL BENAMOU

> It's performance that matters—pacing,
> economies, juxtapositions, aggregations of
> tone, the whole conduct of the shaping pre-
> sence.
>
> Richard Poirier
> *The Performing Self*[1]

The problematic of performance in postmodern culture ranges from questions about shamanism to projections of the human drama playing itself in an expanding universe. But lest this formulation mislead the reader to expect a progress from ritual to high technology, let me restate the problematic as an undecidable argument between presentation and re-presentation, Being and absence, presence and play. Performance, the unifying mode of the postmodern, is now what matters. From the experiments of the Living Theater to the sophisticated mixed-mediations of video, performance has changed the scene of the arts, of painting (since Duchamp), of theater (since Artaud), of poetry (since Olson).

One might ask, what causes this pervading need to act out art which used to suffice by itself on the page or the museum wall? What is this new presence, and how has it replaced the presence which poems and pictures silently proffered before? Has everything from politics to poetics become theatrical?

As Raymond Williams remarked upon accepting the drama chair at Cambridge, we live in a society dramatized by TV: "What we now have is drama as habitual experience: more in a week, in many cases, than most human beings would previously have seen in a lifetime."[2] There is of course so much difference between "seen" on television and "seen" in live performance that "dramatized" loses part of the presence active in presentation or re-presentation. Our society is dramatized by television and at the same time deprived of real drama. Most critics of McLuhan have stressed that difference. Notions of orality, tribal reach, and the global village connecting us with the performance of pre-literate times need redefinition in terms of electronic communication. The powers of

3

performance in the postmodern age are so radically changed from the modern period, not to speak of pre-print, pre-modern times, that if Marx and Jesus had sought exposure via television instead of word or book, most probably neither any Christians nor any Marxists would remain to this day.

Yet, now, it's performance that matters, not only in everyday life, but in areas of culture which one seldom associates with it. Poems and art "events" are performance, to be sure, but criticism itself, no longer content to gesticulate in the margins of texts, also takes hold of a part of the stage, and plays. Free play, or simply play as a Nietzschean affirmation occupying the void left by the death of god, is the common link between most of our means of "extrication," to use Harvey Cox's phrase. We must extricate ourselves from strict positivistic causality, find play in the physical machinery which has replaced the divine order. While the modernist culture hero—such as Eliot in *The Waste Land*—went back to myth and personal symbolism for a stay against the slippage of centers of belief, the postmodern artist performs as a believer in chance operations, the releasing of controls, and collective participation. Indeterminacy in the performance of the universe calls for indeterminacy in authorship at the level of the text. Correction: since this parallelism itself suggests some kind of determinism, an immanent presence increasingly fills the postmodern noria to the inverse ratio of the emptiness of external sources. The "ground of being" is invoked by Heideggerians, who excavate presence at the same time as they extoll decentering.

There is another atmospheric element. Postmodernity exists in a technological society in which machines perform: so also with poems or artworks which no longer aspire to mean or to "be," but literally to "work." Entering the postindustrial age twenty years ago meant that as production became secondary to services and as information tended to be the most important product, performance was measured less in terms of objects made than in terms of organization. A parallel shift from structure to process affects the arts. At one end of the spectrum action painting performs its dance, at the other concept art manipulates paragraphs. Intertextuality and a shimmering horizon of citations replace the hard tactility of the well-wrought text.

Thus, for a beginning, we could accept these three aspects of performance—the dramatization of life by the media, the playfulness of art, and the emphasis on functioning in a technological environment. That things are not that simple, however, will become clear as we read the essays, some of them quite diffident toward postmodernism. Doubt is part of the problematic.

Is this a book? Its groupings suggest a shape, although an open-ended one, since we start with LIMINALITIES, mostly concerned with the

historical roots of postmodern performance, and end with PROJEC-
TIONS of the future. But the last "piece," by Ihab Hassan, was in fact the
keynote address at the Symposium on Postmodern Performance. Hassan's "shaping presence" makes itself felt as origin: he gave the term
postmodern its wide currency, borrowing it from Arnold Toynbee to
characterize a mode of consciousness which he contrasted with the modern.[3] But his essay now moves beyond that boundary to an embrace of
Prometheus as "our performer." To Ihab Hassan, presence is not in the
past, lost in some Arcadia, but in the future, with "the Human, which will
not remain human." Compare with Jerome Rothenberg's opening statement: "the artist becomes, increasingly, the surviving non-specialist in an
age of technocracy." These two visions, one shamanistic, the other
futuristic, frame the discourse of postmodern performance. They represent its outer limits. Within, three groupings: EVENTS, a critique of
non-theatrical performance, SOUNDINGS, a postfreudian theory of performance in film and music, and TRACES, three examples of the new
writing which augments the text of fiction by such a critical increment that
it performs the text either on stage or on the page.

Jacques Derrida writing about literature as an act of questioning, in
what is perhaps the best introduction to the *Book of Questions* by Edmond
Jabès, uncovers the *aporia* of the postmodern, the undecidable problematic of performance which runs through practically all the essays of this
collection. He formulates for us the following acknowledgement of the
aporia:

> Just as there is a negative theology, there is a negative atheology.
> Complicitous, it still repeats the absence of a center when it would be,
> already, better to affirm free play. But a desire for centrality is a
> function of play itself: is it not indestructible? And in repetition or
> playful return, a ghostly center is calling us. Hesitation is infinite
> between writing as decentering and writing as the affirmation of
> play.[4]

What is a book is the question. Modernism solves the problem of negative
theology by the use of symbols and myth, its compensations for a lost
presence; hence an art oriented towards texts and pictures rather than
events and performance. But the postmodern acknowledges what is at
stake: the play of the will that takes place where presence once was.
Nothing is more serious, then, than free play. Jacques Ehrmann's critique
of Huizinga's *Homo Ludens* already denied the binary opposition between
play and seriousness which is a characteristic of Western thought.[5] Between these two propositions, performance as presence, performance as
play, we cannot, perhaps must not, decide.

It all starts in a playpen, with the famous "fort — da" uttered by Freud's grandson while alternately hiding and rediscovering a symbolic spool at the edge of his bed. Freud leaves no doubt about it: theater originates from the pain of disconnection from the mother's breast. Theater originating in pain is also what binds the wound. But that, Jean-François Lyotard argues, is negative theology.[6] Freud's model is the Renaissance stage: the mother/child separation designed as house/stage, presence/re-presentation, sign/reality dualities. But what if a new performance system refutes the curtain, the limelight, the wings, the perspectives of the set (with two vanishing points: God absent in the wings, the King present in his box)? That system is postmodern performance, an energetic theater as a succession of intensities rather than symbolic action based on the presence/absence syndrome. Postmodern performance, which Lyotard admires in the films of Michael Snow, refutes the playpen theory of performance.

Yet, one must ask, is it possible to bring postmodern theory full circle to a reconciliation of the theatrical paradigm, the event still called theater, with the non-perspectival, non-centered, and radically de-symbolized performances called art events, happenings, and now, activities?

The answer given by Herbert Blau resonates, in a sense, with Derrida's question about the indestructibility of the desire for centers of being: art in its public forms ministers to that desire still, and its refusal to do so would mean killing off audienceship—and it has almost done just that, if one judges by the smallness of the numbers interested in the avant-garde. Absence still conditions the actor's performance. An awareness of the symbolic nature of any public show installs around it a space which Blau calls illusion and Victor Turner liminality.[7] To annex or annul the space between life and art, between heightened presence and a bland present, leads to the School of Boredom and its refusal of history. Herbert Blau will say it better than I: "a new solipsism, playful and plaintive, open-ended and recessive, still disinherited, apolitical, vain." And what Victor Turner has taught us all in his marvellously poetic science of social play is that performance projects a human charisma of communal origins into the routinized space established and maintained by the force of structure. Play decenters the authoritarian rule, recenters the egalitarian love. Yet, for all the *participation mystique* which demands fulfillment in our alienated lives, the distance between actor and the public cannot be abolished willfully. It is the hard-won achievement of reflexivity through the history of consciousness which has separated us into an actor and a spectator. Techniques of participation, short of restoring *communitas* in society by some advance to Anarchy, are bound to fail outwardly; but more important, they are resisted inwardly by the postmodern reflexivity: structure is of our mind as well as of our society.

There is also the moot point about the new oral poetry and ritual theater, whether they recover a pre-modern, archaic power of the word for the new shamans, or connect with the "secondary orality" of television, rock and roll, and C.B. radios.[8] To these sources of sound and imagery, postmodern literature has preferred "the non-alignment of voice and writing, which is essential to (the recovery of both) the voice *and* the sign."[9] Its typographical and scriptive experiments may seem futilities performed by privileged elites of the majority in an age of utilities and minorities. But let us not forget the lesson which Deleuze and Guattari gave us from the history of writing: in oral societies, the voice and marks on the body, the first "writing," were independent of each other. Scriptural civilization aligned the graphic system on the linearity of the voice. "The voice no longer sang, but dictated edicts; writing no longer danced, animating bodies, but was fixed on tables, stones, and books."[10] The rest is known: how linear writing served the despotic supremacy of the state. Thus, making the letters dance again and the voice sing independently of any script—small achievements in the glaring light of social injustices—may not be such insignificant performances after all, as they attack the very system of signification on which the state was historically founded.

I leave it to Charles Caramello, who joined the Center with these problems in mind, to write on the postmodern stylistics of performance in his postface. The emphasis on performance, whether demystified as illusionistic or resurgent with symbolic messages, is a pattern of all postmodern art. To recognize the infinite hesitation between presence and play is, finally, the purpose of our collection.

REFERENCES

[1] Richard Poirier, *The Performing Self: Compositions and Decompositions in the Languages of Contemporary Life* (New York: Oxford University Press, 1971), pp. 86-7.

[2] Raymond Williams, *Drama in a Dramatised Society* (Cambridge: Cambridge University Press, 1975).

[3] Ihab Hassan, *The Dismemberment of Orpheus. Toward a Postmodern Literature* (New York: Oxford University Press, 1971).

———, *Paracriticisms: Seven Speculations of the Times* (Urbana: University of Illinois Press, 1975).

[4] Jacques Derrida, *L'Ecriture ou la différence* (Paris: Editions du Seuil, 1967), pp. 432-433.

[5] Jacques Ehrmann, ed., *Game, Play, Literature* (Boston: Beacon Press, 1968), pp. 31-57.

[6] Jean-François Lyotard, *Economie Libidinale* (Paris: Editions de Minuit, 1974), pp. 31-34.

[7] Victor Turner, *Dramas, Fields, and Metaphors* (Ithaca: Cornell University Press, 1974).

[8] Walter J. Ong, S. J., *Rhetoric, Romance, and Technology* (Ithaca: Cornell University Press, 1971), Chapter 12, "The Literate Orality of Popular Culture Today."

[9] Michel Benamou and Jerome Rothenberg, eds., *Ethnopoetics, A First International Symposium* (Alcheringa/Boston University, 1976), p. 138.

[10] Gilles Deleuze, Félix Guattari, *L'Anti-Oedipe* (Paris: Editions de Minuit, 1972), p. 243.

I
Liminalities

New Models, New Visions:
Some Notes Toward a Poetics of Performance*

JEROME ROTHENBERG

The fact of performance now runs through all our arts, and the arts themselves begin to merge and lose their old distinctions, till it's apparent that we're no longer where we were to start with. The Renaissance is over or it begins again with us. Yet the origins we seek—the frame that bounds our past, that's set against an open-ended future—are no longer Greek, nor even Indo-European, but take in all times and places. To say this isn't to deny history, for we're in fact involved with history, with the sense of ourselves "in time" and in relation to other forms of human experience besides our own. The model—or better, the vision—has shifted: away from a "great tradition" centered in a single stream of art and literature in the west, to a *greater* tradition that includes, sometimes as its central fact, preliterate and oral cultures throughout the world, with a sense of their connection to subterranean but literate traditions in civilizations both east and west. "Thought is made in the mouth," said Tristan Tzara, and Edmond Jabès: "The book is as old as fire and water"—and both, we know, are right.

The change of view, for those who have experienced it, is by now virtually paradigmatic. We live with it in practice and find it more and more difficult to communicate with those who still work with the older paradigm. Thus, what appears to us as essentially creative—how can we doubt it?—carries for others the threat that was inherent when Tzara, as arch dadaist, called, circa 1917, for "a great negative work of destruction" against a late, overly textualized derivation from the Renaissance paradigm of culture and history. No longer viable, that great western thesis was already synthesizing, setting the stage for its own disappearance. The other side of Tzara's work—and increasingly that of other artists within the several avant gardes, the different, often conflicted sides of "modernism"—was, we now see clearly, a great positive work of construction/synthesis. With Tzara it took the form of a projected anthology, *Poèmes nègres*, a gathering of African and Oceanic poems culled from

*This is a version of an essay presented at the Wenner-Gren Foundation Symposium, "Cultural Frames and Reflections: Ritual, Drama and Spectacle," held in Burg Wartenstein, Austria, August 27-September 5, 1977.

11

existing ethnographies and chanted at Dada performances in Zurich's Cabaret Voltaire. To the older brokers of taste—the bearers of western values in an age of chaos—this may have looked like yet another Dada gag, but seeing it now in its actual publication six decades after the fact,[1] it reads like a first, almost too serious attempt at a new classic anthology. In circulation orally, it formed with Tzara's own poetry—the process of a life and its emergence as performance in the soundworks and simultaneities of the Dada soirées, etc.—one of the prophetic statements of where our work was to go.

Sixty years after Dada, a wide range of artists have been making deliberate and increasing use of ritual models for performance, have swept up arts like painting, sculpture, poetry (if those terms still apply) long separated from their origins in performance. (Traditional performance arts—music, theater, dance—have undergone similarly extreme transformations: often, like the others, toward a virtual liberation from the dominance of text.) The principal function here may be viewed as that of mapping and exploration, but however defined or simplified (text, e.g., doesn't vanish but is revitalized; so, likewise, the Greco-European past itself), the performance/ritual impulse seems clear throughout: in "happenings" and related event pieces (particularly those that involve participatory performance), in meditative works (often on an explicitly mantric model), in earthworks (derived from monumental American Indian structures), in dreamworks that play off trance and ecstasy, in bodyworks (including acts of self-mutilation and endurance that seem to test the model), in a range of healing events as literal explorations of the shamanistic premise, in animal language pieces related to the new ethology, etc.*

. . . .

While a likely characteristic of the new paradigm is an overt disdain for paradigms *per se*, it seems altogether possible to state a number of going assumptions as these relate to performance. I won't try to sort them out but will simply present them for consideration in the order in which they come to mind.

(1) There is a strong sense of continuities, already alluded to, within the total range of human cultures and arts, and a sense as well that the drive

* When I made a similar point in *Technicians of the Sacred* ten years ago, I attributed the relation between "primitive" ritual and contemporary art and performance to an implicit coincidence of attitudes, where today the relation seems up-front, explicit and increasingly comparable to the Greek and Roman model in Renaissance Europe, the Chinese model in medieval Japan, the Toltec model among the Aztecs, etc.: i.e., an overt influence but alive enough to work a series of distortions conditioned by the later culture and symptomatic of the obvious differences between the two.

toward performance goes back to our pre-human biological inheritance—that performance and culture, even language, precede the actual emergence of the species: hence an ethological continuity as well. With this comes a rejection of the idea of artistic "progress" and a tendency to link avant garde and "traditional" performance (tribal/oral, archaic, etc.) as forms of what Richard Schechner calls *transformational* theater and art—in opposition to the "mimetic/re-actualizing" art of the older paradigm.[2]

(2) There is an unquestionable and far-reaching breakdown of boundaries and genres: between "art and life" (Cage, Kaprow), between various conventionally defined arts (intermedia and performance art, concrete poetry), and between arts and non-arts (*musique concrète*, found art, etc.). The consequences here are immense, and I'll only give a few, perhaps too obvious, examples (ideas of this kind do in fact relate to much else that is stated in these pages):

—that social conflicts are a form of theater (V. Turner) and that organized theater may be an arena for the projection and/or stimulation of social conflict;

—that art has again recognized itself as visionary, and that there may be no useful distinction between vision-as-vision and vision-as-art (thus, too, the idea in common between Freud and the Surrealists, that the dream is a dream-*work*, i.e., a work-of-art);

—that there is a continuum, rather than a barrier, between music and noise; between poetry and prose (the language of inspiration and the language of common and special discourse); between dance and normal locomotion (walking, running, jumping), etc.;

—that there is no hierarchy of media in the visual arts, no hierarchy of instrumentation in music, and that qualitative distinctions between high and low genres and modes (opera and vaudeville, high rhetoric and slang) are no longer operational;

—that neither advanced technology (electronically produced sound and image, etc.) nor hypothetically primitive devices (pulse and breath, the sound of rock on rock, of hand on water) are closed off to the artist willing to employ them.

The action hereafter is "between" and "among," the forms hybrid and vigorous and pushing always toward an actual and new completeness. Here is the surfacing, resurfacing in fact of that "liminality" that Victor Turner recognizes rightly as the place of "fruitful chaos" and possibility—but no less "here" than "there." It is, to say it quickly, the consequence, in art-and-life of the freeing-up of the "dialectical imagination."

(3) There is a move away from the idea of "masterpiece" to one of the transientness and self-obsolescence of the art-work. The work past its

moment becomes a document (mere history), and the artist becomes, increasingly, the surviving non-specialist in an age of technocracy.

(4) From this there follows a new sense of function in art, in which the value of a work isn't inherent in its formal or aesthetic characteristics—its shape or its complexity or simplicity as an object—but in what it does, or what the artist or his surrogate does with it, how he performs it in a given context. This is different in turn from the other, equally functional concept of art as propaganda, at least insofar as the latter forces the artist to repeat "truths" already known, etc., in the service of the total state. As an example of a non-formal, functional approach to the art object as instrument-of-power, take the following, from my conversations with the Seneca Indian sculptor/carver, Avery Jimerson:

> I told him that I thought Floyd John's mask was very beautiful, but he said it wasn't because it didn't have real power [the power, for example, to handle burning coals while wearing it]. His own father had had a mask that did, until there was a fire in his house and it was burnt to ashes. But his father could still see the features of the mask and so, before it crumbled, he hurried out and carved a second mask. And that second mask looked like the first in every detail. Only it had no power. (J.R., *A Seneca Journal*)

(5) There follows further, in the contemporary instance, a stress on action and/or process. Accordingly the performance or ritual model includes the act of composition itself: the artist's life as an unfolding through his performance of it. (The consideration of this private or closed side of performance is a little like Richard Schechner's discovery that rehearsal/preparation is a theatrical/ritual event as important as the showing it precedes.) Signs of the artist's or poet's presence are demanded in the published work, and in our own time this has come increasingly to take the form of his or her performance of that work, unfolding it or testifying to it in a public place. The personal presence is an instance as well of localization, of a growing concern with particular and local definitions; for what, asks David Antin, can be more local that the person?

(6) Along with the artist, the audience enters the performance arena as participant—or, ideally, the audience disappears as the distinction between doer and viewer, like the other distinctions mentioned herein, begins to blur. For this the tribal/oral is a particularly clear model, often referred to by the creators of 1960's happenings and the theatrical pieces that invited, even coerced, audience participation toward an ultimate democratizing of the arts. In a more general way, many artists have come to see themselves as essentially the initiators of the work ("makers of the plot but not of everything that enters into the plot"—Jackson Mac Low), expanding the art process by inviting the audience to join with them in an

act of "co-creation" or to respond with a new work in which the one-time viewer/listener himself becomes the maker. The response-as-creation thus supercedes the response-as-criticism, just as the maker/ particularizer comes to be viewed (or to view himself) as the superior of the interpreter/generalizer. It is this which Charles Olson had in mind when he saw us emerging from a "generalizing time," etc., to regain a sense of the poem "as the act of the instant . . . not the act of thought about the instant."[3] More dramatically, as a contrast between the involved participant and the objective observer, it turns up in Gary Snyder's story of Alfred Kroeber and his Mojave informant, circa 1902, in which Kroeber sits through six days of intense oral narration, the story of the world from its beginnings, and then writes:

> When our sixth day ended he still again said another day would see us through. But by then I was overdue at Berkeley. And as the prospective day might once more have stretched into several, I reluctantly broke off, promising him and myself that I would return to Needles when I could, not later than next winter, to conclude recording the tale. By next winter Inyo-Kutavere had died and the tale thus remains unfinished. . . . He was stone blind. He was below the average of Mojave tallness, slight in figure, spare, almost frail with age, his gray hair long and unkept, his features sharp, delicate, sensitive. . . . He sat indoors on the loose sand floor of the house for the whole of the six days that I was with him in the frequent posture of Mojave men, his feet beneath him or behind him to the side, not with legs crossed. He sat still but smoked all the Sweet Caporal cigarettes I provided. His house mates sat around and listened or went and came as they had things to do.

To which Snyder adds the single sentence: "That old man sitting in the sand house telling his story is who we must become—not A. L. Kroeber, as fine as he was."[4]

The model switch is here apparent. But in addition the poet-as-informant stands in the same relation to those who speak of poetry or art from outside the sphere of its making as do any of the world's aboriginals. The antagonism to literature and to criticism is, for the poet and artist, no different from that to anthropology, say, on the part of the Native American militant. It is a question in short of the right to self-definition.[5]

(7) There is an increasing use of real time, extended time, etc., and/or a blurring of the distinction between those and theatrical time, in line with the transformative view of the "work" as a process that's really happening. (Analogues to this, as alternative modes of narration, performance, etc., are again sought in tribal/oral rituals.) In addition an area of performance using similarly extended time techniques toward actual transformations (of the self, of consciousness, etc.) parallels that of traditional medi-

tation (*mantra, yantra*, in the Tantric context), thus an exploration of the boundaries of mind that Snyder offers as the central work of contemporary man, or Duchamp from a perspective not all that different: "to put art again at the service of mind."

. . . .

For all of this recognition of cultural origins and particularities, the crunch, the paradox, is that the place, if not the stance, of the artist and poet is increasingly beyond culture—a characteristic, inevitably, of biospheric societies. Imperialistic in their earlier forms and based on a paradigm of "the dominant culture" (principally the the noble/imperial myths of "western civilization" and of "progress," etc. on a western or European model), these have in their *avant garde* phase been turning to the "symposium of the whole" projected by Robert Duncan. More strongly felt in the industrial and capitalist west, this may be the last move of its kind still to be initiated by the Euro-Americans: a recognition of the new/old order in which the whole is equal to but no greater than the works of all its parts.

---

¹ "Poèmes nègres," in T. Tzara, *Oeuvres Complètes*, volume 1 (Paris: Flammarion, 1975), pp. 443-489.
² "Towards a Poetics of Performance," in R. Schechner, *Essays on Performance Theory* (New York: Drama Book Specialists, 1977), pp. 108-139.
³ "Human Universe," in C. Olson, *Human Universe & Other Essays* (New York: Grove Press, 1967), pp. 3-15.
⁴ G. Snyder, "The Politics of Ethnopoetics," in M. Benamou & J. Rothenberg, *Ethnopoetics: A First International Symposium* (Alcheringa/Boston University, 1976), pp. 13-22.

[5] To speak further of this "right to self-definition," it underlies, I think, the discomfort expressed by various contemporaries about the increasing use by critics, etc., of the term "post-modernism"—largely that this usage rests on an idea of a dominant earlier "modernism" (Eliot, Yeats, Auden, Tate, Lowell, etc., among the poets), which many of use view as something utterly different. I've already written about this at length in *Revolution of the Word* (my own assemblage of a viable American modernism, 1914-1945) and in "A Dialogue on Oral Poetry with William Spanos" (*boundary 2*, New York: SUNY-Binghamton, 1975). In the latter I set out the differences as follows:

> To begin with, in my own chronology of modern poetry . . . that string of poets you reeled off [see above] is largely out of place. They're 20th century poets, most of them skillful and even intelligent, but working for the most part within very conventional limitations as to form and content—and with varying degrees of hostility to modern poetry. If we were talking about modern painting, you wouldn't throw Burchfield and Grant Wood at me and expect a serious discussion. And my point is that modernism in poetry has to be discussed at its extremes—just as it does in painting—otherwise you don't know if you've gotten past it. Now, by "early" modern poetry I'm talking about the term as it came into use around the First World War, not only in America and England but throughout the so-called western world: *a poetry of changes, experiment, destruction and creation, questioning old structures and inventing new ones, blurring fixed distinctions, opening the domain, and so on*. I'm very grateful for all of that as a beginning, as a paradigm of poetics and creative work in the 20th century; and what disturbs me about most of the poets you mention is that they raised an opposition that tried to halt the modernist ferment, to pull back to a conventional poetics somewhat modified by the modernist turn of events but fundamentally conservative in outlook: a familiar anglo-saxon and class-oriented view of language and high culture.

I still hold by those distinctions and I fear the consequences of a critic-generated "post-modernism" that fails to take something of the sort into account or that sets up false oppositions between "now"and "then." In that context it may be useful to recall that at the Milwaukee Conference John Cage's "post-modern" performance piece was a word-literal series of mesostics derived from Joyce's *Finnegans Wake*, which by an arbitrary dichotomizing (without reference, that is, to the actual views of Cage and others) was being viewed by some as part of the "modernism" to which all of us "post-modernists" were supposed to be reacting. A spot check of the artists and performers present indicated a near unanimity in the matter.

Toward a Postmodern
Hermeneutics of Performance

RICHARD PALMER

When we originally contrasted the performative with the constative utterance, we said that (1) the performative should be doing something as opposed to just saying something; and (2) the performative is happy or unhappy as opposed to true or false. Were these distinctions really sound? . . . Surely to state is every bit as much to perform an illocutionary act as, say, to warn or pronounce.

> J. L. Austin, *How to Do Things with Words*, Chapter 11.

"Did I really fly, Don Juan?"
"You flew."

> Carlos Castaneda, *The Teachings of Don Juan*.

On Performance and Performatives

Performance in drama and music generally refers to the fact that a script or a score must be "realized" in performance in order to "be" at all. Of course, a play can be read silently, and a piece of fiction can be "performed orally." Performance in both cases is also the interpretive articulation of a script or a score.

I would, however, add another dimension to the meaning of the term in light of J. L. Austin's philosophical reflections on "performative utterance" in *How to Do Things with Words*. Austin notes that when I pronounce the words "I do" in certain circumstances, more than just describing something with words, I am *doing* something with them. The saying of the words constitutes a legal obligation; it is an *action* with words. When the judge says "I sentence you," or when I say "I apologize," the words themselves—if the situation is right—do something. Of course, such "speech acts" are able to "do" something only if the situation in which they are used is appropriate. Speech acts have to be understood "in the total speech act situation." In contrast to a logical analysis that treated meaning in terms of propositional truth—an analysis that sought to devise elaborate qualifying phrases that would reduce the ambiguity of natural language—Austin proposed an analysis of the interpretive *situation* in which the words were used—an analysis of the rituals they enacted, the act done in and by the words.

The recent lively interest in speech act theory among American literary theorists testifies to the suggestiveness of what Austin, and after him, John Searle, have done to the formalism, abstractness and objectivist tendencies of much modern literary criticism. For our conception of performance, this means that we must think beyond the categories of mere representation and re-enactment to the "thing done" in the performance itself. Performance is not just an aesthetic act but a moral act, a community act, a celebration of what is being brought to experiential fullness through performance. Performance of a text does not just "say" something; it does something, and we need to reflect more deeply on that doing.

The Postmodern Turn

For all its suggestiveness, Austin's thinking about language does not take the postmodern turn. As Walter Cerf has noted in his penetrating review of *How to Do Things with Words*, one's view of language is related to one's view of man, and Austin remains firmly within the tradition of Western thought in seeing man as the being who uses language to perform certain acts. Even his stated purpose of approaching the total speech act in the total speech situation assumes that the act is a move made by a centered human will, a subjectivity, in a "situation" that is defined as fairly mundane transactions within a field of basically material objects making up a world. Man remains *homo logon echon*, the being that *has* language—the tool of man in his transactions with nature and other men. Man remains the rational animal; language is the instrument of this rationality.

The current vogue among some literary theorists for speech act theory, moreover, is not particularly radical from a philosophical point of view. Its appeal rests on its emphasis on situationality, a thrust of existentialist thought which is taken over without a grasp of the ontological implications of existentialist philosophical thinking. And when existentialist philosophy remains a form of "humanism," such as that embodied in Sartre's "Existentialism is a Humanism," it too continues the trajectory of humanist, subjectist, apollonian thought that has dominated the modern era. Modernity in existentialist garb is still modernity. Philosophical thought takes the "postmodern" turn only when it calls modernity itself, with all its successes, into question.

To call modernity itself into question—that is, to think radically about modernity—means to confront the root assumptions of Western thought *including* humanism (see Heidegger, "Letter on Humanism"). Such thinkers as Nietzsche, Heidegger, Wittgenstein, Foucault, and Derrida have done this with significant consequences for hermeneutics. Of course, the rebellion against modernity has not been confined to the philosophical level. It is reflected in the American "counterculture" movements, the growing ecological consciousness and the revival of the mythic, the occult, the oriental.

So, in referring to postmodernity and the postmodern turn, I am not referring to the literary-aesthetic movements of "modernism" and the countermovement sometimes called "postmodernism." In fact I am not talking about a "movement" at all but something closer to an archeological shift in the presuppositions of our thinking. Or putting the matter in philosophical terms: the issue is the metaphysical basis of our seeing.

A whole series of thinkers have helped us to point our thinking beyond modernity: the tremendous contribution of Nietzsche; the ontological revolution in Heidegger; the suggestiveness of *tonal* and *nagual* in Castaneda; the conception of a healing and transformative function of art in Argüelles; James Hillman's attack on monotheism; the transcendence of logo-centrism in Derrida; the question of visionary reality, especially as suggested in Theodore Roszak; the endless suggestiveness of Ihab Hassan moving at the speed of light; and of course the contributions to hermeneutical reflexivity in Gadamer and Ricoeur. Something radical happens when the question of performance is put in the context of these new currents of thought. The "what" of the performance moves beyond the subjectivity of man.

Perspective and the Genesis of Modernity: Premodern vs. Modern

To gain some sense of the hold which the presuppositions of modernity have on our thinking we must be clearer about what modernity is and where it came from. We must go back to its genesis. Five centuries ago the "new world" did not exist. Going back five centuries we antedate the rise of modern astronomy and modern philosophy. We are at a point before the Reformation in the 1500's, when printing by mechanical means had just been invented. The great voyages of discovery had not yet taken place.

Just at this time there emerges in Western consciousness something that goes to the very heart of modernity, a discovery that was to bring a new sense of space, of spatiality, and of human being-in-space: the rise of *perspective* in drawing, woodcuts, and painting. One can point to many factors in the Renaissance that contribute to the emergence of a new

man-centered view of life, but none more graphically and crucially illustrates and gives foundation to a new hubris than that which caused a
perceptual transformation of the world. As the Swiss cultural historian
Jean Gebser has argued in his *Ursprung und Gegenwart* (1949-52), the rise
of perspective is the key to modernity. Perspective spatializes the world; it
orients the eye in relation to space in a new way. As William M. Ivins, Jr.,
puts it, the rise of perspective represents the "rationalization of sight" (see
his *On the Rationalization of Sight*, 1973). Perspective leads to the founding
of mathematical geometry, which is the prerequisite for modern engineer-
ing and modern machinery. In addition "the most marked characteristics
of European pictorial representation since the fourteenth century have
been on the one hand its steadily increasing naturalism and on the other
its purely schematic and logical extensions. Both are due in largest part to
the development and pervasion of methods which have provided symbols, repeatable in invariant form, for representation of visual awareness,
and a grammar of perspective which made it possible to establish logical
relations not only within the system of symbols but between that system
and the forms and locations of the objects that it symbolizes." Ivins
concludes that "the discovery of the early forms of these grammars and
techniques constitutes that beginning of the rationalization of sight which
. . . was the most important event of the Renaissance." (pp. 12-13) The
combination of the abstractness of numbers as symbols that measure,
with perspective, a way of relating those numbers to the visual world,
leads to a sense of space as measured, as extending outward from a given
point; ultimately the world is measurable. Galileo's maxim, "To measure
everything measurable and to make what is not measurable capable of
being measured!" epitomizes modern spatialized thinking.

Thus, the spatialization of vision has ramifications that extend
beyond the world of art. It has metaphysical and epistemological implications. Modern man begins to dream of reducing everything to measurable
terms, of making everything visualizable, i.e. spatial. And the mind, with
its armory of mathematical symbols—better and more reliable than any
ordinary language—nominates man as the absolute monarch of the
world. The overemphasis on space and extension tends to divide the
world into observing subject and alien, material objects. Materializing
and naturalizing, it tautologically positions the standpoint of materialism
as the natural one. Magic and the occult, outside the reliably measurable,
are consigned to the realm of superstition. Likewise, the assumption that
the word is intrinsically connected to the thing it symbolizes becomes
absurd: it becomes more natural to see words as mere signs for the
material objects in the world. As James Hillman rightly notes in his recent
Re-Visioning Psychology, the decline of Neoplatonism and other mystical
forms of thought in the modern era removes the ground of such an

assumption; he indicates how the nominalism of Mersenne, who was educated in the same school as Descartes, becomes the weapon against every form of animism—which appears as superstition to the modern eye. The division of world into monadic ego and a real world of extension, of material objects, is compatible with Reformation austerity and monotheistic male chauvinism. The line of development is direct between it and ego-psychology. Similarly, modern philosophy from Descartes to Husserl is centered in the observing subject, a model carried over from the standpoint of man in perspectival drawing.

And this is not all. Time itself is perceived in spatialized terms. The most important dimension of time becomes its measurability as a linear succession of nows. Also, since the world is made up of material objects whose meaning is what I as a subject can give them, the sense of the sacred wanes. Realities other than those of extension—other than those that can be measured, spatialized, visualized—become second-class.

In short, the "new world" discovered beyond the ocean may be taken as a metaphor for the more important "new consciousness" that arises out of perspective. This leads to a new spatializing of reality and an ego-centered and materializing view of the world. It is not accidental, but perfectly consistent, that Mersenne campaigned with religious zeal to stamp out the "mumbo-jumbo" of Neoplatonism, the animism of Renaissance alchemy, and the paganism of astrology—views that link man as microcosm to the macrocosm. The new rationalist-modern view of the world as ensemble of material objects at the mercy of the "new man" leaves no room for Neoplatonic views of matter as governed by the spirit, of language as the "mark of the thing," or of history as great cosmic cycles. The new secular and humanistic image of man and its consequent view of his place in the world are expressions of the perspectival model that makes man the measure and measurer of all things. Reformation theology, with its diminution of feminine values, is appropriate for the new secular man of the world. Technologized rationality and the protestant ethic harmonize perfectly: God places his blessing on the individualistic, competitive male who exercises restraint and represses desires in the interest of more "rational" goals: power and control.

The perspectival sense of space, then, is more significant than it might at first appear. The voyages of discovery show man exploring and claiming the surface of the earth in a quite new way, a way made possible by his new mensural-spatial consciousness and his sense of centered selfhood. The frenzy to measure everything and, by extension, to control and to lay claim to everything that is measured, ushers in a new scientific era predicated on the quest for systematic and verifiable knowledge. The methodology of perspective and the measuring eye furnish the means for taking control of the world and for assembling a single body of coherent knowledge about it. And they lay the basis, as we have seen, for the machine age. They lead to the spatializing of time and to the "visualizing" of everything possible—conceptual knowledge takes center stage. The sense of the sacred and the mythic attitude toward man as a part of the whole give way to man's secular project of controlling the world through reason. The "new world" is the new world of spatialized perception— with its attendant ego-centered and materializing view of the world—that arises with perspective.

Some tentative constrasts between the pre-modern European view of things and that which has been definitive now for several hundred years may suggest more clearly some of the premises upon which our thinking is based—perhaps without our being fully aware of the origins or of the implications of these premises. We may then question what a view might be which is neither pre-modern, nor modern, but something as yet undefined. (The following contrasts are influenced by my recent reading of Jean Gebser's *Ursprung und Gegenwart*, to which the reader is referred for more detailed analysis. Although I have drawn freely from Gebser, he is not to be blamed for the errors I make in specific formulations. I should like to stress my hesitancy about these huge statements, which are made for propaedeutic purposes only.)

DIMENSION OF REALITY	MODERN	PRE-MODERN
1. TIME	Time is the medium of personal being, experienced in relation to the cycle of seasons and death (time experienced relationally).	Time is a linear continuum in which processes of change can be abstractly measured and symbolized (time seen in spatial terms).
2. SPACE	There is little sense of space as the medium of one's being; life and world are not defined in spatial terms.	Space is the central dimension in which we think; spatial extension is the measure of what is real.
3. MATTER	Matter is governed by spirit; matter and spirit alchemically interact with nature; microcosm and macrocosm are related.	Matter is basically inert; organic process is autonomous; there is no "spirit" in or behind nature.

4. LANGUAGE	The word contains power; it is a mark or signature of what it names; it retains a mysterious link or connection with what it names.	The word is a label or sign; it is a man-invented designation which can be changed at will; its connection with what is named is conventional.
5. PERSON	A person is a God-created mystery, the combination of spirit and body; seat of a divine spark.	A person is an autonomous living being of undefined origin, a combination of mind and matter; a "subject."
6. TRUTH	Truth is a manifestation of the way of the universe; it relates man to the macrocosm; it articulates being.	Truth is the agreement between a secular fact and a statement about it; it is a verifiable proposition.

Like any set of generalizations, these are subject to qualification, and indeed instances of the opposite can be found in virtually every case. Nevertheless, as Gebser argues in much greater detail, there is a decisive contrast between the archaic, the magical, and the mythic structures of pre-modern consciousness and the abstract, intellectual quality of modern consciousness since the rise of perspective. This he labels the "mental" structure of consciousness. With "perspectival" consciousness has come the materializing or naturalizing of the world, so that matter itself is perceived differently. The chemical elements are neither alchemically rooted in a spirit-world, nor mysteriously attached to their names. Time is routinely conceived in mensural, linear terms. And history, perceived as a straight line that never circles back on itself, becomes the story of man's gradual self-improvement through the exercise of reason. Progress becomes the theme of modernity, as each generation uses the powers of scientific reason to control nature and, thus, to transform the world.

With these developments, the premodern "world" recedes. The mythic sense of the harmony of the whole and the deep appreciation of man as a part of that whole fade, as do animism and the belief in intercourse with nature through spirits. The magic of science with its mechanical devices supersedes the old fashioned magic and uttering of incantations. Of course, the belief in the power of words (the magical power of words to *be* what they utter) fades to a reliance on language as a system for recording experience, as an "instrument" of communication and scientific notation. Any idea of attuning oneself to the cosmic harmony is stripped of meaning when the cosmos is not perceived as alive but as impersonal as a clock, lacking all consciousness and spirit. Only "persons" have spirit, and even this is defined not as a relationship to the mysterious organic movement of the cosmos, but as a perceptual awareness of the objects in one's world. And truth becomes truth-for-man: a body of verifiable knowledge. Its deeper roots—bringing the laws of the cosmos to articulate form—yield to the modern demand for objective verifiability. The worship of objectivity becomes the modern form of idolatry.

The six elements which I have singled out also condition one's view of the hermeneutical situation—that is, the situation of interpreting a text. For they specify the modern *context* for interpretation. A text handed down from a premodern time—such as Biblical texts or those of Greek antiquity, with their rich mythic lore—faces the problem of a modern's predefined sense of reality and truth. This is exemplified in the eighteenth century interpretation of the Bible as still relevant because it gives us "timeless truths"—general and universal laws and principles—or in the twentieth century effort on the part of Protestant theologian Rudolf Bultmann to save the message of the New Testament from modern rejection by arguing that, although the cosmology is mythic, the message has the psychological effect of giving the individual person a sense of "new being," of freedom. In effect, he argues that the Bible is not irrelevant because it has an *existential* message. The "hermeneutical problem" here becomes that of recovering something in the text that can still be meaningful for a modern. But the modern view of language, persons, truth, and the world, places narrow limits on the speaking power of a literary or a sacred text from a premodern time. It also places limits on our view of what literature itself can do: express human subjectivity? give us a vicarious experience of someone else's suffering? We have not given sufficient attention to the effect our limited perspective has on our vision of man and reality and on our interpretation of texts. I believe we need to expand our vision of reality and of our own being (its possibilities, its status) beyond the blinders set on us by the naturalism, the egocentricity, the pragmatism, and the apollonianism of modernity.

But how? I can only offer some suggestions here. We need a sense of time as the dimension of our being, one that enfolds past and future into the present and involves depth and intensity and presence. We need a view of our "selves" and our world that goes beyond mind as the seat of reason and will; we need to perceive mind as medium of being, medium of the historical realization of world, medium through which the miracle of language and of personhood occurs. We need a post-naturalist view of imagination as a holy, an ontological faculty. We need to reclaim the sense of spiritual depth and mystery in life that was available to premodern consciousness but that has faded away under the hegemony of nominalistic thinking. We need a more adequate view of the status, the mystery, the power of language. We need a mode of being-in-the-world that is able to *reconnect* us with now lost sources of spiritual power. We must come to understand the limits of scientific and technological forms of thought without tossing overboard the benefits accrued in our single-minded pursuit of them. We need to study recessive, rebellious, even mad thinkers in our tradition and to listen deeply to what we have heretofore ignored.

We cannot turn back the clock. The modes of thought with which the modern mind displaced the premodern are firmly entrenched today; only a postmodern standpoint that incorporates the benefits of modernity and reclaims what has been lost will work for us. The contrasts I have suggested, however, do indicate three things: (1) Our present view of the world is historically conditioned: the world has not always been seen as we see it and, in fact, is not so seen in many places today. (2) The rise of perspective in the Renaissance brought with it a spatializing of our mental world—our modern consciousness—whose one-dimensional emphasis on extension impoverishes our views of time (of history), of matter, of words, of persons, of truth. (3) We may have paid high spiritual costs for our material progress and mastery of nature. Perhaps if we understand more clearly what we have lost and how that loss came about, if we understand more clearly the limits of modern objectivized thought, we may find a way to transcend those limits and reclaim what has been lost.

Postmodernity and the Hermeneutics of Performance

The six contrasts that I have suggested might be extended, speculatively, into postmodern modalities of consciousness. (Those contrasts were very tentative; these are even more so. As with the first set, I am indebted to Gebser with regard to time, space, and perspective.)

DIMENSION OF REALITY	POSTMODERN
1. TIME	Time may not be abstract and linear but round and whole—an essential dimension of being. It may even be free of space and multiperspectival. Intensive rather than extensive, it may hold both past and future in a unity that adds depth to a now that always is.

2. SPACE

The spatiality of modern thought, dependent on one-point perspective, may give way to a multiperspectival consciousness, a field with several variables. Since the experience of space is tied to that of linear time, a new experience of time would bring a different experience of space.

3. MATTER

A result of perspectival consciousness, the perception of objects as inert matter divorced from the observing subject would disappear. Objects in the world might again take on qualities of life; a new unity of meaning and spirit might be generated between soul and cosmos, self and world.

4. LANGUAGE

Language might become a medium of ontological disclosure in which things take on being through words. I believe Bachelard was right about the creative and ontological character of language, and Heidegger right in seeing language as the "house of being."

5. PERSONS

The modern view of man as encapsulated ego leaves us a subjectivity without depth but with boundless will to power. Postmodern man may again situate himself in relation to larger forces and meanings; the view of personhood derived from Reformation and monotheistic thinking may, as Hillman suggests, give way to Neoplatonist and "polytheistic" views of the self, or self as hermeneutical medium. Man as mask or *persona* through whom gods of love, fury, or friendship, "play" would put "personhood" in a quite different context.

6. TRUTH

As Heidegger has noted, a deeper dimension of the word "truth" is *"Treue"* or loyalty. In postmodern thinking, truth might transcend the merely pragmatic dimension; it might become the loyal articulation, in language, of what *is*. The traditional view of truth as correspondence (between understood fact and

statement) assumes the mediation by which
the fact is given; the postmodern view might
return to the mediation-event itself and its
"trueness" to being. "The deep truth is image-
less," says Shelley; and postmodern truth
may recover the depth of mystery, even of
"untruth."

How do these dimensions relate to a postmodern hermeneutics of
performance? They place the performance-event in a "new world"
context—not the new world of the "modern age" but of the "postmodern." No longer an entertainer, the performer acts as an intermediary,
a hermeneutical link in creation by which "things" rise up in (linguistic)
being. Rilke expresses it eloquently in his *Ninth Duino Elegy*:

H i e r   ist des S ä g l i c h e n Zeit, h i e r seine Heimat.

Sprich und bekenn. . . .
. . . .
(Erde,) Was, wenn Verwandlung nicht, ies dein drangender Auf-
trag?

Here is the time of the *sayable*, *here* its home.
Speak and make it known. . . .
(Earth,) What is your urgent command if not transformation?

Standing in the "here" in which the sayable has its home, the performance causes it to arise invisibly as *word*, to arise in a "transformed" state, in
its "truth" or essence as word. Truth as a "saying" of being comes to event
in the performance. It speaks *through* man *as* language because man is that
hermeneutical being through which such transformation can occur. Relating to something higher (here, Earth is higher than man), he is a medium
of disclosure, or rather of linguistic *being*. Beyond humanism, beyond
autonomy, beyond the subjectivist will to make the world disposable,
beyond objectivist illusions of verifiability, beyond the modern anthropology of secularized man as a "tool-using animal," beyond the
reductionist view of the earth as silent and inert matter to be shaped to the
aimless egoism of modern man, we would find a quite different "hermeneutical situation." Visionary reality, driven underground by modern
modes of thought, would emerge with great power.

For the Newtonian-Lockean man a tree is (to use Blake's scornful words) "just a green thing that stands in the way." Bulldozers and dam-builders will remove it. Yet the loss of visionary reality, the naturalizing of it in the great romantic poets like Wordsworth (see Geoffrey Hartman and Meyer Abrams), is symptomatic of the repression of "enthusiasm" (being filled with God) in the modern age. The recovery of depth modes of interpretation through a reclamation of premodern hermeneutics—allegorical, figural, esoteric forms of interpretation like the Kabbalah—would provide a means of overcoming modern literalism. As Owen Barfield, Norman O. Brown, and James Hillman have said: "Literalism is the enemy." Literalism is the death-in-life mode of thought with which modernity has waged war on the visionary imagination. We need to understand why modern hermeneutics has been so closely tied to literalism, why allegory has gone into eclipse, but also why, very recently, Kabbalah and other arcane modes of interpretation have begun to com-mand our attention. Is it, perhaps, that man is trying to reconnect with the deeper, less "rational" powers and realities of the cosmos?

With regard to a postmodern hermeneutics of performance, I believe a radically fuller view of time, person, language, and so on, will yield a correspondingly fuller view of interpretation. It seems to me that much philosophical reflection on performance has been conditioned by a "mod-ern" understanding of the interpretive situation and has tended to define understanding of a text in external and analytical terms. Such emphasis on verifiable truth and correctness can lead to an insensitivity to the performative *doing* that takes place in *saying*. Recently, theory of oral interpretation has turned to existentialism and phenomenology and liter-ary criticism to "speech act" theory, but these fall short of what I mean by a postmodern hermeneutics of performance; continuing the humanist trajectory, they offer no deeper anchor for performance than the re-enactment of "experience." The issue, precisely, is the character of the "place" of that experience.

Heidegger speaks of *ein erörtendes Denken*—a "placing" form of thought—in *On the Way to Language*. To think is to enter into a dialogue or discussion (*Erörterung*), to find one's way patiently to the "place" of that about which one speaks. My reflections above have sought to find the way to the "place" of performative speaking in a postmodern hermeneut-ical context, to locate "where" the speaker stands (in a metaphorical sense) in his speaking. What is the "place" of performance in relation to the "higher powers" that rule our lives? What is the "transformation" wrought by poetic speaking? What is the ontological status of the experi-ence of hearing a poetical text? What is the "place" of the text? How does the interpreter find his way to that "place"? To interpret a poem is, in a way, to "place" it—to find one's way to its place of power. Perhaps a postmodern hermeneutics of performance will locate the event of interpretive mediation in a place quite different from that it has occupied during the modern epoch. Perhaps it may even restore to the interpreter his ancient shamanic-hermeneutical powers to reveal the hidden, to transform the understanding, even to heal the soul.

SELECTED SOURCES

Abrams, M. H. *Natural Supernaturalism*. New York: Norton, 1971. Regarding the hermeneutical problem in romanticism, see pp. 65-70.

Argüelles, José A. *The Transformative Vision: Reflections on the Nature and History of Human Expression*. Berkeley: Shambhala, 1975.

Argüelles, José A. and Miriam. *Mandala*. Berkeley: Shambhala, 1972.

Austin, J. L. *How to Do Things with Words*. Cambridge: Harvard University Press, 1962.

Bultmann, Rudolf. *Jesus Christ and Mythology*. New York: Scribners, 1958.

Castaneda, Carlos. *Tales of Power*. New York: Simon & Schuster, 1974.

Derrida, Jacques. *Glas*. Paris: Galilée, 1974.

——. *Marges de la philosophie*. Paris: Minuit, 1972.

Fann, K. T., ed. *Symposium on J. L. Austin*. New York: Humanities Press, 1969. Contains the review of *How to Do Things With Words* by Walter Cerf.

Foucault, Michel. *The Order of Things* and *The Archeology of Knowledge*. New York: Macmillan, 1971 and 1974.

Gebser, Jean. *Gesamtausgabe*. 6 vols. Schaffhausen, Switzerland: Novalis, 1975-77. See especially vols. 1, 5, 6.

——. *Ursprung und Gegenwart*. 3 vols. Munich: Deutsche Taschenbuch Verlag, 1973. Originally published 1949-52. Forthcoming as *Origin and Presence* through Ohio University Press, Athens, Ohio.

Hartman, Geoffrey. *The Fate of Reading and Other Essays*. Chicago: University of Chicago Press, 1975.

Hassan, Ihab. *Paracriticisms*. Urbana: University of Illinois Press, 1975.

Heidegger, Martin. *Being and Time*. New York: Harper and Row, 1962.

——. *On the Way to Language*. New York: Harper and Row, 1971.

——. *Poetry, Language, Thought*. New York: Harper and Row, 1971. "The Origin of a Work of Art" contains a major (postmodern) statement on art with the kinds of redefinitions I have proposed.

Hillman, James. *Re-Visioning Psychology*. New York: Harper and Row, 1975. I am indebted to Hillman's discussion of Mersenne, pp. 3-10.

Ivins, William M., Jr. *On the Rationalization of Sight: With an Examination of Three Renaissance Texts on Perspective*. New York: Da Capo Press, 1975. His introductory remarks on the "rationalization of vision" confirm Gebser's argument.

Nietzsche, Friedrich. *Erkenntnistheoretische Schriften*, ed. Jürgen Habermas. Frankfurt: Suhrkamp, 1968.

———. *The Will to Power*. New York: Vintage, 1968.

Ricoeur, Paul. *The Conflict of Interpretations*, ed. Don Ihde. Evanston: Northwestern University Press, 1974.

———. "The Model of the Text: Meaningful Action Considered as Text," *New Literary History*, 5 (Autumn, 1973), 91-117; also in *NLH*, see "Metaphor and the Main Problem of Hermeneutics," 6 (Autumn, 1974), 95-110.

Roszak, Theodore. *Unfinished Man*. New York: Harper and Row, 1976.

Sartre, Jean-Paul. *Existentialism and Human Emotions*. New York: Citadel Press, 1971. Contains the essay, "Existentialism is a Humanism."

Scholem, G. *On the Kabbalah and Its Symbolism*. New York: Schocken, 1965.

Wittgenstein, Ludwig. *Philosophical Investigations*. New York: Macmillan, 1953.

Frame, Flow and Reflection:
Ritual and Drama as Public Liminality

VICTOR TURNER

What, at first glance, could be less close, less akin than drama and reflection? Drama demands a stage, actors, a heightened atmosphere, spectators, the smell of the crowd, the roar of the greasepaint. Reflection is at least one of the things one does with one's solitude. But to counter this opposition an anthropologist tends to think in terms not of solitary but of plural reflection, or, much better, plural reflexivity, the ways in which a group or community seeks to portray, understand, and then act on itself. Essentially, public reflexivity takes the form of a *performance*. The languages through which a group communicates itself to itself are not, of course, confined to talking codes: they include gestures, music, dancing, graphic representation, painting, sculpture, and the fashioning of symbolic objects. They are dramatic, that is literally *"doing"* codes. Public reflexivity is also concerned with what I have called "liminality." This term, literally "being-on-a-threshold," means a state or process which is betwixt-and-between the normal, day-to-day cultural and social states and processes of getting and spending, preserving law and order, and registering structural status. Since liminal time is not controlled by the clock it is a time of enchantment when anything *might*, even should, happen. Another way of putting it would be to say that the liminal in socio-cultural process is similar to the subjunctive mood in verbs—just as mundane socio-structural activities resemble the indicative mood. Liminality is full of potency and potentiality. It may also be full of experiment and play. There may be a play of ideas, a play of words, a play of symbols, a play of metaphors. In it, play's the thing. Liminality is not confined in its expression to ritual and the performative arts. Scientific hypotheses and experiments and philosophical speculation are also forms of play, though their rules and controls are more rigorous and their relation to mundane "indicative" reality more pointed than those of genres which proliferate in fantasy. One might say, without too much exaggeration, that liminal phenomena are at the level of culture what variability is at the level of nature.

Liminality is the term used by the Belgian folklorist Van Gennep to denominate the second of three stages in what he called a "rite of passage."* Such rites are found in all cultures, and are seen as both indicators and vehicles of transition from one sociocultural state and status to another—childhood to maturity, virginity to marriage, childlessness to parenthood, ghosthood to ancestorhood, sickness to health, peace to war and vice versa, scarcity to plenty, winter to spring, and so on. He did, however, distinguish between those rites performed at life-crises, such as birth, puberty, marriage, death, and those performed at crucial points in the turning year, or on occasions of collective crisis when a whole society faces a major change, peace to war, health to epidemic, and so forth. The first set were mainly performed for individuals in secret or hidden places and related to upward mobility. The latter were performed for collectivities, were public in character, and often portrayed reversals or inversions of status or confusion of ordinary every day categories. Van Gennep distinguished the three stages as (1) separation (from ordinary social life) (2) margin or limen (meaning threshold), when the subjects of ritual fall into a limbo between their past and present modes of daily existence; and (3) re-aggregation, when they are ritually returned to secular or mundane life—either at a higher status level or in an altered state of consciousness or social being. I have written at length about initiation rites or rites of status elevation. I am now extremely interested in the other major type of rites. I used to call it "ritual or status reversal," from the fact that in many cultures rituals performed at major calendrical turns portrayed turnabouts of normal social status: the poor played at being rich, the rich at being poor; kings and nobles were abased and commoners wore the insignia of rule. But these ritual reversals are only part of the story. Just as important are the ways a society finds in these public rituals of commenting on and critiquing itself. Here there is not so much the symbolism of birth, maturation, death, and rebirth—that is, of linear developments—but rather the continuous presence of a metalanguage—that is, codes or presentation and expression which enable participants and spectators to realize just how far they have fallen short of or transgressed their own ideal standards, or even, in some kinds of ritual, to call those very ideals into question under conditions of sharp social change.

I have spoken about liminal time. I now distinguish between everyday social space and liminal space. In public metasocial rites we have to do with public liminality, and such rites are often performed in the village or town square, in full view of everyone. They are not secret affairs, performed in caves or groves or in lodges protected from profanation by poisoned arrows. All performances require framed spaces set off from the routine world. But metasocial rites use *quotidian* spaces as their stage; they merely hallow them for a liminal time.

Now the gist of my argument is simply this. That for every major social formation there is a dominant mode of public liminality, the subjunctive space/time that is the counterstroke to its pragmatic indicative texture.

Thus, the simpler societies have ritual or sacred corroborees as their main metasocial performances; proto-feudal and feudal societies have carnival or festival; early modern societies have carnival and theater; and electronically advanced societies, film. I am aware that this is a gross oversimplification, that there are many other performative genres, such as spectacles, parades, processions, circuses, even art exhibitions, and television, and that in each of the four divisions (mentioned earlier) there are many subdivisions. But to get a preliminary hold upon the relationship between social processes and performative genres it is perhaps best to start with bold strokes and attempt to fill in the fine details later.

To look at itself a society must cut out a piece of itself for inspection. To do this it must set up a frame within which images and symbols of what has been sectioned off can be scrutinized, assessed, and, if need be, remodeled and rearranged. In ritual what is inside the frame is what is often called the "sacred;" what is outside, the "profane," "secular," or "mundane." To frame is to enclose in a border. A sacralized space has borders. These may be permanent, in the case of the temple, or situational, as in the case of many central African rituals I have observed where sacred space may be demarcated by an improvised fence or merely by the anticlockwise circling of a tree or cleared area by ritual adepts. Time also enters the framing, since rituals, as Van Gennep has shown, have a well-defined beginning, middle and end. Often audible markers are used: bell-ringing, shouting, singing, percussion sounds. By such means sacred time is dramatically separated from secular time. Ritual time is ordered by rules of procedure, written or unwritten. A ritual contains an explicit scenario or score. Modern views of ritual stress its rigid and obsessional character. But tribal rituals are anything but rigid. One should rather regard them as orchestrations of a wide range of performative genres, symphonies in more than music, comprising several performative genres. These may include dancing, gesturing, singing, chanting; the use of many musical instruments; mimetic displays; and the performance of drama during key episodes. All the senses are enlisted, and the symbolic actions and objects employed are in every sensory code. Since the rise of puritanism we have been inclined, in the West, to stress the pervasively solemn and strict character of ritual. But the majority of rituals still performed in the world contain festive, joyful, and playful episodes and incidents. What Huizinga has called the "ludic" interacts with the solemn in complex fashion. Again, while there are fixed, stereotyped sequences of symbolic action, there are also episodes given over to verbal and nonverbal improvization. Indeed, if we adopt the standpoint of culture history it is clear that full-scale rituals of this sort are the matrix from which later performative genres have sprung, both serious and entertaining.

Rituals have form, but it is a special sort of form which arises after secular social structure has been suspended to allow it to emerge. Pre-ritual and postritual social life is goverened by a multiplicity of laws, rules, regulations, and customs which make up a system of social control. These are for the most part culture's indicative mood, as I have said. But in ritual an even more complex situation comes into being. On the one hand, the framing process, which continues throughout the entire ritual process, since it established and articulates the sequence of phases and episodes composing the ritual, is subject to firm procedural, even rubrical rules. But, on the other hand, the subjunctivity of ritual, that part of it which expresses supposition, desire, and possibility, rather than actual fact, particularly in the central liminal phase, may rather be described in such terms as "charismatic," "numinous," "sacred reality," "*illud tempus*," "a time of wonders," and so on. This is the world of the exhibition of sacra, symbols or a higher reality; of the dramatization of creation stories; of the appearance of masked and monstrous figures; of the construction of complicated shrines; of the revelation of figurines or wall paintings used to instruct and catechize naked or painted novices undergoing initiatory transformation. In times of radical social change, some of these sacred items and symbolic processes burst out of the secrecy of lodges and enter the public arena as part of the repertoire of prophetic leaders who mobilize the people against invaders or overlords threatening their deep culture.

But it is not of initiatory secrets that I would speak here. It is of the great public festivals where public events come under the lens of liminal atten-tion. Such rituals have very frequently a satirical, lampooning, comedic quality. Furthermore, they tend to stress the basic equality of all, even if this involves a status reversal and the setting up of hierarchies of roles, occupied by those who are normally underlings, which caricature the normative indicative hierarchy's power, wealth, and authority. In my book *The Ritual Process* (1969: 178-188) I have mentioned a number of these public rituals, such as the *Holi* festival in the Indian village, *Kishan Gari*, described by McKim Marriott in "The Feast of Love" (1966: 210-212), and the *Apo* ceremony of the northern Ashanti of Ghana, in which there is a reversal of secular social status, and social inferiors are privileged to upbraid and lampoon their "betters." Quite often, however, public ritual dramatizes secular, political, and legal status relationships. Even in those cases, episodes of status reversal, including the direct manifestation of what I have called communitas, the mutual confrontation of human beings stripped of status role characteristics—people, "just as they are," getting through to each other—may strikingly occur. For example, the great ethnographer Henri Junod (1962: 397-404) discusses the major pub-lic rituals of the Thonga of Mozambique, the "*luma* of *bukanyi*" in the following terms: The *nkanyi* from which the ritual derives its name is a large tree bearing a plum-like fruit from which a mildly intoxicating liquor is brewed. Political hierarchy is at first in evidence here, for the rites must be inaugurated by the paramount chief, followed at the district level by sub-chiefs, who pray to their deceased royal ancestors in sacred woods. The term *luma* means that a major restriction is being lifted. Things are being tabooed. No one may gather the fruit or brew its beer until the rites have been inaugurated. When someone *lumas* the ban is lifted. What I have said about the public and visible nature of calendrical ritual—for the *bukanyi* is considered to mark the beginning of the new year—is exemplified in Junod's description of what occurs after the chiefly prayers.

> The young people are now assembled to clean up the public square and all the roads. The ball room must be prepared! The women of the capital start out early in the morning . . . . and they go all over the country gathering the golden fruit; this is piled up in an enormous heap on the public square. The women of the capital brew ten or fifteen huge casks of the precious liquor. . . . A convocation of the entire male portion of the tribe is held in the capital, but the first to respond to the call must be . . . . the warriors of the army, who come in full array, with all their ornaments, and carrying their small clay shields. One cask of beer is selected, into which is thrown the black powder, the great medicine of the land. . . . Now comes the third act: the drinking in the villages. Each district chief must commence to *luma* in the presence of his subjects, and not until he has done so can the people drink freely in the villages (p. 399).

Here I would like to interpolate that the various components of the national political structure, here principally the chiefs and the warriors, have the role of first framing, then punctuating the episodes of the ritual. Structure is used in the service of communitas. The *content* of the ritual relates to the unity and continuity of the nation and the land, transcending all structural oppositions of chief and commoner, men and women. I now wish to return to Junod's account, which stresses the Dionysian *communitas* which is the ground swell of the *bukanyi*, and which here escapes its Apollonian framing by male authority.

> From this moment (i.e. the chief's prayer) there is no further description. Drinking continues day and night, night and day! When the supply is finished in one village, they go to the next. These feasts are the Saturnalia, the Bacchanalia, the carnival of the tribe (here I would criticize Junod's nomenclature: I would reserve all three of these terms for performative genres in societies more complex than the Thonga). During these weeks some individuals are in a continual state of semi-intoxication. Orgies on all sides, songs and dances! . . . How far does sexual license go during *bukanyi*? Not to the point of general promiscuity as amongst the Ba-Pedi (another southern Bantu people) after the circumcision school. However, many cases of adultery occur.

Men and women forget the elementary rules of conduct. They attend to the wants of nature in the same places, which is taboo under ordinary circumstances: *"Nau, a wa ha tiyi,"–"The law is no longer in force"* (p. 401).

But social structure, after its dip in communitas, emerges renewed when the district chiefs send their people to the capital with supplies of "new wine." This is followed by a series of return visits by the chief to villages of his subjects, with further dancing, singing, and drinking.

Junod, who as early as 1912 knew his Van Gennep well, was aware of these polarities of public ritual, although he did not, of course, use my vocabulary: "structure and antistructure," or "social structure and communitas." But he did write that: "These rites are. . . . dictated by the sense of *hierarchy* (Junod's emphasis). A subject must not precede his chief, nor a younger brother the elder in the use of the new harvest, else they would kill those in authority. Such an act is against order" (p. 404). Junod then goes on to stress the idea of *passage*, following Van Gennep: "There is a passage from one year to another. . . . though the *luma* rites do not bear all the characteristics of a true passage rite, like those of circumcision or moving, we may observe in the *luma* or *bukanyi* a kind of marginal period of general license, when the ordinary laws are more or less suspended" (p. 404).

Junod does not mention the use of antistructural process here as a metasocial critique, or, even at the simplest level, as an opportunity for the common folk to speak frankly to chiefs and aristocrats. That this aspect was probably present is suggested by evidence from other Southern Bantu-speaking peoples. For instance, Eileen Jensen Krige (1950) finds it in the Great *Umkhosi* or National First-fruit Ceremonies of the Zulu of Natal. The Zulu, it must be remembered, had largely converted this agricultural ritual into a grand review of the army and a celebration of the military kingship established by Shaka, that genius of war. Nevertheless the agricultural basis remains and the king's song is said to bring rain for the crops. Krige writes:

> A remarkable feature of this review of the army was that considerable freedom of speech was allowed on this occasion, and the king could be insulted with impunity. Various people would leave the ranks of the warriors, who were made to sit down during the discourse, and there (were) free interrogations to which the king (was) bound to reply. Sometimes they denounced him in the presence of all, blamed his acts, stigmatized them as infamous and cowardly, obliged him to explain, destroyed the reasoning in his answer, dissecting them and unmasking their falsehood, then threatening him proudly, and ending with a gesture of contempt (p. 260).

Thus the highest becomes the lowest; the equality of all outside social structure is asserted.

Instances of a similar kind could be multiplied from many standard ethnographies. I will now consider the second major performative genre I mentioned earlier: *carnival*. I should interpolate that growing evidence convinces me that *new* ways of modeling or framing social reality may actually be proposed and sometimes legitimated in the very heat of performance, emerging as a sort of artifact or popular creativeness. That is why public liminality has often been regarded as "dangerous" by whatever powers-that-be who represent and preside over established structure. Public liminality can never be tranquilly regarded as a safety valve, mere catharsis, "letting off steam," rather it is communitas weighing structure, sometimes finding it wanting, and proposing in however extravagant a form new paradigms and models which invert or subvert the old. Carnival is a particularly interesting illustration of this ambiguity. As Natalie Z. Davis has said (*Society and Culture in Early Modern France*, 1975: 97): "Festive life can on the one hand perpetuate certain values of the community, even guarantee its survival, and on the other hand criticize political order." I cannot today discuss in detail how the historical religions of the book (Judaism, Christianity, Islam) have come, by and large, to emphasize the *solemn* in their official liturgical structures, while merely countenancing with some misgiving the *festive* and *ludic*, as parallel "fold" processes fit for fairs and feasts perhaps, but not for "serious" ritual to their major calendrical rituals. But to the eye of the investigator, the "solemn" and the "ludic," often regarded as equivalent to the sacred and the profane by religious professionals, must surely be analyzed as polarities of the *same* ritual field. Solemn liturgies dramatize paradigms of axiomatic value. Festivals and carnivals allow considerable creative latitude for collective scrutiny of the contemporaneous social structure, often with lampooning liberty. People stand back from their lives and weigh their quality. We have seen how in Thonga, Zulu, and other "tribal" ritual, solemn and ludic are interdigitated, penetrate one another. Now at a more advanced stage of the social division of labor we must turn our attention to performative genres that are specialized in the direction of festal play, however rough that playfulness may often be.

Carnivals differ from rituals in the further respect that they seem to be more flexibly responsive to social and even societal change, change in the major political and economic structures. Strictly speaking, "carnival" refers to the period of feasting and revelry just before Lent, including Mardi Gras in France, Fastnacht in Germany and Shrove Tide in England. The popular and probably fictitious etymological derivation "carne vale," "flesh, farewell," hits off its ludic and liminal quality, poised between mundane and solemn modes of living—with more than a hint of desperation. All the things of the flesh, including the "things that are Caesar's," are being brought to the fore of social attention, the pleasurable to be indulged in, and the politically and legally unjust to be given a long hard look. It is perhaps no accident that the two best American historians of carnival in my view, Natalie Davis and Robert J. Bezucha, should consistently acknowledge their debt both for theory and data to Arnold van Gennep, the spiritual father of modern cultural processualism whose *Manuel du folklore français* is as influential for historians as his *Rites de passage* is for anthropologists. Both have studied carnival rather late in European history, Davis in the later middle ages and the sixteenth century, Bezucha in the nineteenth century. Both have worked in France, where change has always been more reflexive, or at least more self-conscious, than elsewhere. I would like to spend some time with these scholars whose data admirably illustrate my case that public liminality is the eye and eyestalk which society bends round upon its own condition, whether healthy or unsound.

Essentially, Davis and Bezucha are interested in the responsiveness to sociocultural change of the various genres, born in the Middle Ages, which Davis has catalogued as:

> masking, costuming, hiding; charivaris (noisy, masked demonstrations to humiliate some wrongdoer in the community), farces, parades, and floats; collecting and distributing money and sweets; dancing, music-making, the lighting of fires; reciting of poetry, gaming and athletic contests—the list in all its forms and variations would be longer than the 81 games in Bruegel's famous painting or the 217 games that Rabelais gave to Gargantua. They took place at regular intervals, and whenever the occasions warranted it; they were timed to calendar of religion and season (the twelve days of Christmas, the days before Lent, early May, Pentecost, the feast of Saint Jean-Baptiste in June, the Feast of the Assumption in mid-August, and All Saints) and timed also to domestic events, marriages, and other family affairs (pp. 97-98).

Natalie Davis concerns herself in her Chapter Four, "The Reasons of Misrule," with one liminal category of French citizens: unmarried men in peasant communities who have reached the age of puberty. "Since village boys usually did not marry until their early or middle twenties in the fifteenth through seventeenth centuries, their period of *jeunesse* lasted a long time and the number of bachelors relative to the total number of men in the village was quite high" (p. 104). For carnival purposes each year before Lent, after Christmas, or at some other time, they elected a King or Abbott from among their midst. This officiant was the head of what was widely called "an Abbey of Misrule" (*Abbé de Maugouvert*), a carnival group put on "by an informal circle of friends and family, sometimes by craft or professional guilds and confraternities, and very often by organizations that literary historians have called 'sociétés joyeuses' (or 'fool-societies' or 'play-acting societies')" (p. 98). Indeed, I well remember how, on Shrove Tuesday in Glasgow, students from the University, dressed in all kinds of bizarre garb, with much transvestitism, used to take over the city and swarm aboard all its public transportation, bullying and cajoling the citizenry into giving generous alms to charity—obviously a latter day Abbey of Misrule in action! The medieval festive Abbeys later came to assume a political nature, and in a remarkable chapter, "Women on Top," Davis shows how males in masks and female garb caricatured female attributes. It was supposed in the carnival frame—which here merely replicated the dominant thought of a patrilineal society—that woman's dominant attribute was "unruliness," or "disorderliness." As Davis puts it: "the lower ruled the higher within the woman . . . and if she were given her way, she would want to rule over those above her outside. Her disorderliness led her into the evil arts of witchcraft, so ecclesiastical authorities claimed; and when she was embarked on some behavior for which her allegedly weak intellect disqualified her, such as theological speculation or preaching, that was blamed on her disorderliness too" (p. 125). The Kingdoms and Abbeys of Misrule had "officers" who presided over their carnival behavior. Among these roles, played by men, were "Princesses and Dames and especially Mothers; we find Mère Folle in Dijon, Langes, and Châlon-sur-Saône; Mère Sotte in Paris and Compiègne; and Mère d'Enfance in Bordeaux. . . . . . In all of this there was a double irony: the young villager who became an Abbott, the artisan who became a Prince directly adopted for *their* Misrule an object of *licit* power; the power invoked by the man who became Mère Folle, however, was already in *defiance of natural order*—a dangerous and vital power, which his *disguise* made *safe* for him to assume" (pp. 139-40).

What one sees here in Davis's material is evidence of an institution originally commited to maintaining a cyclical repetitive order, in which the natures and virtues of the sexes as structurally classified are clearly figured. Nevertheless, although *both* male and female offices of the Abbeys of Misrule may be said to belong to the *liminal domain* of carnival, the female ones are *quintessentially* liminal, since they represent persons who, even in the mundane "indicative" world, by reason of their status inferiority and marginality, have a "subjunctive" penumbra reinforced and reduplicated in the carnival setting. The danger here is not simply that of female "unruliness." This unruliness itself is a mark of the ultraliminal, of the perilous realm of possibility of "anything *may* go" which threatens any social order and seems the more threatening, the more *that* order *seems* rigorous and secure. The powers of the weak—to curse and criticize—set limits on the power of the strong—to coerce and ordain.

The subversive potential of the carnivalized feminine principle becomes evident in times of social change when its manifestations move out of the liminal world of Mardi Gras into the political arena itself. Natalie Davis has written at some length of peasant movements and protests by other kinds of groups, in which men, clad in the carnival "drag" usually associated with *Mère Folle* and her *Infanterie*, putting on feminine "unruliness" so to speak, projected the carnival right of criticism and mockery into situations of real, "indicative" rebellion (p. 147).

She gives several instances of how "ritual and festive inversion" was put to new overtly political uses (p. 147). In the Beaujolais in the 1770's, male peasants blackened their faces and dressed as women "and then attacked surveyors measuring their lands for a new landlord" (p. 147). In England, in 1629, (the so-called) "Captain" Alice Clark, a real female, headed a crowd of women and male weavers dressed as women in a grain riot near Maldon in Essex (p. 148). In 1631, in the dairy and grazing sections of Wiltshire, bands of men rioted and leveled fences against the king's enclosure of their forests. They were led by men dressed as women, who called themselves "Lady Skimmington." In April 1812, "General Ludd's Wives," two weavers dressed as women, led a crowd of hundreds to smash steam looms and burn a factory in Stockport (p. 148). Among other examples, Davis cites the "Whiteboys" of Ireland, who, for almost a decade, from 1760-70, dressed in long white frocks and with blackened faces, "set themselves up as an armed popular force to provide justice for the poor 'to restore the ancient commons and redress other grievances'." She says that these "Ghostly Sallies" were the prototypes of the "Molly Maguires and the Ribbon societies of the nineteenth century" (p. 149). What has been happening, of course, is that the rebellious potential of the unruly female persona hitherto confined to the "play" world of carnival, has been put to new use by men in the traditionally masculine realm of political action. As Davis writes: "On the one hand, the disguise freed men from the full responsibility for their deeds and perhaps, too, from fear of outrageous revenge upon their manhood. After all, it was 'merely women' who were acting in this disorderly way. On the other hand, the males drew upon the sexual power and energy of the unruly woman and on her license (which they had long assumed at carnival and games)—to promote fertility, to defend the community's interests and standards, and to tell the truth about unjust rule" (p. 149).

Another historian who has made use of popular festivity not only as an index, but also as an agency of sociocultural and political change is Robert Bezucha, of Syracuse University, whose period for intensive study is the Second Republic in France. In a paper delivered at the Davis Center at Princeton in 1975 he followed Maurice Agulhon (*La République au village*) (1960: 265-66) in tracing a double evolution in popular "mentalité" during the early nineteenth century in France from traditional to progressive in political life and from *folklore* (in the French sense of this term, that is, as the nexus of traditional customs, beliefs, and practices—Americans might call it "folk culture") from *folklore* to modernity in daily life. These processes, though parallel, were not synchronized, so that when villagers wished to express an advanced political idea, they often did so within the context of a *folkloresque* event. In doing so they carried further the normal lampooning license of the carnival, of which Van Gennep has written: there is "the temporary suspension of the rules of normal collective life . . . one profits from this period of traditional license to mock the constraints of the State and the Government to which the collectivity submits in normal times" (1938-58, Vol. I:xx; Vol. III:981-82). How far they carried it may be seen from the fact that most of Bezucha's data were drawn from reports by *Procureurs Généraux* in the Archives Nationales on incidents officially classified as *affaires politiques* that occurred on Mardi Gras or Ash Wednesday (the key days of the *Carême-Carnaval* cycle) between 1848 and 1851. Carnival contained many traditional symbols and symbolic actions; these were used in new ways to express political attitudes, while new symbols, such as the Phrygian caps of the French Revolution, were introduced into carnival processions. Bezucha also records instances of the transvestitism discussed by Davis, but this has ceased to be a dominant symbolic motif by the time of the brief Second Republic. Let me give two examples from Bezucha's talk; one represents a critique from the Right, the other from the Left, of the rapidly changing political scene from Louis Napoléon's Revolution of 1848 to his proclamation of himself as Emperor in 1852—a period characterized by increasing repression of the rural masses. The first comes from a report on the town of Uzès in the department of Gard in southern France ("Popular Festivity and Politics During the Second Republic," pp. 12-13). The year is 1849.

> February 21 was Ash Wednesday. On this day in the Midi of France, the young people belonging to the popular class (*la classe du peuple*) are accustomed to hold a burlesque divertissement whose theme is the burial of Carnival. They cover or blacken their faces, don bizarre costumes, arm themselves with kitchen bellows, and go through the streets of the town, one after the other, each trying to use the bellows on the person in front of him. At the head of the procession, they carry a mannequin called *Carimantran* (*Carême entrant* the arrival of Lent) which they dance around at each stop and end by throwing into the water.
>
> This year, its authors, since they belong to the legitimist party (seeking the restoration of the Bourbon dynasty) have not neglected to give to the festivities a significance which was insulting to the Republic. In place of a bellows, each of them carried a broom, and at a signal they all began to sweep, raising a cloud of dust, while at the

same time singing a song called "The Song of the Sweeps"
(*Ramoneurs*).

But what gave the parody an extremely clear meaning was another
smaller group of persons preceding the sweepers and who, by the
various emblems they wore, obviously represented the Republic (i.e.
the government of Louis Napoléon). One of them rode a wretched
nag and held a dirty tricolored flag which from time to time he let trail
on the ground behind him.

From time to time the sweepers would draw close to this flag bearer,
pretending to hit him with their brooms and to force him to descend
and give his place to another. In addition, five or six persons on foot
and wearing clothing of various colors, in contrast to the completely
white costumes of the sweepers, marched in front of them with an
issue of the journal *La Reforme* displayed on their chests. Thus, it
seemed that the white troupe was sweeping away the tricolored flag
and those gathered around it.

Here, again, we have an instance of improvisation during performance
itself—of the introduction of a new element—broom replacing bellows;
and critical commentary on current events. Bezucha fills in for us some
features of the relevant historical and cultural contexts (pp. 13-16). He
sees in the *danse des soufflets* (dance of the bellows) an instance of a class of
Ash Wednesday snake dances popular in southern French towns, which
Van Gennep believed were themselves parodies of the processions of the
pénitents, the religious fraternities of Provence. In these dances there was
much ritual tranvestitism. Masked youths dressed in women's petticoats
or nightshirts amused the spectators by trying to grab the persons dancing in front of them, whether to set his skirts on fire or strew him with
ashes. But the 1849 carnival at Uzès made additional use of old custom.
The Gard department has witnessed religious conflict from the Camisard
wars of the seventeenth century to the White Terror of the restoration.
After the Revolution of 1830, the Protestant elite of Uzès had gained
control of the town's administration and National Guard. When Guizot, a
Protestant, fell in 1848, power went over to their old foes the impoverished Catholic majority. The Protestants feared that a third restoration of the Bourbons was imminent. In other towns, this group might
have been "men of Order"; here many supported the Left, "the democratic and social Republic," as a means of opposing a government they
distrusted. As in so many small towns, at Uzès, religion, politics and
social structure formed a single sociocultural field. Even before the Carnival, "the Republican cafe" had assaulted dancing Catholics with billiard
cues, while Catholic youths retaliated by attacking Protestant homes and
businesses—why does this script seem so familiar these days? Bezucha
summarizes the events of 1849 as a "popular demonstration by the Right
against an elite on the Left. The costumes of the sweepers were indeed

traditional, but the color white also symbolized the legitimist, Catholic party. Their dance was a customary one, but by substituting brooms for bellows and adding a tricolored flag and a few copies of a newspaper they changed the meaning of the parody. Its theme was no longer the burial of Carnival, rather the burial of the Republic . . . this mechanism of innovation set off a chain of violence" (pp. 15-16).

Color symbolism plays a clear role here. I wish I had time to speak more about it, for I have written extensively on the initiatory significance of what I can only consider the culturally "primary" colors, white, red, and black in studies of tribal cultures. But it is importantly used in provincial France during the Second Republic, as Bezucha's second example demonstrates. This case is from a procureur's notes on Ash Wednesday 1849 in the town of Issoire in the Puy-de-Dôme, in the north. Here the Whites are put down and the Reds prevail.

> On the 21st of this month a masquerade thusly composed appeared on the main square of Issoire: an individual wearing bourgeois clothing, his face covered with a mask of white material and holding a cattle pik in his hand, pretended to be a herdsman driving cattle. Behind him were two persons joined together by a yoke and dressed like workers, their faces covered by masks of red material. Following them came a cart pulled by a horse and containing five or six persons supporting a straw dummy which in this part of the country is called *Guillaume*. The allegory was highly transparent: the bourgeois aristocracy was forcing the *people* [emphasis in the original text] under the yoke of its power.
>
> At the same time in another part of town, another group of maskers was going about in a cart; one person wore a red bonnet and carried a wooden staff which he jabbed into the side of a straw dummy which was wearing a white bonnet. This last masquerade was the opposite, or rather the complement, of the first allegory: it was the *people* in turn taking its vengeance by the destruction of the aristocratic bourgeoisie.
>
> Finally, elsewhere in the town, a band of young peasants went about shaking their fists, singing, and shouting *A bas les blancs*! (p. 16).

Issoire had the reputation of being a turbulent town, strongly anticarlist and hostile to the bourgeoisie. The color symbolism had potent cultural meaning here too. Red was not only contra-Carlist but also pro-revolutionary. If white and Right stood for order, red and Left stood, not for disorder, but for a new order based on the (often bloody) overthrow of the old order. The figure of Guillaume, the Straw Man, is interesting. Traditionally he was a buffoon or clown, who represented Turncoatism, like the Vicar of Bray in the English song. He was the person who put opportunism before principle. In Bezucha's interpretation (p. 18) he had ceased to be, as he once was, "a symbolic representation of carnival," with its plasticity of commentary as against the rigidity of a structure accepted by all, but was now "the personification of the maskers' enemy, the so-called bourgeois aristocracy." He was petrified in a new structural role—if only in the labile world of carnival.

Four days after this Ash Wednesday parade, which still preserved many traditional features, a local chambrée or Republican club mounted a procession, presumably to celebrate the first year of the Republic, which represented a conscious combination of traditional carnival allegory and elements of the *fêtes révolutionnaires*, the official pageants staged in the 1790's. As Bezucha describes it:

> In a horse-drawn cart decorated with red cloth, green garlands, and the motto *Honneur au travail*, rode a costumed figure representing Liberty, her (his, for Liberty was played by a man) hands on the shoulders of The Worker and The Farmer. Behind Liberty stood her children, Genius and Instruction; next to here were two men, one with a large open book and the other with a sign reading *La République fera le tour du monde*. The cart was led by a villager dressed as a Roman herald and followed by the figure of Time.
>
> An honor guard of ten persons preceded the cart and behind it came five persons in chains: one was dressed as a priest or jesuit, a second in white, a third in black, and final two as nobles wearing signs marked Privilège in their hats. Completing the procession was a crowd of perhaps one hundred and fifty men, marching arm in arm and singing *La Marseillaise* and *Le Chant du départ*. As they passed the home of the retired subprefect, a peasant was heard to shout *Vive le sang!* (pp. 18-19).

The thought of the guillotine must have made shivers run down several backs that night! Indeed, in other Mardi Gras parades recorded by Bezucha from that period, symbolic guillotines were taken on procession on carts. At Schirmeck in the Bas-Rhin department, for example, one such "guillotine" was accompanied by an "executioner," wearing a red belt and smeared with a colored substance imitating blood. The procession stopped outside the homes of local notables, while the group shouted "Long live Robespierre! Long live the guillotine!"

The examples of public liminality I have given—calendrical rites in tribal cultures and carnivals in post-feudal and early modern culture—stress the role of collective innovatory behavior, of crowds generating new ways of framing and modelling the social reality which presses on them in their daily lives. Here all is open, plurally reflexive, the folk acts on the folk and transforms itself through becoming aware of its situation and predicament. I now want to turn to a major reflexive genre, which in keeping with its origin in cultures which recognize the category of "the individual" as the significant decision-making and ethical unit, attributes to individuals the authorship of its scenarios—I refer to stage drama. But stage plays are, of course, as much public as private performative modes.

They involve actors, audience, producers, stagehands, often musicians and dancers, and, most of all, their plots and messages are communicated by various written and oral networks to a general public which varies in span and composition from society to society and epoch to epoch. It is a moot point whether plays derive from rituals—as carnivals clearly do—or whether they originated in the retelling of hunting and headhunting adventures, with pantomimic accompaniments. In either case they are liminal phenomena, with a good deal of reflexive commentary interwoven with the descriptive narrative.

In considering drama, we should consider flow. There can certainly be flow in ritual and carnival, but it is not so central to these genres as framing and plural reflexivity. What is flow? My colleague at Chicago, the psychologist Mihaly Csikszentmihalyi, has recently devoted a whole book (1975) to the study of this elusive concept. For him flow is a state in which action follows action according to an inner logic which seems to need no conscious intervention on our part; we experience it as a unified flowing from one moment to the next, in which we feel in control of our actions, and in which there is little distinction between self and environment, between stimulus and response, or between past, present, and future. He sees flow as a common, though by no means inevitable experience when people act with total involvement, whether in play and sport, in the creative experiences in art and literature, or in religious experiences. He assigns to flow six attributes of distinctive features, marking it off from other interior states.

1. Action and awareness are experienced as one.

2. Attention is centered on a limited stimulus field: in games by formal rules and such motivational means as competitiveness. Rules, motivations, rewards, the will to participate are seen as framing devices, necessary limitations for the centering of attention.

3. Loss of ego: the "self" which is ordinarily the broker between one person's actions and another simply becomes irrelevant. The actor, immersed in the flow, accepts the framing rules as binding which also bind the other actors—no "self" is needed to bargain about what should or should not be done or to "negotiate" about the meaning to be assigned to actions.

4. The actor finds himself in control of his actions and environment. He may not know it when "flowing," but reflecting on it "in tranquillity" he may realize that his skills were perfectly matched to the demands made upon him by ritual, art, or sport. Outside the framed and willingly limited flow situation such a subjective sense of control is hard to attain, due to the enormous number of stimuli and cultural tasks that press on us. If skills outmatch demands, boredom results; if skills are inadequate, anxiety—hence the book's title.

5. Flow usually contains coherent, noncontradictory demands for action and provides clear, unambiguous feedback to a person's actions. Culture reduces flow possibilities to defined channels, for example, chess, polo, gambling, prescribed liturgical action, miniature painting, a yoga exercise, attempting a specific ascent by well-tested rock-climbing techniques, the practice of surgery, and so forth. One can throw oneself into the cultural design of the game, art, procedure, and know whether one has done well or not when one has completed the round of culturally predetermined acts. Flow differs from everyday activities in that its framing contains explicit rules which make action and the evaluation of action unproblematic. Thus cheating breaks flow—you have to be a believer, even if this implies temporary "willing suspension of disbelief," that is, choosing to believe that the rules are in some way axiomatic. If many forms of play or ritual occur in liminal space-time, that time is framed by rules that give credence to whatever make-believe or innovative behavior, whatever subjunctive action, goes on within the frame.

6. Finally, flow is what Csikszentmihalyi calls "autotelic," that is, it seems to need no goals or rewards outside itself. To flow is its own reward: it is to be as happy as a human being can be—in one sense the specific rules that trigger and frame flow, whether of chess or a meditative technique, are irrelevant. This, Csikszentmihalyi concludes, is important for any study of human behavior, since if it is true it follows that people will deliberately manufacture cultural situations and frames which will release flow, or, as individuals, seek it outside their ascribed statuses or stations in life, if these are, for one reason or another, "flow-resistant," that is, conducive to boredom or anxiety.

It is obvious that flow is an ingredient in any kind of successful cultural performance. But what is its relationship to frame and reflexivity? Let us first consider Erving Goffman's recent views on framing as expressed in his *Frame Analysis* (1974). Frames, for him, are "the principles of organization which govern events" (p. 10). They are divided into a number of types: *natural frames* refer to unguided events, while social frames refer to "guided doings" (p. 22). Ritual, carnival, and stage drama would be "socially framed." Frames may also be *primary*, where the interpretation of meaning is imposed on a scene that would otherwise be meaningless (p. 21), a view close to that of the phenomenological sociologists such as Schutz, Garfinkel and Cicourel. Here social life may itself be seen as an endless negotiation about which cultural frame of meaning should surround and account for a given bit of behavior. I do not think that flow can often occur in relation to primary framing unless it can be shown early that there are prior shared understandings about, say, the moral or aesthetic values of a given event or action, for negotiating often divides action from awareness. Goffman speaks of such performative genres as movies and the theater as *secondary* frames. He also uses the term *fabricated* frames where an activity is managed so that one or more others has a false belief about what is going on, as in the frame created by a confidence trickster (p. 83).

Now I would argue that in Goffman's terms, while ritual, carnival, and theater are all socially framed guided doings, the first two genres, since they are more deeply located in *social structure*, defined by Peter L. Berger and Thomas Luckman as the element of continuity or objectification of reality (*The Social Construction of Reality: A Treatise in the Sociology of Knowledge*, 1966), owe their flow qualities to the degree to which participants identify themselves with the traditional scenario—the procedural outline—which itself may constitute a reflexive metacommentary on the history of the group—while flow in stage drama comes from the fidelity with which actors convey the dramatist's *individually*-based appraisal of the social structure. In all cases, the actors themselves are not reflexive, since reflexivity inhibits flow, but in the flow of their mutually interconnected performances they convey the reflexive message of the scenario or script. Part of the potency of a "great performance" comes precisely from this: the author *reflects*; the *actors flow*. There is a fruitful tension between the opposites. The audience is "moved." A cultural problem is irradiated into full visibility for the audience to reflect upon passionately. In ritual and carnival it may not be too fanciful to see social structure itself as the author or source of scenarios. The cases presented by Natalie Davis and Robert Bezucha are interesting because we can detect in them social structure divided against itself; one part authoring the downfall of another in mime and mask. No longer is social structure relatively solidary; class and gender have become self-conscious, reflexive, and one part of the social system employs formerly shared cultural symbols to provide a critique of others. It is at this point that collective reflexive genres seem to become clumsy instruments of periodic self-appraisal for modernizing societies. Here Goffman's notion that transformation may occur between frames—a process he also calls "keying," the "set of conventions by which a given activity, one already meaningful in terms of some primary framework, is transformed into something patterned on this activity but seen by the participants to be something quite else"—may be relevant. Carnival—or ritual—may key into stage drama. The former seems to have happened, for example, in the case of the *Commedia dell'Arte*, whose actors, masked virtuosi of spontaneous stage business, flourished in the atmosphere of the great fairs, such as the Fair of Saint-Germain and the Fair of Saint Laurent in Paris. The *Noh* play of Japan, which took its present form in the fourteenth century seems to have developed out of several earlier performative genres. One was *Gigaku*, a form of entertainment brought from Korea early in the seventh century A.D., which "made

use of music, dance, masking, and miming and was often of a satirical
nature, but was part, nevertheless of religious festivals" (Henry W. Wells,
"Noh" in *The Reader's Encyclopedia of World Drama*, 1969:602). Other major
theatrical genres have carnivalesque origins, such as Greek comedy
which has been conjectured to originate in a processional celebration with
a song or dance at entrance, a debate or dispute, and an address to the
onlookers—characters are ridiculed and represented as absurd or offen-
sive. Medieval European comedy has been held to have been affected by
the carnivalesque Feast of Fools, which itself derived in part from the
Roman Saturnalia. H. J. Rose thus describes the Saturnalia (1948:77):
"During it there were no social distinctions, slaves had a holiday and
feasted like their masters, and all restrictions were relaxed . . . civilians
and soldiers alike celebrated it, it was usual to choose by lot a Lord of
Misrule (*Saturnalicius princeps*, 'leading man of the Saturnalia') and gifts
were exchanged."

Stage dramas are genres that I would be inclined to call "liminoid,"
"liminal-like," rather than "liminal"; that is, they are historically connected with and often displace rituals which possess true liminal phases,
and they also share important characteristics with liminal processes and
states, such as "subjectivity," escape from the classifications of everyday
life, symbolic reversals, destruction—at a deep level—of social distinctions, and the like; nevertheless, liminoid genres differ from liminal
phases in ways which indicate major differences in the societies of which
they respectively constitute major modes of reflexive stocktaking.

Liminoid genres—which would include the writing of novels and essays, the painting of portraits, landscapes and crowd scenes, art exhibitions, sculpture, architecture, and so on, as well as individually written
plays—contrast with liminal phenomena in the following ways. Liminal
phenomena tend to dominate in tribal and early agrarian societies; they
are collective, concerned with calendrical, biological, and social structural
cycles; they are integrated into the total social process; they reflect the
collective experience of a community over time; and they may be said to
be "functional" or "eufunctional," even when they seem to "invert"
status hierarchies found in the nonliminal domain. Liminoid
phenomena, on the other hand, flourish in societies of more complex
structure, where, in Henry Maine's terms, "contract has replaced status"
as the major social bond. Where people voluntarily enter into relationships instead of being born into them. Perhaps they begin to appear in
what Georges Gurvitch calls "city-states on their way to becoming em-
pires" (of the Graeco-Roman, Etruscan and Umbrian type) and in late
feudal societies. But they become really prominent mainly in Western
Europe in nascent, capitalistic societies, with the beginnings of industri-
alization and mechanization, and the emergence of socioeconomic

classes. Liminoid phenomena may be collective (and, when they are so, are often derived, like carnivals, parades, spectacles, circuses, and the like, from liminal predecessors) or individually created—though, as I said, they have mass or collective effects. They are not cyclical but intermittent, generated often in times and places assigned to the leisure sphere. Liminoid phenomena, unlike liminal phenomena, tend to develop apart from central political and economic processes, along the margins, in the interstices, on the interfaces of central and servicing institutions—they are plural, fragmentary (representing, in some cases, the dismemberment, or *sparagmos*, of holistic, pivotal, pansocietal rituals) and often experimental in character. Furthermore, since they are often assigned to individuals as scenario writers they tend to be more idiosyncratic and quirky, more "spare, original and strange" than liminal phenomena. Their symbols are closer to the personal-psychological than to the objective-social typological pole. Cliques, schools, and coteries of liminoid authors and artists emerge, but these are bonded more by optation, by choice, than by obligation—in the liminal case, persons *have to* undergo ritual by virtue of their natal status. Competition emerges in the later liminoid domain; individuals and schools compete for the recognition of a "public" and are regarded as ludic offerings placed for sale on a free market—at least in nascent capitalistic and democratic-liberal societies. Liminoid phenomena, unlike liminal, do not so much *in*vert as *sub*vert quotidian and prestigious structures and symbols. This subversive quality inheres in many structural and antistructural perspectives, for example, ritual liminality reasserts itself against secularization in the manifestos of Antonin Artaud. Let me quote here and there from *The Theater and Its Double* (1958):

> Where alchemy, through its symbols, is the spiritual Double of an operation which functions only on the level of real matter, the theater must also be considered as the Double, not of this direct, everyday reality of which it is gradually being reduced to a mere inert replica— as empty as it is sugar-coated—but of another archetypal and dangerous reality, a reality of which the Principles, like dolphins, once they have shown their heads, hurry to dive back into the obscurity of the deep (p. 48).

Here Artaud seems to see theatrical reflexivity as being a confrontation of modern quotidian reality with the "inhuman" (to use his term) depth of the fecund and primordial depths of a "cosmos in turmoil," subverting thus our glib acceptance of surface, rational realities. Subversion for Artaud implies a curious "retribalization," not disakin to Jung's. We seek for replenishment from the myths which coil within us and must out. For Artaud, Oriental theater, for example the Balinese, had a therapeutic effect: it broke "through language in order to touch life." Subversion often takes the form of rational critique of the established order—from various structural perspectives: didacticism is explicit in the theater of Shaw, Ibsen, Strindberg, and Brecht, implicit in the work of Pinter, Becket, and Arrabal. Drama, and other liminoid genres and media, exposes the injustices, inefficiencies, immoralities, alienations, and the like, held to be generated by mainstream modern economic and political structures and processes.

Of course, liminal and liminoid phenomena have always coexisted, though in various ratios. Religions, clubs, fraternities, secret societies, in modern societies, have their initiation rituals with liminal phases. In tribal societies, there are liminoid games and experimental practices in art and dance. But the trend from liminal to liminoid is discernible, as are those from status to contract, mechanical to organic solidarity, and so on.

Putting our initial terms together we might say that liminal genres put much stress on social frames, plural reflexivity, and mass flow, shared flow, while liminoid genres emphasize idiosyncratic framing, individual reflexivity, subjective flow, and see the social as problem not datum.

Postscript

I have recently been in earnest dialogue with Dr. Richard Schechner, co-Director of the Performance Group, who is both a theorist of drama and a producer of plays—outstanding in both capacities. Dr. Schechner, like Jerzy Grotowski, is professionally concerned with the relationship between ritual and drama. Grotowski's article "The Theatre's New Testament" is, indeed, included in a volume published in 1976, *Ritual, Play, and Performance*, edited by Schechner and Mady Schuman. Grotowski, quite frankly, regards his theater as a type of *rite de passage*, an initiation rite, for modern man. For him "it is necessary to abolish the distance between actor and audience by eliminating the stage, removing all frontiers" (p. 189). The play is to become the liminal phase of an initiatory scenario directed to the spectator (hardly a spectator any more, rather a participant) "who does not stop at an elementary stage of psychic integration, content with his own petty, geometrical, spiritual stability, knowing exactly what is good and what is evil, and never in doubt. For it was not to him that El Greco, Norwid, Thomas Mann and Dostoyevsky spoke, but to him who undergoes an endless process of self-development, whose unrest is not general but directed towards a search for the truth about himself and his mission in life" (p. 188). Clearly, it is to the modern individual Grotowski addresses himself, to the man confronted by a preponderance of "liminoid" genres. But Grotowski wishes to "reliminalize" or "retribalize" if not all modern men, at least that handful which could constitute a cult group of shamans. In answer to the question: "Does this infer a theatre for the elite?" Grotowski answers: "Yes, but for an elite which is not determined by the social background or financial situation of the spectator, nor even education. The worker who has never had any secondary education can undergo this creative process of self-search, whereas the university professor may be dead, permanently formed, moulded into the terrible rigidity of a corpse. . . . We are not concerned with just any audience, but a special one" (p. 188).

Grotowski's anti-intellectual bias, evidenced here, is not the most important component to his Poor Theater, heir to the Polish Laboratory Theater of Wroclav. His is a sort of secular Franciscanism with, indeed, latterly, the requirement that neophytes must travel to a sacred mountain in Poland, as pilgrims, on foot, to work with his core group of actor-adepts, if they wish to be "stimulated into self-analysis" (p. 189). Clearly, Grotowski is still working within a liminoid frame, since he is prepared to admit the validity, however limited, of other types of theater. But within this frame he wishes to use what the anthropological eye clearly detects as a sequence of initiatory rituals as a means of creating a community of "saved" persons, who in finding themselves through the psychic discipline and carefully designed physical exercises of Grotowski's rehearsal procedures, also find others, thus gradually disseminating what Berdyaev would have called "an aristocracy of the spirit" throughout a world of "alienated" individuals. The liminoid character of his enterprise is revealed by his reversal of the tribal ordering—in which liminal rites indicate antecedent social structures and form thresholds between significant states and statuses of those structures. Grotowski uses his "rites" (I use quotes to mark their liminoid character as the constructions of a postmodern man) to create first existential communitas, then normative communitas. He begins with the "threshold" and generates the structures on either side of it. This is how the founders of millenarion movements have operated—Wovoka for the Ghost Dance, Isiah Shembe in South Africa. Evangelizing fervor pervades Grotowski's vocabulary: "the theater's New Testament," the "holy actor," "secular saints like Stanislawski"—even though he protests that one must not take the word "holy" in a religious sense (p. 190).

Schechner now takes a more detached stance towards this ritual/theater issue. For him "the entire binary 'efficacy/ritual-entertainment/theater' is performance." "Performance," the generic term, comprehends "the impulse to be serious and to entertain; to collect meanings and to pass the time; to display symbolic behavior that actualizes 'there and then' and to exist only 'here and now'; to be oneself and to play at being others; to be in a trance and to be conscious; to get results and to fool around; to focus the action on and for a select group sharing a hermetic language, and to broadcast to the largest possible audiences of strangers who buy a ticket" (p. 218). However, I think that if we are to prehend more fully than before the dynamics of sociocultural process, we have to see cultural performances as constituting the reflexivity of human groups and to see growing reflexivity embodied in a developmental sequence of cultural genres. Schechner's "performance" is a fairly precise labelling of the items in the modern potpourri of liminoid genres—but it indicates by its very breadth and tolerance of discrepant forms that a level of public reflexivity has been reached totally congruent with the advanced stages of a given social form—Western capitalist liberal democracy.

As a personal footnote I would like to add that I see the liminoid as an advance in the history of human freedom. For this reason I relish the separation of an audience from performers and the liberation of scripts from cosmology and theology. The concept of individuality has been hard-won, and to surrender it to a new totalizing process of reliminalization is a dejecting thought. As a member of an audience I can see the theme and message of a play as one among a number of "subjunctive" possibilities, a variant model for thought or action to be accepted or rejected after careful consideration. Even as audience people can be "moved" by plays; they need not be "carried away" by them—into another person's utopia or "secular sacrum," to use Grotowski's phrase. Liminoid theater should present alternatives; it should not be a brainwashing technique. As Blake said: "One Law for the Lion and the Ox is Oppression."

REFERENCES

Agulhon, Maurice. *La Republique au village*. Paris: Plon, 1960.

Artaud, Antonin. *The Theater and Its Double*, tr. M. C. Richards. New York: Grove Press, 1958.

Berger, Peter L. and Luckman, Thomas. *The Social Construction of Reality: A Treatise in the Sociology of Knowledge*. Garden City, New York: Doubleday Anchor Books, 1966.

Bezucha, Robert. "Popular Festivities and Politics During the Second Republic." Paper delivered at the Davis Center, Princeton University, 1975.

Csikszentmihalyi, Mihaly. *Beyond Boredom and Anxiety*. San Francisco: Jossey-Bass, 1975.

Davis, Natalie Z. *Society and Culture in Early Modern France*. Stanford: Stanford University Press, 1975.

Goffman, Erving. *Frame Analysis*. New York: Harper and Row, Colophon Books, 1974.

Junod, Henri. *Life of a South African Tribe*, vol. I. New York: University Books, 1962. Originally published in 1912-1913.

Krige, Eileen Jensen. *The Social System of the Zulus*. Pietermaritzburg: Schuter and Shooter, 1950.

Marriott, McKim. "The Feast of Love" in M. Singer, ed., *Krishna: Myths, Rites, and Attitudes*. Honolulu: East-West Center Press, 1966.

Rose, H. J. *Ancient Roman Religion*. London: Hutchinson, 1948.

Schechner, R. and Schuman, M., eds., *Ritual, Play and Performance*. New York: The Seabury Press, 1976.

Turner, Victor. *The Ritual Process*. Chicago: Aldine, 1969.

Van Gennep, Arnold. *Manuel du folklore francais contemporain*. 7 vols. Paris: Picard, 1938-1958.

Wells, Henry W. "Noh" in *The Reader's Encyclopedia of World Drama*. New York: Thomas Crowell, 1969.

II
Events

Letting Be Be Finale of Seem:
The Future of an Illusion

HERBERT BLAU

There was very good reason for St. Augustine, Tolstoy and other penitent geniuses to have had their suspicions about the theater. If it's not obscene, and it is (I shall come back to that), it is a Platonic Cave, shadows upon shadows performing. The overlays of illusion can be demoralizing. If one dwells upon it, there is something alarming in the most normal theater event, the more normal the more alarming. I mean what we grant and what we take for granted. The habits of mind are so long ingrained they are unexamined. They exist in and out of the theater. The consciousness we have inherited from theater accumulates, determining behavior and expectancy in everyday life. We meet each day as if a curtain were rising, although it rarely occurs to us to ask why, in the theater, the curtain that wasn't there should have been there. Out of what queer longing did it come? The language of theater—its grammar of motives and rhetoric of appearances—has filtered through history into perception. Outside the theater we see as if we were inside, the world gradually seeming what it is not. We come to see what we have seen like the photograph which tries to fix it, by negatives, coming up with only a surface. What is there is not there. What is there is an evanescence, an escapement, a slippery clockwork. The theater is the most *time-serving* of forms, literally, functionally, and metaphysically. It is by nature unreliable.

The sum and substance is a moving fiction, a lie like truth, a mere cast of thought. The more we think about it the more we are teased out of thought. All its strategies are deceptions. No matter how the theater denies it—for instance, becomes strange, as in Brecht, to be objective—its power is the power of a thoroughly laminated illusion. The obfuscation is deliberate. It is surely illicit. Which is why—at the Symposium on Postmodern Performance—I summoned up Iago's view of reality as "Seeming, seeming" while describing my own most recent work as a reflexion on appearance through a process we call "ghosting."* In the disease of seeming, the ghosting is homeopathic.

---

*See "Seeming, Seeming: The Disappearing Act," *The Drama Review*, 20, 4 (December 1976), 7-24.

The present essay was delivered at UW-M later in the year.

Once the mind is let loose on the inescapable content of illusion in the form, it can turn insidious, as in Genet. In the dead middle of *The Balcony*, there comes an impeccable emissary from the Power Structure, presumably to explain what's happening. A dramaturgical necessity, he seems extruded from the opacity of the play, forced up like a cipher from the Void. The mind, demanding explanations for the razzle-dazzle allegorical pornography of the previous scenes, awaits the Word. The Envoy is (or claims to be) an agent of the missing Queen. He seems quite at home in the Funeral Studio, ravaged by revolution. Instead of clarifying things, however, the Envoy impacts obfuscation with obfuscation, like pure illusion. Embroidering on the absence of the Queen, he says the Queen is at her embroidery. Does she exist? She is occupied with becoming entirely what she must be, either engaged in an infinite meditation heading rapidly toward immobility, or picking her nose. The explanation is mummy's cloth, the Envoy is a death-bringer, killing with words. When the ambiguities (seem to) cease, he is exposed as a thug, an ineffectual phony among the phonies in the brothel who play out, in dread, their fantasies of power.

We are among them—hypocrite voyeurs—contributing to the illusions, unmoored and vulnerable. Genet plays with the power behind the scene, so to speak (and we do), which is—whether we admit it or deny it—the power of illusion; which is—even when the structure is exposed—the sustaining power of all performance.

Think of it: the systems of information within the systems of information, even at a more obvious level, that we take for granted in a theater event. We bring not-entirely examined fictions from life to support the probable impossibilities of the art. Think of all the tacit agreements around the play and in the rehearsal process—if the play is rehearsed or if it's improvised or if it's something other than a play, the latest mutation of a Happening perhaps, some hybrid that is not-quite-life—the whole conglomerate of supposition, arrangement, plotting and pretense out of which an act of performance is made. Consider simply an object in front of your eyes: on stage it is no longer simple. A real chair used for a real chair in a "realistic" setting remains, though a real chair, a *sign* for a chair. It is what it is not though it appears to be what it is. The real chair may also be, by convention, something other than a chair. If we move from object to action, the thing is immediately complicated: a faked kiss may seem a real kiss and a real kiss may obviously seem faked or less obviously seem real, as between any two actors the faked kiss may develop in the heat of performance, as we say, into something more real.

Those who have followed the history of non-matrixed performance events outside of regular theaters have a repertoire of stories about real things that looked staged up to and including murder. There is a similar history in the conventional theater, somebody from an audience periodically jumping into the scene to assault or embrace an actor whose imitation seems only too much what it is. Once you imagine the possibilities that have been realized in actual performance, either accepted as a matter of course or developing unbeknownst, you see what a queerer system of unquestioned information is endorsed within a performance than is covered by the mere willing suspension of disbelief. The endorsement is part of the process of acculturation. It is also structured into the illusions by which we live. "Sancho," says Don Quixote to his skeptical consort, "if you want me to believe what you saw in the sky, I wish you to accept my account of what I saw in the cave of Mentesinos. I say no more."

The tradeoff, all things considered, may be the only means of psychic survival. It is (if you think about it) as shocking as it is amusing. "Pretend, pretend that you are just and true," says Alceste to Célimène in Molière's play, "And I will do my best to believe in you." We collaborate by laughing in perpetuating the deceit. We carry over the experience of our own relationships—and the necessary duplicities on which they are built—to establish the credibility of the thing being performed. If we don't laugh, we may miss the point of its appalling brilliance. The truth is it takes just as much truth to play credibly false as it does to appear indubitably true; and sometimes to convince others (and even ourselves) that we are true we have to play at being true. The illusions by which we live are the illusions by means of which we sustain the fiction. Or is it the other way around? Ordinary life imitates its formulations which are drawn, in time, from ordinary life. Theater is one of the formulations, perhaps the most summary of all. The exploitation of the circularity makes the theater seem suspect, but from its own perspective the more it does it the better it is. So, what's real?

If the theater were real, we wouldn't bother with it. When it's not real, we complain. The confusion depends of course on how we're using the word real and the degree of illusion which makes it so. We abandon that illusion at our peril. Some new modes of performance, in theater and the other arts, have put illusion up for grabs: either it's nothing but or not at all. Both attitudes, oddly, seem to intensify the Renaissance conceit inherent in Shakespeare's Globe and expressed by John Donne, that "the whole frame of the world is theater." We have seen through the sixties a passage from concern with the psychopathology of everyday life to the conscious theatricalization of everyday life. There was theater all over the place, in politics, in fashion, in therapy, and in the histrionic emphasis on life-style. In the process, there was some fudging on the word *frame* or a desire to wrench it quite from its fixture. The period of radical activism was a period of revived illusions. Perhaps the wildest illusion of all is the one that really believes—as Don Quixote does not, as Shakespeare did not though he wrote it—that all the world is a stage, failing to see through the seeming that not even theater is all theater.

What makes anything theater? Thinking makes it so. The same Fall which brought consciousness into the Garden brought the first actor. I tried to show (in "Seeming, Seeming: the Disappearing Act") how thinking, in my own work, recycles itself between the illusions of theater and the realities of the world, the realities of the world and the illusions of theater, arriving at a kind of theater whose express subject is the *dis*-appearance of theater; that is, the appearances from which theater is made and upon which it reflects are conceptually elaborated and in turn reflected upon until there is a denial, or refusal, by means of theater of the distressing and maybe crippling notion that in life there is nothing but theater. "I could be bounded in a nutshell and count myself king of infinite space," says Hamlet, "except that I have bad dreams." In developing *Elsinore*, we were particularly interested in those dreams. The performance consists of image upon image replicating, exhaustively, until it returns to that nothing in the nutshell which is the source of theater, but resists being theater in the living end.

The idea of reality as Total Theater is fortified in our time by the illusions coming to us—as we become disturbed by the mental fixations of the categorical West—from the metamorphic experience of the Far East, where reality in its Oneness is held to be a performance in which identity has a thousand faces. The release from duality is of short duration as our sense of distinction wavers. The expanding illusory universe curves back, haunted, through the electronic media. The superflux of imagery is further manipulated by the image-making propensities of our politics. The result is that our hold on reality, whatever it is, is further attenuated. We feel very much the immanence of the idea that life is a dream or a play-within-the-play-within, the series stretching as far as reflexive thought conspires with the after-images. No appearance can be taken at face value. Or in desperation we create theories of value that are entirely based upon appearance. No wonder we are ready to believe everything, and nothing. The conspiracy theories that arise with or without evidence around great public events, such as the assassinations, are virtually unavoidable in this context. What scandal is being performed? After Watergate, everybody seems to be working at the problem of credibility. It is no wonder—despite Jacques Ellul's caution that they are *not* the same—that we tend to collapse the illusory political universe, where policy is a masque of pretense, with the elusive old perceptual problem of the philosophers, "who say we do not know the external world except through the intermediary of our senses and have no guarantee that our senses do not deceive us, or even that the external world exists and that, in any event, we can perceive the world only through images . . . . There is a world of difference," says Ellul in his book *Political Illusion*, "between experimental knowledge of a fact and knowledge of it as filtered through the verbal screen. Diogenes already answered the question." But the fact is that many contemporary artists haven't believed him.

We are familiar in postmodernism with the many ingenious efforts to break down the barriers between art and life—should there have been the illusory appearance that there was any real difference to begin with. John Cage's 4'33" of silence was designed to let music arise out of the illusory difference, passing indistinguishably from one to the other, cancelling the difference, as Robert Wilson's 12-hour long presentation of *The Life and Times of Josef Stalin* also did. Wilson's highly graphic surrealist theater piece begins with a 5' wordless speech/song by Queen Victoria (pure fiction) played by the "director's" 90-year old grandmother (pure truth?). People were expected to come and go during the performance, and even possibly to fall asleep. This was not preferred but it was acceptable. I suspect it was similarly acceptable when Cage did his reading of *Writing through Finnegans Wake* at the November symposium. About that performance, an *aside* (as we say in the theater) that may become more relevant as we proceed:

We saw in that event how thoroughly, despite all theory, the reception of performance is still bound up with certain pernicious (Erving Goffman's word—I prefer to call them illusory) qualities that also establish the credentials if not the credibility of performance: charisma, presence, reputation or notoriety; in short, star-quality. This is true even in the avant-garde, as Andy Warhol has dexterously demonstrated in making an uninterrupted performance of his life-in-art to his great and creditable prosperity. When Cage did his version of *Finnegans Wake*, we had a compounded irony: the archetype of obscurity in literature being presented by the tutelary deity of indeterminacy in music, and managing to find in the process (I think it was part of the *process*, counted upon now as it once couldn't be) a perfectly passive and acquiescent audience who out of some combination of courtesy and intimidation accepted the premises of performance even when they were bored.

In explaining his structural principles for *Writing through Finnegans Wake*, Cage had indicated that it was a work, given how much he had written, which might have gone on for 12 hours, and after about a half hour or so when it looked as if it might (admiring nevertheless the aplomb and achievement and unfailing *zazen* good humor of John Cage) I walked out. I didn't do so in protest or to set an example; there was nothing in the occasion that warranted that. My only justification has something to do with the time-serving aspect of performance, its temporal dependency, if I may get theoretical again in self-defense. Since I had stayed around (even through boredom) in the days when John Cage needed it, I felt I could satisfy my needs when he didn't. If it were to be as he suggested like a reading of the Koran, I thought I might return the next morning to look in on the worship as, on Christmas Eve, an unbeliever might attend a Mass.

I am analyzing the occasion of *Writing through Finnegans Wake* as a performance because I also think it important to point out, as we discuss new forms, how much harder it is within the ethos of postmodernism and the preemptive capacity of bourgeois culture to work powerfully at the acceptable center of performance than it is when you're a guerrilla at the margins. Cage had a remarkable situation—one which we have all desired or fantasized—and that is to have a large receptive and reasonably sophisticated audience ready for anything. When we do, however—when the audience's ears are, as Cage says in the epigraph to *Silence*, "in excellent condition"—it seems more difficult to say anything of exceptional consequence. We almost require the resistance. Of course, this was also an occasion for celebration, a testimonial. But: the one characteristic of Cage's performance that might have been more devastatingly ironic than we realized was the actual manner of the reading. At long last, Cage—who has certainly endured and is still enduring his quota of superciliousness from others, and outright rejection—assumed the paternal role and reduced us all to children at last, as he read in a voice suited to bedtime stories his redaction of Joyce's loquacious phantasm of the rude awakening, which circles back river-runningly on itself.

There are various shadings and motives in the art/life syndrome. There is the abandonment of old formal properties in order to facilitate the interchangeability of art and life. There are forms which suggest ecological feedback, life in art, art in life, restitution by recycling, as in Newton Harrison's lagoons or Joseph Beuys' self-exposing political pieces. There is the differential preservation of the *appearance* of art, as in the socio-declensions of the new participatory Activities of Allan Kaprow. The following, from his *7 Kinds of Sympathy*, might be performed in the home environment of the participants:

A, writing
occasionally blowing nose

B, watching
copying A blowing nose

continuing

(later)

B, reading A's writing
occasionally scratching groin, armpit

A, watching
copying B scratching

continuing

Etc. This is more like an experiment in quasi-guided behavior, Skinnerism absorbed or subverted into the widening context of the old Happening. Kaprow is in fact studying here the primary and secondary messages, the artful increments and involuntary encodings of the participants, in which they mix up the socially acceptable and the elusively or obsessively private. The conception is influenced by Goffman's studies of behavioral discourse and the presentation of the self in everyday life (which drew its terminology from conventional theater and drama). There is a script and careful preparation in which the participants are briefed, and the artist doesn't want to relinquish his art entirely to the slipstream of experience as it simply happens. This Activity, however, is at the edge of a disappearance into something other than what was once art. It is not unusual, even in more definite art contexts, to conceive of performance as a "personal inquiry," but for Kaprow "It would reflect that everyday meaning of performing a job or service, and would relieve the artist of inspirational metaphors such as 'creativity' that are tacitly associated with making art, and therefore theater art." It is not difficult, he adds, "to see performance aspects of a telephone conversation, of digging a trench in the desert, of distributing religious tracts on a street corner, of gathering and arranging population statistics, and of treating one's body to alternating hot and cold immersions."

No, it is not difficult to see the performance aspects, nor has it become difficult to bring such performances back alive from life to art by restoring the idea of the frame, or by shifting it. Kaprow knows that: "The framework tells you what it is: a cow in a concert hall is a musician, a cow in a barn is a cow." He prefers to stay closer to the life-as-it-is, however, working in non-art modes and non-art contexts, ceasing even to call the work art, "retaining instead the private consciousness that sometimes it may be art, too." And sometimes not. It's chancy, to say the least, but not quite Cage's "indeterminacy" which, as practiced, was setting the stage for chance. Art and performance have always, of course, referred themselves back to life when they were in danger of going stale, when the gestures became through long repetition mere pale relics of the thing itself. But what has recently been happening on the blurred margins between art and life is not quite the pressing of art back upon life that was the empirical insistence of the old realism and naturalism. Nor is there the determination to respond to the pressure of insistent fact, as in the charge given by Wallace Stevens to the performing imagination. Kaprow would probably dismiss the imagination as another inspirational metaphor which has damaged art or been used up. But, as Stevens indicates in his statements on the poetry of war, we live in an age when the enormity of fact almost corrodes the reality and value of art. When reality is *that* real, we don't like to bother with it either.

I cannot help feeling that in the attempt to unify life and art by obscuring the difference there is another order of illusion, which is to say another way of evading life. There is a world elsewhere, it should be out there, but we don't really know where, so it keeps coming back to where we are, a new solipsism, playful and plaintive, open-ended and recessive, still disinherited, apolitical, vain. The old modernists—Marx, Freud, and Joyce—told us that history is the nightmare from which we are trying to awaken. The post-modernists would sometimes rather forget about it.

The tendency is either to bypass history or reverse it. In the paradoxical quest of the modern, that's normal. We are always reminded, or should be, that the avant-garde is not far out but way back, reactionary. There is a desire for the elemental, to purify the words of the tribe, to dance us back the tribal morn, to find the little child who passes through the eye of the needle into the kingdom of heaven or some more intimate secular paradise. Clear the altar, sweep the stage. Grasp the root. *Per*-form: to carry through to completion, furn sh forth, finish, perfect. There was something lost or abandoned that needs to be recovered so that the action can be resumed. Where's the action? they asked in the sixties. In the fifties, we waited around for it in *Godot*. "Nothing to be done." *Pause. Do.* So far, so good. The void is there to be filled. Make your scene. Live the moment. Do your thing. Put your body on the line. We are still more or less doing it, as we can see in Kaprow's Activities, but—to my mind—with a certain weakening of perception in the loosening phenomenology of performance. Habits form in thin air as they do in stricter climates; the culture scraped away is space for other accretions. We learn, for instance, that objects can be camouflaged on the surface as they were once obscured in the depths. What is *just there* may not be very much, and the body that's there on the line may tell its quota of lies.

There was surely good reason for the released and non-matrixed forms which disavowed the old behavioral illusion of reality and its structured disguises. But for all that, and total exposure too, the result has often been parody, paranoia, mythotherapy and melodrama, illusion's revenge upon itself. There is something hollow at the center, and it is not the void. The widening perimeters of theater include a lot of emptiness, and the theatricalization of experience keeps us, at times, from seeing it. For the fact is, the danger of accepting all history, all reality as histrionic is that, ultimately, you do miss its deeper drama. That has happened in every period where spectacle subsumes reality and participation is up for grabs, as it was finally in the admirable but lamentable communitarian anarchy of The Living Theater. "We wanted to make a play," said Julian Beck in the published version of *Paradise Now*, "which would no longer be an enactment but would be the act itself, . . . an event in which we (the actors) would always be experiencing it (the play) not anew at all but something else each time." The something else was the unaccomodated self, the increment of solipsism that thinks if you substitute the *is* for the *as if* you have a revolution, which is what made the political urgencies of the group a misguided mess as performance careened out into the street, presumably annihilating the boundaries between art and life. The Power Structure is more adept at game theory. Paradise now, reality tomorrow.

At its best, the desire of art increasingly given over to performance is to collapse the painful dualities with which philosophy has struggled from its inception: mind/body, form/content, truth/illusion, spirit/matter, art/life; always, however, keeping a cliff-hanging finger on the critical difference. The potency of performance may almost be measured by the acuity of that perilous act. If there is something reactionary in the drift of performance back toward life, it may also be regressive. We see both tendencies in the shamanistic concerns of Richard Schechner, who admires the performances of the aborigines, which transform states of being so there is "only one reality." One wonders about that. What we know is only that we do not know. Schechner has recently gone on a walk through India to pursue it further, and I admire him for that. But as Lévi-Strauss has shown in *Tristes Tropiques*, the pathos of the anthropological quest is that the very capacities the anthropologist needs to see correctly prevent him from being what he wants to see. He is, to the degree he remains true to what he is, forever alienated from what he wants to know. I suspect myself that what we have among the aborigines is the *illusion* of one reality, the performance *structure* changing, even intensifying the quality of that illusion, however organically developed the performance may be as a seasonal rite or a sacramental occurrence which incrementally happens as an outcome of daily living. Whatever it is for the aborigines, it is mere dreamscape for us; and all our efforts in the sixties to imitate spirit-voices and the trance states of the aborigines have ended up in the percussive exaltations and illusion of communitas that Mircea Eliade has called "family shamanism."

We have in recent years been very foolish about ritual in performance. If there has been anything but a mockery of it, I haven't seen it. As for communitas, Schechner knows the work of the anthropologist Victor Turner, who writes in *Dramas, Fields, and Metaphors*: "Communitas in ritual can only be evoked easily when there are many occasions outside the ritual on which communitas has been achieved." I don't see them either. Nothing but fractures, factions, fragments, and splintering vested interests, all of which contribute to the general powerlessness. Against that we have to oppose all the "necessary perspective" we can get "on the desire for a return to the will"—to use Jean-François Lyotard's phrase on new performance modes. That requires, I assume (lest the apocalypse really come), all the rational intelligence at our disposal. The kind of factitious and manipulative ecstasy that came up in *Paradise Now* and *Dionysus in 69* has gone out of fashion; yet the regressive impulse is still there, the desire to reproduce through performance some more fulfilling earlier state of being, some avatar of the old *homo ludens*, still polymorphous perverse. It is a desire we all share to some extent, to remain a child forever. We see this impulse reflected in the very sophisticated self-abusive performance pieces by Vito Acconci, such as *Seedbed*, in which Acconci can be heard over an amplifier masturbating below a sloped ramp in a gallery; or more specifically even in *Trappings*, where Acconci situated himself in a closet surrounded by foam, shawls, flowers, toys—and used his penis as a playmate and doll, dressing it, speaking to it, trying to dissociate it as a separate being. "An occasion for self-sufficiency—expanding myself," he said, "so I don't have to go outside of myself." The solo follows the failure of the renewed communitarian dream.

Exposing the drama back in the closet may still be a refusal of the Freudian Reality Principle, though it may offer a perspective on the desire for a return of the will. I want to say more about that in a moment; but what is it, first, that Freud asks of us that we seem to be rejecting? It is to confess, as he puts the case in *The Future of an Illusion*, man's (and woman's, for all the resurrection of the Great Mother) "utter helplessness and his insignificant part in the working of the universe." Freud adds in his characteristically unillusioned way: "But, after all, is it not the destiny of childishness to be overcome? Man cannot remain a child forever: he must venture at last into the hostile world." For this task, the only residual faith is "a certain measure of appropriateness" in our mental structure to attempt to understand the alien and hostile world which we are trying to know. Whatever the age of man, the intellect is still relatively young—though it has been much debunked for failing to do what instinct, which has been with us I suppose from the primeval slime, has also failed to do.

Acconci's performance is as pure a solipsistic act as we are likely to find. "Whatever the solipsist *means* is right," said Wittgenstein, not what the solipsist says or does. The solipsistic self is a tautology—all assertions curving back upon themselves in a kind of metaphysical redundancy. If the self is neither body nor soul but only self, not anything else in the world, it is only a metaphysical subject—it vanishes behind the mirror of thought. In gaining perspective on the return of the will, one has to take stock of that vanishing. The self's fiction empties itself out, as in the masturbation of *Seedbed*, in order to be itself, like the replenishing and replenished void of the Tao. The self-aggression is a negative capability. It would seem as if in this mirror there is only one future, and that is the future of an illusion. Solipsism, so seen, is an idealism arising from brute fact. There is only what is there is there is there, and that's all. . .

I have circled back to Lyotard who, in his lecture at the November symposium, tried to deflect the Freudian perspective on the will by examining "The Unconscious as *Mise-en-Scène*." I am speaking from memory, but as I remember he showed how Freud's structure of the unconscious was, so far as it can be said to be a theater, derived from nineteenth-century Viennese opera and theater. That is not entirely accurate, as Freud's Oedipus complex came from diverse sources. He was enormously affected by Dostoyevsky, for instance, who took charge in the nineteenth century of what was most harrowingly Shakespearean in the history of western theater. The closet drama was where the action was, the demonic having gone into the novel. Freud saw it there. But no matter. Let us follow Lyotard, who concluded his lecture by shifting the *mise-en-scène* from theater to film. In that displacement, he left one crucial element behind—and that in fact *is* drama (which is only in loose talk equated with theater). Showing his own wide range of reference as a philosopher, Lyotard cited an extraordinary film by Michael Snow, in which by a kind of phenomenological exposure we are even made aware of the apparatus by which the film was made. Snow had built for this purpose a DaVincean instrument which panned over a landscape while a convex lens made it possible to show the base upon which the camera stood. There was a shadow on the landscape. I don't recall whether it was the shadow of the tripod or the shadow of the cameraman. The shadow was, however, first of all a shadow, and the system appears to be (even the shadow) almost like the game of chess according to Duchamp, a perfect system or system of "perfect information." It seems to resist psychologizing. But the shadow is still troublesome to me. It reminds me that there might be somebody there, more than shadow, or surface—for the film presents a surface only, presumably undisguised by animistic or anthropomorphic projections.

I am not satisfied. I am not satisfied in the way Stevens suggests when he says that "the poetry of a work of imagination constantly illustrates the fundamental and endless struggle with fact." The fact is—as with the absent boy in Beckett's *Endgame*—there is a terrible desire to see someone there. And as Stevens says relevantly to that fact, too, "Nothing will ever appease this desire except a consciousness of fact as everyone is at least satisfied to have it be." So: put the case. I see a landscape, I want a man. Fact. That, too, is a time-serving desire; which is to say, I have been, like others, irritated by the excess of psychology in our theater, our art, our habits of mind. I have worked my own depredations on the convention of character in theater which is psychologically based and about which, in the acting process, we have to "excavate" the unconscious, to use Freud's archeological term. But new realities, or views of them, conceptions, styles, perspectives on the return of the will are as much the result of (provisional) exhaustion as of discovery. When something comes to the end of the road it doesn't mean it's going nowhere. True, destinations inhabited too long may induce paralysis, especially if there's the shadow of some superhuman figure over the way—Milton with the Epic, Shakespeare with the drama. In order to liberate ourselves from what has become troubling custom or overpowering or vapid form, we proclaim not only new freedoms and a change of heart, but new truths, structures, and even existential data. Yet if, by whatever devious means, old forms return, it's because they were never absent to begin with, as Genet shows in *The Balcony*. The disturbing truth appears to be we are the same old performers of the hour. Things come around. Human needs being what they are, we find that new needs are a recycling of old denial. What was not absent was just strategically ignored, scrupulously overlooked or refused validity on what could only be a trial basis. We look for breathing space, exemption, a new geography. The new perspective on the return of the will is a familiar coign of vantage, an open landscape which, we discover, has its margins, as every continent a land's end. Then, the turning back, the turning in: last year's freedom is another structure. It was already in the mind.

So, on Snow's landscape, there is a man. (I am tempted, having mentioned Stevens, to say a Snow Man, which is to say a man minimal, who hears nothing that is not there and the nothing that is—and knows that life itself is a poverty in the space of life.) Unless the technique is going to reduce the human presence (as it can in film) to a mere thing among things, the old Freudian questions are going to return like the repressed. Or, to use the language of *Hamlet*: "Who's there?" "Nay, answer me. Stand and unfold yourself." In short, we are back through this perspective on returning will to memory and curiosity, projection and lamination, the desire to know more, to identify where the person came from, history and biography, and all the old incriminating and maybe crippling problems of the ego. The *mise-en-scène* passes out of the frame and back into the realm of the unconscious. We are not where we were. However much we would like to free ourselves of the obtrusive screen and selfish claims of the ego, it comes back to haunt us.

So it is in my own work (and I will not repeat what I've said at length about that). Form is the ceaseless reflexive uroboric passage back into the ego, preparing for the leap outwards, then only to be driven back like the creature of Kafka's *The Burrow* into the underground (that is, the unconscious as *mise-en-scène*) because reality feels realer that way ("Stay, illusion!") as it does in Kafka's story, which was the basis for many of the performance concepts that determined *Elsinore*. The creature of the burrow—a mode of consciousness not a character, almost totally solipsistic—has created an intricate labyrinthine defense mechanism, hidden from the world. Yet it is desperate about what's out there, tempted by it, in fact moves outside the burrow, but is driven back in panic, helplessly, realizing finally that there may be no way to hide, there are countless others ("Nay, answer me."), many burrows converging, all the similarly frightened identities encroaching, accumulating like some great rough beast slouching but not, alas, to Bethlehem to be born.

All the talk of going beyond Freud, so far as I can see—whether by structuralism, chance operations, objectism, projective verse, environmental theater, or the false participatory democracy of open forms, you name it—hasn't gone in that respect, though they do provide perspectives, anywhere yet. "In the fight between you and the world," says Kafka, "back the world"—and if you look at the world it seems to be that we are still juggling purpose and randomness, determinism and will, the diachronic and synchronic, being and becoming and all the successions of selfhood seeming between. Which is to say the wires are still crossed, the messages still scrambled, and the *mise-en-scène* still inscrutable. The terms of what we're juggling are not merely polarities but soulmates, indivisible and insoluble. In this performance, chance has, maybe, the last featuring blow at events, as it does in that great paradigm of human motives developed in the mat-weaving section of *Moby-Dick* or in the use of the pirate ship in *Hamlet*. But by no means does it have the last word. Chance made strategically central in art or human affairs—is bound to be reductive, a far cry from the whole story. The same is true of self and surface. The task is still to read the indecipherable writing on the immutable wall. Problems of destiny are still more entrancing and urgent than problems of chance (I stress this because of the dominant ethos at the November symposium, and in much postmodern performance), because it is within the compass of destiny that one requires perspectives on the desire for a return of the will: ". . . an unpleasant suspicion persists," says Freud in *The Future of an Illusion*, "that the perplexity and helplessness of the human race cannot be remedied. This is where the gods are most apt to fail us; if they themselves make fate, then their ways must be deemed inscrutable. The most gifted people of the ancient world dimly surmised that above the gods stands Destiny and that the gods themselves have their destinies." It is out of that perception, I think, that performance was born, dramatically. When, in the most terrible desire for performance—that is, the consummate, completed action—there is paralysis of the will, the best and most immaculate response may be the most moving poetry that Shakespeare ever wrote, the two simple words: Let be. But we're not even satisfied with that.

The endless struggle with fact has by no means ended since Stevens wrote what he did during World War II. Letting be was never the finale of seem, only a nuance, the readiness which may not be all but as much as we've got if we're lucky to have that. The imagination of disaster, one of those literal metaphors of the century, is still as much with us as ever, however much we'd like to say let's move on to something else. In whatever ways art transforms reality, reality doesn't always oblige art. The outgoing president recommended to the new president that we go ahead with the Trident and the B-1 programs and, like the creature of the burrow, keep our defenses up and weapons stockpiled. Nuclear overkill, which dropped out of the headlines for a while, is still woefully on the scene. The military industrial complex which Eisenhower warned against when he left office is now complicated (and obfuscated) by linkages with the new multinationals and the development of an arms industry with eager markets in the Third World that would make Shaw's Undershaft bloat with envy. It does make George Kennan—formulator of the Cold War policy of Containment—blanch at the prospect of the Bomb being available, willynilly, in the OPEC countries and, perhaps, to terrorists.

The illusions of performance are still horrifically entwined with the performance of illusions. The profession of theater, as it normally exists in this country, is part of the Gross National Product. The activism of the sixties looked to the reorganization of human relations to achieve a redistribution of human resources so that power and coercion would not be necessary to enforce a common existence. Some of the newer performance modes still attempt to reflect this desire. They are admirable, though we have seen an abrupt end to that renewed utopian illusion. What we strove for in the radicalism of the last generation was, as Freud puts it for all such striving, a golden age, "but it is questionable if such a state of affairs can ever be realized." It pains us to accept this verdict, but we have seen no evidence in human history to overturn it. Coercion and instinctual renunciation almost seem synonymous with the idea of culture. It may be the ground for the very idea of performance. Why? As Angelo says in *Measure for Measure*, "We are all frail." One last message from Freud: "it does not even appear certain that without coercion the majority of human individuals would be ready to submit to the labour necessary for acquiring new means of supporting life." The sweat of the brow is as out of fashion as the rational intelligence.

We go at our own hazard. The yielding up of boundaries is always a risk, whether between playing space and spectator space, reality and illusion, theater and life. The yielding up has the apparent advantage of any holism. There is a unitary illusion, but it may be a further illusion, and less valuable than the one which insists, without being slavish to categories, that some distinctions are worth keeping, must even be ferociously kept.

Take just one performance idea that still persists out of the abated turmoil of the sixties: the desire for participation, which is a function of the desire for an extended community, both positive values. "I don't see any middle ground," writes Schechner in his book *Environmental Theater*. "Either the audience is in it or they are out of it. Either there is potential for contact or there is not. I don't deny that the spectator in the orthodox theater feels something. Sure he does. *But he cannot easily, naturally, unconsciously, and without embarrassment express those feelings except within idiotically limited limits*." Aside from the fact that it sometimes encourages idiotically limited feelings, this is a nearsighted view of theater conventions. What is natural and unconscious varies with expectation and mores, and any design of consequence is a responsive evolution. The proscenium theater arrangement does have limits and it has been abused; but it is an available perceptual field, not merely a foolish structure of class consciousness and invidious design. The limits are what is useful, depending on what you're looking for, and how. I have often found behavior at the Performance Garage or other environmental theaters artifical, self-conscious, constrained, improbable, falsely focussed or unfocussed, and lacking the potency of concentrated reflection which one can experience in an orthodox theater, depending on who does what with the convention. For that's what it is, available, site and structure in potential, ready to be seized by an idea. I don't deny the validity of the other experience, but see no primacy in either convention.

Anything is possible in the theater. Anything. Years ago, when I was studying "dramatic art," they said certain things couldn't be done on a stage. All of them are quite doable, like shifting place and time. Still, they were right for the wrong reasons. The power depends not only on what we do, but on what we disallow. The orthodox theater—and I am not recommending that we go back to doing old-fashioned plays, don't get me wrong—accomodates accident in consequential ways. There is a pressure in the medium which demands tribute. It keeps you honest. Open forms—the happening, the multimedia event, things non-matrixed—ordinarily lack that pressure. In approximating, with strangeness, the more random texture of life outside the theater, they want the sense of consequence that life seems to require, and provide, even when it's lost its savor or is, as in darkest Beckett, on the edge of not-existing. When the pressure is not in the recognized conventions of the form, it must be resolutely supplied by the artist. There are of course works that manage this; for instance, Denis Oppenheim's recent multimedia installation at the D'Arc Gallery (January 17-February 21, 1976), where he reconstructs a vision of death as a dream of his 7-year old daughter. A puppet (representing the artist?) lies facedown dangling off the far edge of a large oriental rug, which floats above the floor of a darkened space. There is a knife stuck in its back. A TV monitor on the floor in a corner shows an identical knife, thrown and thrown again into an ambiguous slowly revolving surface. We hear a child's voice. It speaks disjointedly about the knife spinning in her dreams, a carpet travelling through space. She seems to be the lifeline of her father's art, whose limits in the reach toward life are suggested by the edge of the carpet. The child doesn't seem frightened; she seems to find it beautiful. The piece is called *Search for Clues*. It is very intelligently conceived and executed. Our function in the space is controlled. It is organized for perception, though in a sense we participate.

What we usually find, however, in abandoning the performing space to whoever cares to enter, without such control, is that many of those who enter have nothing to say there, little to bring, or so little as not to be worth even their own attention. Very often, insisting that they be expressive, the work doesn't give them a chance. When everyone, of course, is onstage, there is likely to be no consciously seeing eye, no sense of contrast, a diminished capacity for judgment, the tokenism of wholeness without the actuality, since wholeness depends on our classifying powers as well as our willingness to throw over classifications. We lose our sense, when everything is theater gratis, of the right thing in the right place. In fact, we lose our power of choice. It may be a better solution—for all our feeling that all is seeming—to act on the equal and opposite feeling that it isn't so. Or, we can juggle both illusions with discretion: choose the separateness of the stage or its apparent continuity with life, depending on what life depends on—which may be nothing or something or whatever we care to make of the life that gives life in the ambiguities between.

Going over the edge of the carpet or denying the separateness of the stage comes out of the desire to replace the idea of re-enactment with the idea of the spontaneous act, to make things happen in performance not as if for the first time but *for* the first time. The idea is attractive but has the liability which the ethic of immediacy has always had in American life. It makes of every moment either a crisis or a banality. It melodramatizes. It can become psychotic. In the end, by erecting attitudes of great moment around everything, whether of consequence or inconsequence, it tends to trivialize experience. It's not that the notion of immediacy or spontaneity is wrong, only that the structures of immediacy have become too recognizable. We have developed conventions of spontaneity like the tradition of the New. We look for mediation again whenever the immediacies are exhausted. The logic of spontaneity is a function of time.

As we continue to explore the possibilities of new forms, it's important to understand where the life-giving power came from in the old— especially in those which appeared in their time to be breaking down conventions and preparing the ground for us. Yesterday's innovation, in the accelerated pattern of breakthroughs, may not serve us in the same way. It has an unstable half-life in the most atomized sense. But go back a bit further, to Pirandello, say, in the theater: the framed action of a Pirandello drama enables him to ask questions about the reality of be- havior and action *outside* the frame; that is, real questions about real life, if you'll excuse that maybe illusory insistence. He deploys the stage's illu- sion of reality against the world's reality of illusion—the stage world is both real and unreal. It is real *as* theater. In contemporary theater, this corrective insight is often surrendered misguidedly, and the result is an impoverishment of resources, injuring the very instrument of perception. The effort to break the illusory spell of theater by merging event and spectator succeeds, if at all, in substituting a vague and loose-minded theatricality for theater. The reality of both worlds is surrendered without a third world solution. The adage goes: if you're not part of the solution you're part of the problem.

So much of what passes for new kinds of performance gets in its own way. We want to be careful as audacity cares. The theater is after all obscene, always was. The root is the Greek word *skene*. *Ob* means against—so, against the scene. There is in every performance an aggres- sion against the scene of performance as a value, a breakdown of unity, a de-realization (this doesn't and cannot happen at the movies because of the absence of the human presence), the parsing out of the scene into definiteness and categories. In the history of theater itself, the scene invariably tends toward fragmentation, closure, loss of outwardness and a sense of the infinite behind. Perspective was fake infinity. With Racine, in the traditional theater, the scene becomes a hothouse, a suffocating system, narrowed and specious, introverted and private, profound in self-consumption; like appetite, the universal wolf, the scene eats up itself. The scene is cannibalized by realism in time and has to repossess itself in its fullness. The pressure toward a surface makes you wonder what's behind. The scene remains obscene. The obscene submits what should be kept private to public scrutiny. In that act, the value of the private may be reduced. That is the perversity of theater. We can't afford to fool around.

Let me see if I can bring this to some conclusion by perhaps raising some more problems. Those of us in the theater, as opposed to other types of performance, dream of an old exemplary drama. But everytime we look back at what it was, we see the enactment of our humiliations. The divinity that shapes our ends, whether for tragedy or comedy, has a demonic face. There is no way to see it as benevolent. As the greatest dramas know, the worst returns to laughter, the imbecile rupture of disbelief. Victimization is relative. The hero who seems in the old drama to be mastering his destiny is mastered. The slave acts the slave for his master, becoming the image of his own reality. (I am speaking here, too, of the evolution of the actor who was a slave.) The pretense is the form by which he coexists with his oppression. The difference between the reality and the pretense is the measure of credibility; the more credible the pretense the more endurable the reality. Illusion, in this sense, is survival. (The idea is sequestered in every play, but it emerges as the subject matter of *The Wild Duck* or *The Iceman Cometh*.) At least that should be so. But as the pretense exposes the reality—which it does to the extent that it becomes real or credible or true (any of those words we use as standards)—it may become unbearable. The illusion bursts with the truth that feeds it. The actor, therefore, who exceeds his role creates a new illusion for the sake of bearing it—one which redefines the potentiality of the social order itself, though it may destroy (obscenely) the propriety of the theater form. The drama is by nature conservative, which is what disturbed Brecht and caused him to develop the theory of Alienation. His view was that the cadences and apparent inevitabilities of the tragic sustained, for all their imaginative glamour, the grip of the status quo. Brecht recognized that comedy, not content with the way things are, is more corrosive. Laughter requires a subversive distance. But when we fear the worst, we realize, as did Kafka, that no distance is far enough. The form is trapped inside the form.

It is this idea which hangs heavy today over the art of acting and over the very idea of performance, for which theater (as even Cage admits) remains the paradigm. The same curiosities about human nature persist and people still like to see themselves enacted. But it's all in the family, only too familiar, and even if more sophisticated, self-evident. There is also the continued liking of a good story, though new performance modes reject narrative, in part because the real story seems untellable. These are pleasures, however, not be be denied. Yet time in the theater is dreary for some of us, perhaps out of vanity. Perhaps we only think we've seen it all before. Behavior is the problem; for the purposes of art it seems exhausted. Mostly, we *have* seen it, because since the Renaissance so much of life-as-we-know-it has gotten around, first in art, then in the media. Where the stress isn't on behavior now, it is usually so artless or formalistic, as in Wilson and Foreman, so engineered—even if improvised · however exquisitely—that it doesn't satisfy our sense of the actor's potentiality. The actor also doesn't like settling for being a function, a manipulable cybernetic bit of a conception (so, too, in the New Dance) fed in on the computer card. But potentiality for what? The secret is still in the creating of that which was not there before being made present in the actor's body. It has to do with the summoning up of powers, and this may still require the breaking of taboos—as Chris Burden does in body art when he has himself shot or crucified on a Volkswagen. We can understand the urgency to extremes. But it also depends, as Burden's self-victimizing events do, on a frank acceptance of the conventions being used—in the theater, the clear realization that a play is another and nether-reality. As Theseus says of the play put on by the artisans in *Midsummer Night's Dream*: "The best in this kind are but shadows; and the worst are no worse, if the imagination amend them." The actor is, to use another term from Stevens, a figure of capable imagination. Everywhere, there is the unceasing slough of brutish fact, the stink of mortality. In performance, that's the undeniable center of gravity. It's the imagining that lifts the weight. The actor says: I refuse the banality I know I am.

We act according to nature. The aim is to separate the liberation of what one is (the desire for) from the determination to be what one can never be, even with the purest returned will. We deal with the ingrained, which is no simple determinism. What is basic, we hear, is that we are genetically coded, with inimitable fingerprints. There are all kinds of performance but, like the faded score for the dance inscribed like a mandala on the floor of the Theater at Epidaurus, that's Destiny; the illusion which is our future.

REFERENCES

Jacques Ellul, *The Political Illusion* (New York: Alfred A. Knopf, 1967), p. 116.

Allan Kaprow, "Non-Theatrical Performance," *Artforum*, XIV, 9 (May 1976), 45-51 *passim*.

Judith Malina and Julian Beck, *Paradise Now* (New York: Vintage Books, 1971).

Victor Turner, *Dramas, Fields, and Metaphors* (Ithaca: Cornell University Press, 1974), p. 56.

Vito Acconci, quoted in Max Kozloff, "Pygmalion Reversed," *Artforum*, XIV, 3 (November 1975), p. 35.

Sigmund Freud, "The Future of an Illusion," *The Standard Edition of the Psychological Works*, Vol. XXI, pp. 5-56 *passim*.

Wallace Stevens, *The Palm at the End of the Mind*, ed. by Holly Stevens (New York: Vintage Books, 1972), p. 206. A prose statement on "The Poetry of War."

Richard Schechner, *Environmental Theater* (New York: Hawthorn Books, 1973), p. 37

Performance as News:
Notes on an Intermedia Guerrilla Art Group

CHERYL BERNSTEIN

That the Symbionese Liberation Army until now has been undetected as a performance group is largely due to the somewhat overcharged rhetoric of their overt content as well as their deliberate avoidance of any recognizable art context in which their work might be framed. These notes are offered as a preliminary attempt to understand the significance of their work and its relationship to performance as it has been evolving over the last decade or so.

In an art-historical sense, the first segment of their long, still unfinished piece, the food sequence, was singularly retrospective, stressing the group's roots in vanguard tradition. On the formal level, it looked like just one more of the many "proposal" pieces of the late 60's and early 70's; but, typically for the SLA, this proposal both commented on and refuted the then-popular proposal form. The difference lay not only in the fact that this proposal was realized (the distribution of food), but also in the essential concept that without an active audience, the work could not be considered complete. Utilizing extremely simple, but effective, materials (a tape recorder and half of a driver's license), the piece not only mobilized the entire San Francisco Police Department, millions of Hearst dollars, several charity organizations, food wholesalers and, of course, scores of the needy, it also set into motion the whole of the communications industry. I will return to their choice of the news as their exclusive artistic medium, but for the moment, I want to focus on the very peculiar kind of risk they undertook at the outset of their work—a risk that set the aesthetic and art-historical terms in which the group would henceforth operate.

In performance art, the artist is more exposed than ever before. The literal identification of artistic risk with the act of risking one's body or one's civil rights has become familiar lately in the work of such artists as Chris Burden, Rudolf Schwarzkogler, Tony Schafrazi and Jean Toche.[1] Of course, much earlier Marcel Duchamp risked—if not his life and freedom—the disclosure of his artistic intentions in a series of (usually incomplete or failed) endeavors that looked more like business ventures than art activities. The appearance of the SLA as a guerrilla political group both adopted the Duchampian gesture and escalated it—and in so doing directly addressed the still unresolved issue of art *vs.* non-art that has preoccupied the art world since the late 50's.

Among the most lucid expositions of the paradox of non-art, Allan Kaprow's well-known 1971 essay, "The Education of the Un-Artist," undoubtedly contributed to the atmosphere in which the SLA piece was conceived. In that essay, Kaprow examines the strategies of artists who seek to liberate themselves from the institutionalized art world. These are the artists who, some or all of the time, "operate outside the pale of the art establishment, that is, in their heads or in the daily or natural domain."[2] Such are the "earthworkers," "Happeners," and Conceptual artists. However, these "non-artists" always report their activities to the art establishment, which duly records them in its art pages. Thus, while they work outside the galleries or museums, they operate completely within the art world in the social sense. Without recognition from that world, their acts have no meaning. In this, they are as dependent on the established art context as were the Dadaists, who never left it in the first place.

To this tradition, Kaprow opposes the notion of the un-artist. Unlike the non-artists, un-artists would be socially invisible *as artists*. They would "give up all references to being artists of any kind what ever,"[3] would outwardly adopt other professions, and would utilize television and other media. Un-artists would still be vanguard artists, but by disguising rather than declaring their esthetic intentions, they would transcend the paradox of older non-art. Anyone familiar with the SLA piece must concede its debt to Kaprow's ideas, but the brilliant tactics of this intermedia guerrilla group and its refinement of the issues Kaprow raises (not to mention its solution to the problem of avoiding detection as an art group) places it squarely in the ambiance of the post-60's. Nevertheless, and not withstanding Kaprow's terms, the essential point of reference here is still the Duchampian mode and the dialectics of art and non-art.

One of the most successful aspects of the SLA piece is its ability to be read as a completely autonomous event unrelated to any kind of art, complete with a politically self-explanatory intent. At the same time, its overt content functions as a unifying metaphor that resolves itself as a negation of political action—perhaps the only way that art can define its limits and maintain its identity in modern, bourgeois society. It is significant that the SLA chose the guise of a militant political group at the very moment when such militancy was demodé, ripe for un-artistic appropriation. The strategy here recalls early Pop art, whose iconography of cheap ads and comic book graphics was equally antithetical to serious art. And just as the Pop artists utilized these highly rhetorical forms in a way that contradicted their original purpose, the apparent content of the SLA piece functions as a self-subverting mask that signifies something other than its overt intent. The resultant negation, a classic vanguardist strategy long before Pop, points to the central meaning of modernist art, which aims inexorably at its own self-transcendence: the abolition of art. And like so much avant-garde art of recent years, the SLA evokes in order to liquidate the idea of art as communication. But the SLA's art practice goes beyond these other forms of vanguardism in its commitment to a self-imposed dichotomic model of perception that systematically develops the dissonant as both a necessity and reality.

The paradox is made evident not only by the un-art disguise, but—less transparently—by the multiple references and anticipations of recent avant-garde art.[4] The video segment (the bank robbery), which used the concept of planned chance (the "given" installation of the bank cameras), is perhaps the most obvious. The fire sequence, which, in Los Angeles, pre-empted national network news broadcasts, critically commented on the work of Chris Burden, Vito Acconci and other performance and body artists who engage in physical risk or "operate" on their own bodies[5] (Patty Hearst's prison operation also belongs in this category). Also noteworthy is the narrative element of the piece—the metaphor of the artist as fugitive and then prisoner is especially wry; and the theme of metamorphosis (the Duchampian disguises and false names) is pointedly apt. More subtle is the open-ended structure on which the narrative is hung. At this writing, it is still viable—Patty is still "news" and the legal fate of those accused of harboring the fugitive artists in Pennsylvania is still unresolved.

The use of the press as a means of distribution for art also has precedents in vanguard art. Joseph Kosuth made extensive use of the ad form, renting space in the non-art as well as the art press. The SLA, however, reversed the relationship between the advertisement and the news item by becoming the news. The group thereby avoided the expense of advertising and at the same time made their work available to a vast audience, even "framing" it on the home TV screen. The strategy not only utilized television as a closed feed-back system, it also drew large numbers of people into the work as active participants. Indeed, the ongoing process initiated by the group involved not only Justice Department officials and law-enforcement agents, but numerous private citizens, most notably the hostages and the many "witnesses" who testified on television concerning the whereabouts of Patty Hearst and the Harrises during the flight sequence.

Another facet of the piece in which the SLA's particular style is revealed with special clarity is the FBI "wanted" poster. The self-conscious reference here of course is to Douglas Huebler's well-known *Duration Piece No. 15, 1969.*[6] That work consisted of an FBI "wanted" poster to which the artist attached a signed statement guaranteeing to pay a reward for information leading to the arrest of the suspect (the amount of the reward dwindled month by month, reaching zero in a year). Typically, the SLA both simplified its model and clarified its implications. Huebler carefully kept his identity distinct from that of the suspect (who, not incidentally, was wanted for armed bank robbery and worked sometimes as an artist). The SLA version, by suppressing the separate identity of the artist and firmly tying it to that of the suspect, literally enacts what, in the Huebler work, is barely a suggestion (the artist-as-outlaw theme). At the same time, the FBI is slyly engaged in the process of documenting the piece, which bears only one signature—that of FBI Director Clarence Kelly.

The choice of the news as artistic form deserves closer scrutiny. On one level, the whole nation becomes art consumer; but more importantly, by accepting the news spectacle as it finally appears, the group could avoid the deceptive distortions that arise when the actuality of the work differs from its recorded form. Since the news itself is identical with the work, that is, since the SLA does not exist except as news, this distortion was impossible. Moreover, the multiplicity of news agents active as reporters insured the piece the shifting values and impermanent ground characteristic of performance art. The video segment, for example, recorded by the "found" or "readymade" feedback installation system of the bank, is actually a series of stills; but aired on national TV, it took on the classic look of grainy vanguard video. The point here is that without the news, this segment would have remained incomplete. Consistent with the overall strategy of the group, however, is the fact that while the press became an unknowing collaborator with the avant-garde, the SLA itself did not compromise its work by disclosing its identity as an art group.

Unlike other performance and conceptual artists who stress the abstract perceptual structures of their work by avoiding an "interesting" look, the SLA overlaid and disguised its commitment to abstraction with dramatic and moving information that partly obscured it. In the excitement of the FBI search, it was easy to miss the complex unfolding time-space structures that constitute the substance of the work. The widening geographic configuration of the piece became perceptible in the tracings inscribed on the map by mobile FBI agents, here transformed, in the spirit of Duchamp, into covert agents of art—in a sense, double agents. But the most brilliant stroke of all was the decision to make the funding of the work an integral part of it: the piece largely financed itself through the bank sequence and the ransom, the latter a kind of parody of the conventional grant that funds so much of today's performance art.

More than any other feature of the work, however, the use of the news media as framing underscores the issue that the work as a whole dramatizes: the inability of modern art to signify its given content as truth. By adopting a set of political ideals that are transparently incredible, the

SLA negated the idea that art can communicate life ideals at all. This becomes clear as the piece unfolds its meaning. To understand its deeper, formal significance, the viewer must first recognize that the group's apparent political identity is a camouflage. This recognition also involves a negation—a mental act of destruction (clarified by the fire sequence) in which the camouflage is stripped away—burned off, as it were. It constitutes the central dialectical moment of the piece as a whole, whose underlying time-space configurations triumph and emerge into full view only after having consumed the manifest political subject matter. Thus, art appears as a transcendence and dialectical resolution of political aspirations, and it attains its most absolute value only when we have fully recognized the futility of political action. Indeed, at that point, the point where we now find ourselves, political action itself can be no more than art performance. The many references to advanced art with which the SLA laced their work frankly avow what Roland Barthes has identified as the central paradox in the literary world: "In spite of the efforts made in our time, it has proved impossible successfully to liquidate literature entirely."[7] Indeed, the advanced consciousness and creative disobedience of the SLA points not to the liberation of art from this impasse, but to the problematic existence of art itself in the modern world.

[1] Chris Burden regularly endangers himself physically and legally (see Robert Horvitz, "Chris Burden," *Artforum*, May, 1976, 24-31). Schwarzkogler is the German performance artist best remembered for his last piece in which he mutilated himself sexually and, within hours, died from the wound. Schafrazi is the artist who defaced Picasso's *Guernica*. The artist Toche was arrested in March, 1974, by the FBI after he publicly acclaimed Schafrazi's act as a "conceptual art work" and called for the kidnapping of (unnamed) members of the museum establishment. The FBI acted on a complaint of Douglas Dillon, President of the Metropolitan Museum of Art (see *Artforum*, November, 1976, p. 8 [letters]).

[2] Allan Kaprow, "The Education of the Un-Artist, Part I," *Art News*, February, 1971, 28.

[3] *Loc. cit.*, 30.

[4] It is a little-known fact that Patty Hearst was an art history major at Berkeley at the time the SLA piece was begun.

[5] Max Kozloff, "Pygmalion Reversed," *Artforum*, November, 1975, 30-37.

[6] Reproduced in Ursula Meyer, *Conceptual Art*, New York, 1972, 138-39.

[7] Roland Barthes, *Writing Degree Zero and Elements of Semiology*, Boston, 1970, xxi-xxii.

III
Soundings

The Unconscious as Mise-en-scène

JEAN-FRANÇOIS LYOTARD

First of all, I should make clear what I mean by the word "mise-en-scène." "Mettre en scène" (to stage) is to transmit signifiers from a "primary" space to another space, which is the auditorium of a theater, cinema, or any related art. I offer a classic example: one evening, at the Paris Opera, we are listening to *Der Rosenkavalier*, by Richard Strauss. This is a "performance"; of what is it made? Singer-actors on stage, musicians in the orchestra pit, stage-hands and light crew in the wings, all are following a large number of prescriptions. Some of these are inscribed in certain documents: the libretto by Hoffmanstahl, the score by Richard Strauss. Others can be solely oral, from the director Rudolf Steinbock—as in stage directions for the actors or directions for the lighting and scenery. This simplified example enables us to distinguish three different phases of the staged work.

The final phase is the performance we are attending. It consists of a group of stimuli—colors, movements, light, sounds. This ensemble which besieges our sensory body "tells" it a story—in this example, the story of *Der Rosenkavalier*. The performance steers us along a course composed of a series of audible intensities, timbres, and pitches; of sentences and words arranged according to expert rhetoric; and of colors, intensities of light, etc.

The initial phase of the work (but is it a work at this point?) is characterized by the heterogeneity of the arts which will be used to put the performance together: a written drama, a musical score, the design of the stage and auditorium, the machinery at the disposal of the theater, etc. We have here groups of signifiers forming so many messages, or constraints in any case, belonging to different systems: the rules of the German (or better, Austrian) language, the rules of the prevalent rhetoric, and those prevailing in Hoffmanstahl's writing on the one hand; and on the other hand, the constraints of musical composition and Strauss' own relation to those constraints, etc.; nevertheless, even in this initial phase, there is something which limits the disorder that could result from such a heterogeneity—this is the single reference imposed on all the messages which make up the work: the story of *Der Rosenkavalier* itself.

87

But what is this story itself, this reference, if not an effect of reality produced by a certain combination of various signifiers contributed by the different arts? It is the very function of this kind of mise-en-scène to create this effect of reality, the story, to make it the apparent motive of the work. The mise-en-scène cannot succeed unless a great number of new decisions are made, decisions not prescribed by the writer, the musician, or the designer; the mise-en-scène must specify the execution of such and such a narrative sequence in the finest detail, and that implies the detailed coordination of the orchestra's actions and those of the singer-actors, together with the lighting effects controlled by the light crew.

The intervention of the director is thus no less creative than that of the poet or the musician; but it is not on the same level as theirs. The director's intervention is a subsequent elaboration of their product. In this sense, the mise-en-scène is subordinate to the noble arts of drama, music, etc. But inversely, the mise-en-scène takes hold of the text, the score, and the architectural space and it "gives life," as they say, to these signifiers. "Give life" means two things: 1) the mise-en-scène turns written signifiers into speech, song, and movements executed by bodies capable of moving, singing and speaking; and this transcription is intended for other living bodies—the spectators—capable of being moved by these songs, movements, and words. It is this transcribing on and for bodies, considered as multi-sensory potentialities, which is the work characteristic of the mise-en-scène. Its elementary unity is polyesthetic like the human body: capacity to see, to hear, to touch, to move. . . . The idea of performance (in French: la représentation de ce soir, this evening's performance) even if it remains vague, seems linked to the idea of inscription on the body.

I might add that I would find the same essential characteristics were I to analyze the function of mise-en-scène in films, at least in the great Hollywood productions of the thirties. If I have taken my example from the operas of Richard Strauss, it is only to remain in the cultural context which was Freud's. The important thing in this context is that mise-en-scene consists of a complex group of operations, each of which transcribes a message written in a given sign system (literary writing, musical notation) and turns it into a message capable of being inscribed on human bodies and transmitted by those to other bodies: a kind of somatography. Even more important, and less dependent on the classic context, is the simple fact of transcription—that is, the fact of a change in the space of inscription—call it a diagraphy, which henceforth will be the main characteristic of mise-en-scène.

Psychoanalysis is first of all an interpretative method. In any interpretative method there is the presupposition that the data to be interpreted simultaneously display and conceal a primary message which the interpreter should be able to read clearly. The interpreter unravels what the director has put together. In several studies, *The Interpretation of Dreams* (*Die Traumdeutung*) in particular, "A Contribution to the Study of the Origins of Sexual Perversions," and at the end of the analysis of Schreber's paranoia, Freud ventures to put forward the single or various possible readings of the messages hidden in symptoms such as paranoid delusion, fantasies, and dreams. We know that for Freud desire is what gives utterance to these primary messages, whereas the unconscious is their director and gives them a disguise in order to exhibit them on the stage. The accent is on deception. In colloquial French one says to a hypocrite: "arrête ton cinéma, cut the act."

This presupposition raises a difficulty, both theoretical and technical, which comes straight from the preceding notion of mise-en-scène. If it is true that symptoms, obscure as they are, result from the mise-en-scène of transparent libidinal messages, their interpretation then requires operations closer to deciphering than translation. For translation consists, at least in principle, in transcribing linguistic signifiers into other linguistic signifiers, while referring to a signified supposedly independent of the two languages. But when we trace the symptomatic "performance" back to the elements which, in principle, constitute its primary phase, we must shift from one register of inscription (the register of somatic symptoms in the case of conversion hysteria, for example) to an entirely different register (in the example, the register in which the desire of the patient is supposed to "speak"), that is, a linguistic register which is clearly intelligible. This transcription encounters at least two difficulties: 1) when we say that desire "speaks," are we using metaphor to say that desire is not nonsense? If so, it does not follow that the meaning of its expressions (the symptoms) is of a linguistic nature. If not, that is, if desire really speaks a language, then we must elaborate its grammar and vocabulary, which brings us to the second difficulty: 2) the operations that permit one to deduce the primary message from its performance do not seem to be rule-governed, as Freud himself acknowledges. The transcription of a libidinal message into symptoms seems to be achieved through irregular, unexpected devices. We may say, and Freud himself says, that the unconscious uses all means, including the most crudely fashioned puns, to stage desire. That seems likely to cut short interpretation, properly speaking.

Let us consider the case of dreams. Freud clearly distinguishes the three phases of representation we described for mise-en-scène. Dream-thoughts (*Traumgedanke*) constitute the primary data (the libretto, the score) which are supposed to be perfectly legible. Freud calls the "performance" dreamcontent (*Trauminhalt*), that is, the narrative told by the patient on the stage of the analyst's couch. The dreamwork (die *Traumarbeit*), which turns dreamthoughts into dreamcontent, is the equivalent of mise-en-scène. According to Freud, this mise-en-scène works by means of a set of four operators: condensation, displacement, the taking into consideration of suitability for plastic representation, and secondary revision. It may be that these are universal operators for mise-en-scene. But it is certain that contrary to the hypotheses of Jacobson and Lacan they are not linguistic operators (especially those a translator would use). Even if for certain ones (condensation and displacement) we can find equivalents in language, we would not find them on the supposedly primary level of enunciation but on the very complex level of rhetorical or stylistic formulation, as Benveniste has shown. Yet that level already implies a certain mise-en-scene in the writer's or speaker's practice. Actually, these "levels" exist only in the fiction of structuralists: the most simple utterance carries with it a primitive rhetoric. Its being uttered, its arrangement have already made it a diminutive stage.

Still another observation on the way in which Freud, from the outset, formulates interpretation. The two basic ideas of mise-en-scène and interpretation are like the recto and verso of the same principle, which is a principle of distrust. In the presence of a dream or a symptom, in the presence of data in general, one decides to be wary: This datum, one thinks, does not say what it says; it is deceptive. This is the principle that Nietzsche identified perfectly as at the origin of the desire of knowledge. One must not be deceived just as in ethics one must not deceive. According to this principle, mise-en-scène is only the implementation of deception which in return gives rise to the counter-effect of truth on the part of the interpreter, the search for causes and errors, the correction of the data. Yet we can ask, along with Nietzsche, why is it better not to be deceived than to be deceived? And above all: aren't we surely deceived by our heeding only distrust?

Die Traumdeutung was completed in 1899. Twenty years later in 1919, Freud published the analysis of a fantasy called "A Child is Being Beaten." We are interested in this text for two reasons. At that time, Freud had completely revised his first typography of the psychic apparatus and was revising his libido theory (theory of instincts). It was in 1920 in *Beyond the Pleasure Principle* that he worked out the theory of death-instincts and the theory of general repetition.

We are dealing with a much more sophisticated hypothesis about the messages of desire than the one developed in *The Interpretation of Dreams*. Moreover, the analysis of "A Child is Being Beaten" is conducted in such a systematic way as to provide a veritably microscopic dissection of the unconscious as stage director.

It is a fantasy very common with women. Its appearance coincides with masturbation; and acknowledgement of the fantasy is made difficult by a strong feeling of shame. The fantasy consists in a kind of scene or tableau vivant where the patient, placed in the position of spectator, sees an adult authority figure (a school-master, a teacher) flogging some young boys. With the help of his patients' recollections, Freud "discovers" that this scene hides another one, which he sums up with the sentence: "The father is beating the child (that I hate)." This first phase constitutes the primary message, whereas the scene: "A child is being beaten" is similar to the final performance. In between there is the mise-en-scène.

But it is not as simple as this. Between the first and the last phase, Freud says, it is necessary to postulate an intermediate phase which he calls: "my father is beating me." Phase no. 2 is not related to any recollections mentioned by the patients. It results from a construction (*Konstruction*) built by the analyst. In brief, the whole process is *not* achieved in two steps but three steps to be enumerated in the following "chronological" order: 1) the father is beating the child that I hate; 2) my father is beating me; 3) a child is being beaten.

It is impossible here to examine in detail all the transformations that succeed one another from the first phase of the fantasy to the last one. I will limit myself to two observations.

First, Freud disassociates the different components of the scene for each phase, just as we disassociated the components of the mise-en-scène that were music, libretto, lighting, etc. I mean that from one phase to the other, each component is dealt with in a specific way. He writes: "Beating-phantasies have an historical development which is by no means simple, and in the course of which they are changed in most respects more than once—as regards their relation to the author of the phantasy, and as regards their object, their content, and their significance." (*Collected Papers*, II, p. 178) When Freud speaks of the *relation* of the fantasy to the patient, he refers to her position in relation to the stage: Is she on the stage or in the audience? She is a spectator in the first phase, and she seems to be so in the third; but she is an actress in the second: it is then *she* who is the child that is beaten. With the word *content* Freud refers to the clinical manifestation in which the fantasy is one symptom among others (as Jean Nassif says): phase no. 3 seems to be sadistic, like phase no. 1, and phase no. 2 masochistic. The *object* is the sex of the victim: either a boy or a girl in phase no. 1; always boys in the last phase, but in the intermediate phase, it is the patient herself as a little girl. And with *significance* Freud refers to the value in terms of affect of the act of beating: Is a person flogged through love or hatred? If my father beats the child that I—his daughter—hate, then he loves me. But if, as in phase no. 2, my father beats me, it is to punish me because he hates the incestuous love I feel for him. In the third phase the masochistic component is maintained, but enveloped in sadism: The value of the final scene in terms of affect is ambivalence.

We see that we need a great number of operations, each of them working on a particular component in phases 1 and 2, in order to arrive at the result of the final performance. And in this sense, Freud's analysis is an important contribution to the understanding of mise-en-scène, at least in the still traditional form we defined in the example of Richard Strauss. We also realize that these operations are entirely misleading. For instance, from "the father is beating the child that I hate" to "my father is beating me," it is necessary that the patient, who was a spectator, become an actress, that the love of the father be turned into hatred, that the hatred for the other child be changed into the hatred the little girl feels for herself, that the initial jealousy, which perhaps is not even sexualized, be replaced by a drive with a strongly anal component, that the sex of the victim be changed (from male to female), along with the position of the patient in relation to the stage. Likewise, to get from sentence no. 1 to sentence no. 3 requires linguistic transformations: the active voice in "The father is beating the child" becomes the passive voice in "A child is being beaten," the determinant *the* in *the child* is turned into *a*, and the part of the father is finally deleted.

After *The Interpretation of Dreams*, Freud elaborated a great number of these operations, particularly in the various studies which make up the *Metapsychology* published in 1914.

It is these operations which we find explicitly or not in the transformations undergone by the tableau of the fantasy "A Child is Being Beaten." Since these operations are, according to Freud, characteristic of the unconscious, it is indeed the unconscious that stages the discourse of the young girl's desire and this mise-en-scène, far from being a translation, would be the transcription of a pictorial text of virtual bodies, with effect on the real body of the spectator (masturbation). Somatography requires both the exhibition and the concealment of the initial message.

The time has come to make a second observation on the nature of mise-en-scène in this text of Freud's compared to what it was in *The Interpretation of Dreams*. Are we able to speak here of fantasythoughts as Freud, in 1900, spoke of dreamthoughts? Can we identify a primary message of equally primary signification underneath the fantasmatic performance—something akin to the wish: that my father love me? Certainly not. What stands in the way is the considerably greater importance which Freud attached to the dynamics and the economy of drives. In 1900, dreamthoughts could be rather simply formulated because the conception of the desire which gave them utterance was itself rather simple: this desire was more a wish, *ein Wunsch*, than a force. The distinction could be made rather clearly between what desire "said," even secretly, and what the unconscious mise-en-scène made it say in the dream's manifest content. But in our text of 1919, it's an entirely different matter: not only are these operations of mise-en-scène much more complex than the four operations described in *The Interpretation of Dreams*, but desire is no longer conceived of as a wish, but as a bloc of forces, in the sense of a dynamics. These forces are called instincts, or better, drives. They are characterized by their impetus or by their aim (to love or hate, for example), by their object, that is, by whatever elements these forces lay siege to or invest. But drives are never observable in themselves; they are always represented and by three kinds of representatives: words, images, and affects.

I will not develop here the question of representing drives on the symptom-stage. The important point is that drives themselves can undergo genuine metamorphoses. Freud lists four of them in "Drives and their Vicissitudes" (1915): 1) reversal into its opposite (love is transformed into hate, for example); 2) the turning round upon the subject's own self (for example, the love for a person who has passed away is transformed into love for oneself through griefwork; or sadism is transformed into masochism); 3) repression, and finally 4) sublimation; these last two further affecting the outcome of metamorphoses of drive-representatives.

In the case of the beaten child fantasy, we have seen that what separates phase one and phase two, for example, is not only stagework involving representatives, it is also and above all a working which affects the objects and aims of the drives themselves: the change from sadism to masochism implies the reversal of active pleasure into its opposite, passive pleasure, and the turning round of the initial object of the drives (the other child) upon the subject of the patient. Therefore it is not the director's interpretation of the libretto and the score which is modified, it is the libretto and score themselves which have changed between the two phases to the point of expressing the opposite of what they were "saying." A second, entirely different mode of desire has annexed itself to the primary mode.

Will we be able to say that this second phase of the fantasy represents the first phase? That the girl's masochism is a mise-en-scène on her initial sadism? We would have to suppose that the messages of desire are not elementary but that they are already performances and that they have been worked at by a kind of pre-mise-en-scène. But this pre-mise-en-scène would then deal with nothing but the "drive-text," if we can still go on speaking thusly, and it would be much more archaic than the mise-en-scène we have spoken of up until now, which was concerned only with drive-representatives. Finally, it would be necessary to explain why, in order to be represented, the initial sadism must be transformed into masochism.

Sometimes Freud lets himself be carried away by this vertigo of representation and causality which keeps endlessly multiplying mise-en-scène, changing representeds into representatives of other representeds.

However, the properties which Freud acknowledges in the drive-processes prohibit our following him along this line. They indicate the opposite direction. In numerous texts, Freud insists on the fact that the logical, spatial, and temporal properties of the "primary processes," which are the metamorphoses of drives, do not fit into the categories of rational thought. From our perspective, this means that primary messages, subsequently staged by a set of transcriptions, do not "speak" at all. I will give only one example of these texts; it concerns the temporality of drives and it can be applied perfectly to the case of the beaten child fantasy. It is a passage from the 1915 article "Drives and their Vicissitudes":

> We may split up the life of each drive into a series of "thrusts" distinct from one another in the time of their occurrence but each homogenous within its own period, whose relation to one another is comparable to that of successive eruptions of lava. We can then perhaps picture to ourselves that the earliest and most primitive drive-eruption persists in an unchanged form and undergoes no development at all. The next "thrust" would then from the outset have undergone a change of form, being turned, for instance, from active to passive, and it would then, with this new characteristic, be superimposed upon the earlier layer, and so on. So that, if we take a survey of the tendency of drives from its beginning up to any given stopping-point, the succession of "thrusts" which we have described would present the picture of a definite development of the drive.
>
> The fact that, at that later period of development, the drive in its primary form may be observed side by side with its (passive) opposite deserves to be distinguished by the highly appropriate name introduced by Bleuler: *ambivalence*.

This text, as well as those works of Freud that echo it, is of great importance for our problem. A drive-siege never lets up; the opposite or inverse investment which accompanies it does not suppress the first, does not even conceal it, but sets itself up next to it. All investments are, in this way, contemporaneous with each other: one loves and hates the same object at the same time and in the same respect, which is contrary to the rules of intelligibility and chronology.

If such are the space, time and logic of drives, then the desire of the woman who fantasizes the beaten child is not a clear message; it is composed of three drive-investments that 1) are logically incompossible, 2) are simultaneous, and 3) concern the same regions of the body. Therefore we must not say that the unconscious stages the message of desire. We must at least say that desire is not a legible text, and that it need not be given a disguise by a mise-en-scène in order to be represented, since it eludes interpretation on its own, due to its dischronisms, its polytopisms, and its paralogisms.

If we follow this direction which Freud indicates here and there starting in 1920, it is thus the distinction between the discourse of desire and its being disguised by the mise-en-scène of the unconscious which tends to become inoperative. For that reason, the idea of mise-en-scène tends both to expand itself inordinately and to overextend itself to the point of vanishing. And it is in this way that it becomes congruent with the theatrical, critical, artistic, and perhaps political inquiries which make up what Ihab Hassan calls "post-modernism" and which Freud's explicit and implicit esthetics resolutely ignores.

In conclusion, to illustrate this orientation, I shall use the example of an already classic work from the visual arts Underground which permits a good approach to the problem of mise-en-scène in a contemporary context. My goal in choosing this work is to make clear *a contrario* just how much the Freudian conception of the unconscious and even desire depends on a particular esthetic, that of official late nineteenth century Viennese theater and opera. If we are attentive to what is going on now, notably in the most audacious inquiries in the most recent arts, and if we bring their lessons back to Freud's discourse, not only will it seem necessary to diminish the import of his discourse but we will also better understand what are the stakes of "post-modernism" as a whole. What is at stake is not to exhibit truth within the closure of representation but to set up *perspectives* within the return of the *will*.

La *Région Centrale* is a "film" by Michael Snow, shot in Canada in 1970-71. A special device designed by the film-maker allows the axis of the camera to be positioned in all possible directions around the point where the camera is connected to the device. This device is itself attached to a mobile shaft which can also turn in every direction around a swivel joint attached to the body of the apparatus. Finally, this apparatus is fixed to the ground. The lense can thus scan every plane passing through all the points of the sphere of the shaft's movements. Because camera and shaft rotate independently of each other, the final speed resulting from their velocities can vary. The setting of the focal distance is synchronized with the motion of the lense so that the images are always legible. The apparent velocity of transition from one image to another varies with the distance of the objects. The apparatus is placed on an elevated platform which overlooks a forest skyline and a landscape with lakes on one side, but on the other side the view is limited by a rocky ridge. The zenith and the nearest patch of ground, including the base of the apparatus, appear in the shot for the same reason as do all the horizontal planes.

The film is presented as a series of continuous sequences. Each one is accorded a unit of velocity and a unit of greater complexity due to the distinctness of the respective movements of camera and shaft. The scanning thus proposed by Michael Snow lasts about three hours in all. The spectator's gaze is carried along supple and irregular trajectories explored by the lense and carried away on a both infinite and bounded voyage that opens up every perspective on sky and ground to the gaze. Not only do the angles and distances change continually but also the light and color. No sounds assist in interpreting the images, with the exception of a weak signal which indicates changes in the program of the apparatus' movements.

It would take too long to examine the work Michael Snow has done on each of the parameters of traditional cinematographic representation. May three remarks be sufficient:

1) The stage, in its usual sense, supposes a stage-frame, a picture frame, an image-frame, that demarcates three regions with its edge: the unreal space, Freud would say fantasmatic or oneiric, where the action takes place; the real space where the spectators are; and the hidden space where the theater machinery is concealed. Because of this framing, this kind of mise-en-scène implies a complementary unframing. Michael Snow's apparatus eliminates framing: he lets us see what traditional framing excludes from the shot, including the machinery itself. And owing to the fact that he dispenses with the wings, the orchestra pit, and the idea of a meaning hidden underneath appearances, he abandons the principle of distrust.

The device which produces *La Région Centrale* belongs to a paradoxical logic related to that of the sophists and Nietzsche: there is nothing but perspectives; one can invent new ones. The statement that there are only perspectives includes itself among them, just as Snow's camera aims itself at its own base. With such a logic, the function of language is no longer to signify a given object, and the function of the image is no longer to deceive by means of false recognition. Language is not made for telling the truth and film is not made to disguise truth on a fantasmatic stage. Both are inexhaustible means for experimenting with new effects, never seen, never heard before. They create their own reference, therefore their object is not identifiable; they create their own addressee, a disconcerted body, invited to stretch its sensory capacities beyond measure.

2) The closure of the movements of Snow's camera results in all the images' referring to a same space, but the infinite variety of scannings results in their all being different. There we have the visual equivalent of the Freudian metaphor of drive-eruptions: many different figures, a closeup of a pebble, a lake on the horizon, a cloud, are all packed into the same region by the camera.

This region is central because all the figures smash themselves on Snow's film due to the coagulent, contripetal, materialist force of the lense's journey. But the bloc of figures thus stockpiled remains without stable identity, and that is due to the fact that the images are not actually taken from a fixed center but by a lense whose very complex movement results from the composition of two movements, those of the camera and shaft. The accumulation of figures on the film succeeds in not constituting any identifiable geometric space, such as a stage should be so that a story may be enacted there. The center of the region is a labyrinth.

3) The time of *La Région Centrale* breaks with that of narration: the film doesn't tell any story. Not only is there no action rolling along, but any unrolling of images is at the same time their being rolled around each other because of the closure of the lense's movements. Or else, but it is still the same thing, the film tells all the tales born of all the images it shows. At every moment, the spectator has the possibility of isolating a single view and of using it to start telling a story about skylines or forests, or the stuff of the earth, or the clouds in the sky, etc.; all of these budding stories form an immense chatter in which we find all times mixed together (for example, astronomical, geological, and technological time). Here again, whether the accent is placed on the atemporality of the film or on the multitemporality of these stories, we encounter an equivalent of the dischronisms of Freud's primary processes, and we understand why Michael Snow preferred the weak and, properly speaking, drive-like sound which gives a rhythm to the movements of the apparatus, to any utterance, no matter how bizarre.

Can we say that mise-en-scène has disappeared from such a spectacle? The mise-en-scène by a Rudolf Steinbock or a libretto by Hoffmanstahl and a score by Richard Strauss—yes (if at least we ignore the frame of the movie screen). But not mise-en-scène as somatography, and not as diagraphy either. For nothing prevents us from saying that here the camera is the interpreter of a text, namely, the program which Snow fed into his machine and whose written signifiers the machine transforms into movements and into emotions on the spectators' bodies.

Are Snow's instructions analogous to the discourse of desire and are the machine's operations analogous to the mise-en-scène of desire by the unconscious? This could be stretching the analogy a bit. Snow's filming machine cannot be compared to Freud's machine of the unconscious unless we underline the strange character of the operations they perform, one on drive-material, the other on visual material. And if we can say that Snow's program of movements is a result of desire, it would be on the condition of understanding desire not as a set of instructions promoted by some love- or hate-wish but as the will to create realities. This double restriction is sufficient to displace the problematic of the unconscious and mise-en-scène from Freud to Nietzsche and beyond.

When the force used to stage something has no goal other than to make manifest its potentiality, when it is the same force that produces and implements the most sophisticated programs and machines, the distinction between desire and the unconscious disappears entirely. By the same token, works must not be taken as symptoms symbolically expressing a concealed discourse, but as attempts to state perspectives of reality. Interpretation must in turn give way to descriptions of devices. As for these descriptions, they are no less prescriptive in nature than works; they continue and eventually reroute the perspective-creating potentialities these works contain. Inversely, the time has come to consider the would-be symptoms as artistic creations.

Instead of our interpreting the mise-en-scènes of the unconscious, we should use these works to set up perspectives of realities with an eye on enjoying heretofore unexperienced intensities. The machines which are drawn into play are, essentially, no longer the machines of illusion and memory, but apparati for experimentation which permit us to quarter sensibility and draw it out beyond this old body.

Translated from the French by Joseph Maier

The Disposition of the Voice*

> The voice is never represented: it represents, it is the act of a presence which represents itself. (D. Vasse)

> Theatre is the art of playing with division, by introducing it into space by means of dialogue. (M. Blanchot)**

This is a recorded message. Yet it does not reproduce my voice, the voice that I hear, myself, as I speak to you now, as I am writing this paper. It represents it, yet it does not re-present it. It does not record it for future representation, it puts it on record, for future reference. Guy Rosolato, "La voix," *Essais sur le symbolique,* Gallimard, 1969 (Henceforth designated as Rosolato I).

The voice, meanwhile, does and does not become silent. It cuts its groove, trace, into the text of which I am saying that, in this particular case, it represents the voice. Were I to read the text in front of you, pretend I am speaking it for the first time, the situation would be reversed. I would be voicing, giving voice to, a text written prior to the performance, the very text I am writing at this minute. And even if I was pretending to improvise—having for instance learned my text by heart—my voice would only be an instrument, second to the written text, and I would be in the same relation to it as an actor to his lines. But even then, as Rosolato indicates, the voice would hardly be a mere instrument. It would produce its own effects, have its own resonances. The voice has to do with fantasy (*le fantasme*) and myth, John Vernon, "Language and Writing," *American Review,* 22 (1975).

Rosolato I, 287-288.

---

*Translations of quoted passages are my own, unless otherwise indicated.

**La voix n'est jamais représentée: elle représente, elle est l'acte d'une présence qui se représente. (D. Vasse)

Le théâtre est l'art de jouer avec la division en l'introduisant dans l'espace par le dialogue. (M. Blanchot)

but it is perhaps in the dramatic metaphor that we can attempt to anchor some remarks on the apparatus (*dispositif*) called the voice; remarks that, by holding together several levels of attention, would aim at complicating the issue a little.

I

Jacques Derrida, *De la grammatologie*, Paris: ed. de Minuit, 1967, 33 and *passim*.

J. Derrida, *Speech and Phenomena*, trans. by David Allison, Northwestern University Press, 1973, 76.

Nothing is closer to me than my voice: the consciousness of the voice is consciousness itself. "Phonic signs ('acoustical images' in Saussure's sense, or the phenomenological voice) are heard by the subject who proffers them in the absolute proximity of their present. The subject does not have to pass forth beyond himself to be immediately affected by his expressive activity. My words are 'alive' because they seem not to leave me: not to fall outside me, outside my breath, at a visible distance; not to cease to belong to me, to be at my disposition 'without further props. . .' " The voice is present, presence itself. Freedom itself, too, and freedom of the language: a discourse which does not have to borrow its signifiers from the world, and hence is never in danger of being dispossessed of them.

Grammatologie, 238.

Absolute presence: the words exist as they are spoken, then vanish in thin air leaving no trace of signifiers behind, no body, leaving us in the immediate presence of the signified. Self-presence, "apparent transcendence" of the voice. *Auto-affection*: from myself to myself. I do not even have to speak to you, as long as I hear myself. I do not even have to *speak*: I can sing, scream, mutter, speak to myself in silence.

Speech and Phenomena

But if I speak, something else takes place: the voice itself can only be immediate presence inasmuch as language, the phenomenological "body" of the signifier, seems to fade away at the very moment it is produced: an absence for a presence. But *speech* differs. In speech we can never say that the body of language is totally absent. It absents itself, yet it leaves a trace. It is at best present-absent. For speech is not voice. It is a voice that has run over and through language: "a wading through language, a wading that occurs inside as well as

J. Vernon, *op. cit.*, 215.

outside of the body." And language like any system of meaningful signs, is something other than pure presence. It differs, and it *defers*: differance is the spacing-out, the constitutive delay and insistence, that which will not be denied its temporality and its power of deferment, what happens when the voice runs through the body of language, becomes speech and writing (*ecriture*).

&

&   &

The voice is inextricably bound up with bodies: the body of language, the body of the speaker. "Between body and language." The voice belongs to the body, is *produced* by it. It is one of those emissions of the body which, in Freudian psychology, play such an important part in the structure and manifestation of desire and fantasy: "the products of an underground operation, of a metabolism which, once they have fallen out, become objects distinct from the body, without its qualities of sensitivity, reaction and excitability, and which acquire a value which interests the desire of the other." Lost objects, *a* objects in Lacanian terminology.

The voice speaks of the body: of its dualities (interior/exterior, front/back, eye/ear, etc.). It speaks of the unconscious drives and fantasies. *Trieb*: drift, drive. The voice has to do with flows and desires, not with meaning. It belongs to the realm of what Barthes calls *signifiance*, that is to say signification *before* it coalesces, before it emerges, of signification nascent, floating. That is why the voice cannot really be apprehended through "scientific" discourse. The most "extreme" manifestations (silence, scream) of the voice dramatize this metaphoric relation to the unconscious drives. However, let us not be mistaken about it, if the voice gives access to metaphorical representations of drives, it is only through the logic of a system of signifiers which act as "desire traps."

G. Rosolato, "La voix: entre corps et langage," *Revue Francaise de Psychanalyse*, 1974, 1, 75-94 (henceforth designated as Rosolato II).

Rosolato II, 78.

Daniel Charles, "John Cage ou la voix symbole du temps," *L'autre scène*, I0 (1975).

Rosolato II, 93-4.

II

"*Between* body and language": it is hard to con-

Ivanka Stoianova, "La voix-silence et le corps," L'autre scène, 10; 37-44.

ceive of a voice without a reference to a signifier, and in particular to language. Yet, conceived it must be, as music and poetry, marginally, show us. Cage, Mauricio Kagel, Dieter Schnebel, de-construct "silence" and speech to free music from the fetters of the signifier's organization. A-verbal musical voice, "silence-voice," which allows us to listen to sound

D. Charles, op. cit, and "Nature et silence chez J. Cage," Le langage, Neuchatel: Bâconnière. 1966.

rather than sense, to the inchoate exploration of sound untamed by syntax (Daniel Charles has shown the parallel with Heidegger's definition of Ursprache).

The voice has to do with loss, fall from the body. Yet it also has to do with the return to origins, to the dream of an Ur-language, a corporeality of language which Vico, Heidegger and Norman O. Brown celebrate. The voice, in this respect, is regressive. Mythically, it aspires to an original state, that of the "first men," before they became enslaved

N. O. Brown, Closing Time, 73.

by words, when they were "entirely immersed in the senses, buffeted by passions, buried in the body." Individually, being an expansion of the body and a metaphor of fantasy, the voice follows fantasy's regressive pattern, and gives expression to traces of unconscious desires and constructs dredged up from the past.

The voice goes back, and forth: a go-between, an

Rosolato I, 294-9.

intermediary. A transmitter that makes dual, dialectical relations possible, on all levels: linguistic in general (the problem of enunciation: the "voice" of the verb): analytic, "as it leads through myth and fantasy, toward the superego with its judgments of

Ibid., 302.

'interior' voice, and beyond it toward the id and its drives."

Denis Vasse, L'Ombilic et la Voix, Seuil, 1975, 14.

In-between, because it can only be defined as "the relationship, the distance, the articulation between subject and object, the object and the Other, the subject and the Other." In-between organism and organization, the body biologic and the body politic, "so that neither the biological body nor the body of language could possibly be conceived with-

Vasse, 21.

out it, in spite of the fact that it belongs properly neither to the one nor to the other." Passage, tunnel, passing-through (traversée). Enigma: "Enigma

because it can be construed neither as the locus of
presence, nor as the knowledge (*savoir*) of representation. It is the unceasing relation between the two,
which cannot be reduced to either of the two orders
it articulates, precisely *because* it articulates them."   Vasse, 215.

III

The philosophical status of the voice is complex
and involves a series of oppositions and enigmas. Is
that what gives it its special appeal, its fascination
(both as a 'real' production and as a critical concept)? We indicated that the voice was always an-
chored in desire, and more precisely that its effect
was to situate the subject in the desire of the other.
There is no such thing as a neutral voice, a voice
without desire, a voice that does not desire me. If
there was, it would be an experience of absolute
terror. But even as it is, and even though it may
charm, the voice frightens and disturbs. Is it because the voice gives us nothing to *see*, because it
has no mirror-image? Speaks of loss, of an absence?
But it also brings pleasure, an unparalleled ecstasy.
How is it that some voices hold us spellbound,
come through mouth, record or print to haunt and
thrill? Because the voice affirms that ecstasy is possible, can be attained through discourse. It tells me
that I too can attain it, that I am not forever excluded
from it, that some sort of ecstasy (*jouissance*) is to be
had in the attainment of my self-image. The voices   Charles Bouazis, "L'ex-
that thrill us allow us to apprehend their power of   cellence de la voix," *Es-*
dissociation. They themselves are not concerned   *sais de la sémiotique du*
with diction, expressive effect. They let something   *sujet.* Bruxelles: Edi-
through which has to do with origin and loss, and   tions Complèxe, 1977.
the determination of a space where ecstasy is possi-
ble. Beyond words, the heterogeneity of signifiers,
the voice determines an enclosure, ambitus. There
it keeps watch over signifiers and over the signifier
of signifiers (the Phallus in Lacanian parlance). This
"transcendental signifier" is that which guarantees   Jacques Derrida, "The
the unity of signifier and signified, underneath and   purveyor of Truth,"
beyond all signified-effects (*effets de signifié*). Thus,   *Yale French Studies,* 52
as Derrida shows, the danger of returning to a   (1975) (a translation of
metaphysics of "pure presence," of the immediate   "Le facteur de la ver-
is always lurking when one discusses the voice.   ité," originally in
     Poétique, 21).

IV

Is there then no way we can help being brought round full circle? Daniel Charles sees a possibility of approaching the problem differently, through the later works of Bachelard and Heidegger: the voice as the "vertical connection" between Earth and Sky, that which establishes instant relation between contraries (Bachelard speaks of "the androgynous moment"). Charles, after Cage, interprets verticality as *intensity*. A vertical connexion which is an experience of pure time, "time degree zero," a yet unstructured time. From those remarks we conclude that a meta-(or para-) discourse on the voice has (at least) two vanishing points. We would be tempted to say that one is more theoretical, the other more geared to performance and creation, except that it would not be quite true (the so-called theoretical aspect becomes performance, performance is always a theoretical statement). If, however, for clarity's sake, we decide to distinguish between them, we turn to the work of Gilles Deleuze and Jean-François Lyotard for the theoretical vantage point. Their work is sufficiently well-known to make a discussion here unnecessary. Gilles Deleuze's contribution to the question of the voice is indirect but essential; it is to be found in the concept of nomadism, in the critique of depth (and height) and the freeing of surfaces which he conducts in *Logique du Sens* and *L'Anti-Oedipe*. With that, Deleuze has given us powerful instruments to re-examine the function of the voice. A passage on nomadism, for instance, quoted by D. Charles, appears to be analogous to the shift in intensity, the abrupt and static vertical connection which the voice effects: "The nomad is not necessarily somebody who moves: there are travels in which one does not move, travels in intensity, and even from a historical point of view nomads are not those who move like migrants, on the contrary they are those who do not move, and who start nomadizing in order to stay in the same place and free themselves from codes." Another concept which serves in Deleuze's work to describe the ability to free oneself

D. Charles, *L'autre scène, op. cit.*, 35.

Logique du sens, Paris: ed. de Minuit, 1969 (in particular "26ème serie: du langage," "27ème série: de l'oralité").

G. Deleuze, "Pensée nomade," in *Nietzsche aujourd 'hui?* Paris: U.G.E., 1973, 176 (quoted by Daniel Charles, *op. cit.*, 36).

from codes is what he calls humour. That too is relevant to our study: "For if irony implies the co-extensiveness of being with the individual, or of the I with representation, humour implies that of sense and nonsense; humour is the art of surfaces and replicas (*doublures*), of nomadic singularities and of the aleatory point which is always being moved, the art of static genesis, the knowledge of pure event or 'the fourth person singular'—signification, designation and manifestation being suspended, depth and height abolished."

Logique du sens, 166.

J-F. Lyotard has carried further the research into shifts of intensities, decoding and recoding of flows (*flux*) with direct relevance to drama and voice. Lyotard has written little on drama itself (apart from "la dent, la paume"), but many of his analyses bear on theatricality (*la théâtralité*) and how avant-garde music, painting and criticism can subvert that concept on which the Western theory of representation rests. The key words again are shifts, jumps in intensity; errance, mobility; *dispositif* (sometimes translated as apparatus but better rendered perhaps as *disposition*). Lyotard makes us aware that drama, vocal music, the cinema, whatever their particular aesthetics, are complex systems, screens, filters, apparati designed to capture and transform energy. The essay on drama mentioned is a radical critique of dramatic theory and practice based on signs and semiotics, on the representative value of signs, and it is a plea for a "theater of energies" (*un théâtre énergétique*).

"La dent, la paume," *Des dispositifs pulsion-nels*, Paris: U.G.E., 1973. Tr. "The Tooth, the Palm," *Sub-Stance*, No. 15, pp. 105-110.

V

That the voice will be an essential element of such a theater hardly needs to be emphasized. What is perhaps worth another brief turn of the screw is the consequences on the medium itself of the theoretical forays I have so sketchily surveyed. It will have been noted that the voice we refer to is a migratory notion: now a vocal production, now a psychoanalytic concept, now a kind of metaphorical support for pure time, mobility, intensity (a name perhaps for the unnameable?) Conversely

Roland Barthes, *The Pleasure of the Text*, trans. by Richard Miller, Hill and Wang, 1975, 66-67.

and symmetrically, this volatile concept plays havoc with the clear distinctions between media and genres, as well as between reality and representation. Roland Barthes in *Le Plaisir du Texte* speaks of "writing aloud" (*l'écriture à haute voix*) as the hallmark of the radical shift we have been approaching by a devious path. The last paragraph of his book is worth quoting in full since it does more than introduce us to the last rung of our spiral: "*Writing aloud* is not expressive (. . .) It is carried not by dramatic inflections, subtle stresses, sympathetic accents, but by the *grain* of the voice, which is an erotic mixture of timbre and language, and can therefore also be, along with diction, the substance of an art: the art of guiding one's body (whence its importance in Far Eastern theaters). Due allowance being made for the sounds of language, *writing aloud* is not phonological but phonetic: its aim is not the clarity of messages, the theater of emotions; what it searches for (in a perspective of bliss) are the pulsional incidents, the language lined with flesh, a text where we can hear the grain of the throat, the patina of consonants, the voluptuousness of vowels, a whole carnal stereophony: the articulation of the body, of the tongue, not that of meaning, of language. A certain art of singing can give an idea of this vocal writing; but since melody is dead, we may find it more easily today at the cinema. In fact, it suffices that the cinema capture the sound of speech *close up* (this is, in fact, the generalized definition of the 'grain' of writing) and make us hear in their materiality, their sensuality, the breath, the gutturals, the fleshiness of the lips, a whole presence of the human muzzle (that the voice, that writing, be as fresh, supple, lubricated, delicately granular and vibrant as an animal's muzzle), to succeed in shifting the signified a great distance and in throwing, so to speak, the anonymous body of the actor into my ear; it granulates, it crackles, it caresses, it grates, it cuts, it comes: that is bliss [jouissance]." This beautiful page, in its allusion to drama, cinema, and voice, summons the name of Marguerite Duras, novelist, dramatist, director and film-maker. It is toward her and the fascinating quality of her work that this whole commentary has been directed from the start. Yet I shall say relatively little about her and content myself with having led you to the door. Like many other people, I was jolted into awareness of the importance of what she is doing by her film, *India Song* (and its twin or ghost film, *Son Nom de Venise dans Calcutta désert*). *India Song* (the text and the film) quite literally *effects* something new in the use of voice and dramatic space.

Duras' use of voices has to do with memory and loss of memory (*l'oubli*). We learn from G. Rosolato that the voice "gives physical manifestation to ancient images reconstituted by an *evocation* from fantasies. It (the voice), being an extension of the body as diversified as the face, becomes the depositary of the desires and intentions of a past, which give it its singularity." M. Duras explicitly conceives *India Song* as just such a dream of voices and desires: "The voices do not address the spectator or reader. They are absolutely autonomous. *They speak among themselves. They do not know they are being heard.* The story of that love, the VOICES knew it, or read about it, a long time ago. Some of them remember it better than others. But none of them really remembers it, and none has quite forgotten it either. One never, at any time, knows *who those* VOICES *are*. Yet, by the way they have, each of them, of having forgotten or of remembering, they make themselves known to us more deeply than through their identity."

In her "Notes for the theater about setting," M. Duras emphasizes the creative—or destructive— power of her conception of voices and the immediate consequences on scenic space: "The setting should be both that of loss of memory and that of vacillating memory, that is to say a place with incidents of light, points of intense luminosity, holes of darkness, breaks (. . .) a place which one enters via the memory and loss of memory of the women, of the voices." The voices, then, are from the start the element through which the text and the film come to life. It would take a separate study to analyze the workings of the voices as generative principle. But it

Rosolato II, 83.

India Song, Gallimard, 1973, 147.

M. Duras, in *Marguerite Duras*, Collection Ça/ cinéma, Albatros, 1975.

is interesting to note how M. Duras worked with
her actors in order to destroy the traditional relation
of actor to voice, of voice to spectator/reader. In a
discussion with Xavière Gauthier, M. Duras explains how she avoids the "abject proximity" of
direct sound. She often has the actors record their
lines so that when they play their scene, they can
hear their own voice returning to them (M. Duras
says *revenant*, which also means a ghost).

X.G.: They listen to their own voice?

M.D.: Yes, while they were acting, they listened to
their own voice.

X.G.: That again must have something to do with
death. Their voices are like voices from beyond the
grave. It is the voice which is from beyond the grave
(*revenante*).

M.D.: Yes, but I don't know whether it is not also
concerned with cinema itself. There was something
in silent cinema which has been lost forever. There
is something trivial, vulgar in direct sound.

X.G.: In realism?

M.D.: Yes, the inevitable realism of direct sound,
and the dishonesty it represents. So you see, when
they speak and hear their own words, the words
have infinitely more echoes. I mean, while they are
supposed to be speaking their words, at the very
same time, they could be saying something entirely
different. The field opens up, the field of speech

*Marguerite Duras, op.
cit.*, 80-1.

opens up infinitely wide. I think that's what it is,
and because of that, everything takes on a dual
dimension."

Those voices, those which return to us from before, from another time, are radically cut off from
our demand, our need to fasten on to them and
invest them with our desire. They will never give us
satisfaction. They don't have a body (the speakers
are never seen, or at least, never seen *while* they are
speaking). They are *off*, unstable, always somewhere else. Yet, like a powerful current, they leave
marks. They burn. Although they are without a
visible body, they are profoundly physical. Although they will not acknowledge *our* desire, they
are voices of desire. The drama of the two female
voices, in particular, is intensely sensual. Here

perhaps is the best actualization of what Barthes calls "writing aloud." Not only the grain, the stereophony of the flesh, but the powerful currents, gusts, shudders of desire which run through the voices.

A new relation is established between sound and image, an amplification of the space *between* them. (M. Duras has carried the exploration even further in *Son Nom de Venise* . . . . in which the same sound track as in *India Song* is used on different images, mainly shots of deserted places, perhaps some of the locations used in *India Song*). The voices in *India Song* are not simply an aid to, a commentary on, the images. They disrupt the images, shatter them. Scenes and voices do not coincide, the words are not spoken by the bodies present on the screen. It is they (the bodies) which seem a creation of the voices. M. Duras transforms the use of off sound. Those voices are no longer *expressive* of something (the interiority of a subject, the knowledge or the consciousness of a central intelligence). What is challenged is not only the primacy of character and image, but also the more modern variations on it, in order to substitute a different logic: the logic of memories *other* than the writer's: "The voices do not speak to the spectator or the reader. They are totally autonomous. They speak between themselves."

Because of this different logic and circulation of desire, *India Song* is perhaps the first cinematographic and textual disposition of *another* scene, in which reader/spectator, writer/director, text/film, characters/actors are equally implicated, equally affected; where no central, omnipotent subject pulls the strings, orders and reorders. With all the importance it is given, it is a wonder that the voice does not become a fetish. But it never does: desire runs from one object, one "person" to another, carrying danger and death to all (including the viewer). M. Duras renounces fixed narrative space, in order to explore what literally cannot be said: not the mystical unknown or attainable, but what is always taking place on another scene, in between words, elsewhere. In her exploration I see the most radical attempt to date to deconstruct "theatrical" space (the "depth" J-F. Lyotard talks about), filmic and narrative order (hierarchy of images and sound, linearity of images, the role of bodies and voices), to alter the relation between writer, word and reader, to cancel, displace, the subject as referent. That she effects through a profound reconsideration of the "affectiveness" of the voice. The question she asks is: What happens when voices are freed from the conventions of what E. Benveniste calls "written-spoken" discourse, in order to become something that literally does not concern you, even though it affects you deeply? Marguerite Duras approaches the exploration of pure desire, pure intensity and horror, allowing us to hear some echoes of what Maurice Blanchot calls the "neutral" voice, "a voice that one could describe as outside discourse, outside language":

"within the neutral space of narrative, the speech bearers, the subjects of actions—those who used to be called characters—fall into a relation of non-identification with themselves: something is happening to them which they can only invest by divesting themselves of their power to say 'I,' and what is happening to them has always already happened to them: they can only account for it indirectly, as the loss of memory of themselves, that loss of memory which introduces them into the present without a memory which is that of the narrating voice."*

M. Blanchot, L'entretien infini, Gallimard, 1969, 564.

*"Dans l'espace neutre du récit, les porteurs de parole, les sujets d'action—ceux qui tenaient lieu jadis de personnages—tombent dans un rapport de non-identification avec eux-mêmes: quelque chose leur arrive, qu'ils ne peuvent ressaisir qu'en se désaisissant de leur pouvoir de dire "je," et ce qui leur arrive leur est toujours déjà arrivé: ils ne sauraient en rendre compte qu'indirectement, comme de l'oubli d'eux-mêmes, cet oubli qui les introduit dans le présent sans mémoire qui est celui de la parole narrante."

*We dedicate this
blank page to
Lawrence Sterne*

New Music: Utopia AND Oblivion

DANIEL CHARLES

1 - Let us take as a point of departure Nam June Paik's statement about the difference between RECORDING and RETRIEVAL: "Retrieval," he writes, "is much quicker with Chinese characters. You can record (write) quicker in English but you can retrieve (read) quicker in Chinese. One is retrieval-oriented, the other is recording-oriented—but you read more than you write." Thus to perform (= to read) means to be Chinese-like, oriented toward Retrieval (not = recording). As Cage says, why should we put any kind of relations between to compose (= to write) and to perform (= to read)?

Quoted by Gene Youngblood, *Expanded Cinema*, New York, Dutton, p. 261.

2 - But there is a third way to make music anyway: to listen to it. What will be the status of LISTENING, if it is to be involved neither in recording nor in retrieving? Following Cage's argument, to listen must be a different type of music-making—an affair of discipline, and/or of tranquility (= the central emotion, according to Coomaraswamy's theory of Indian *rasa*). So that we have to try to define it as that which, differing from both recording and retrieving, MAKES THE DIFFERENCE between them. The public listens to the interpreter, who listens to the composer, who listens to the sounds themselves; but to listen to the sounds is at last what the public is doing, so maybe we have the opportunity of a short-cut: to perform music would be then, simply, to listen to the sounds without having to write them or even retrieve them. That seems to be the lesson of Charles Ives—that IS the lesson of John Cage.

"When asked why, God being good, there was evil in the world, Sri Ramakrishna said: To thicken the plot." John Cage, Silence, Middletown, Connecticut, Wesleyan University Press, 1961, p. 63.

cf. System and Structure: Essays in Communication and Exchange, London, Tavistock, 1972, Chapter XIII, "Order from Disorder," p. 395-412, passim.

Wilden, loc. cit., p. 404.

Wilden, loc. cit., p. 405.

Wilden, loc. cit., p. 398/399.

Wilden, loc. cit., p. 409.

3 - At this point, we have to "thicken the plot," as Sri Ramakrishna said. And (for example) to comment upon the status of that "difference." Anthony Wilden's theory of memory may help us here. Wilden suggests we refer to Hegel's *Er-innerung*, i.e. to Memory, the Derridian theory of Trace and Writing: "Just as the memory trace is for Derrida the INFORMING OF FORM, so the distinction between organism and mechanism, and between man and nature, is for Hegel the explanation of improbability or SURPRISE VALUE, both of which, of course, are technical synonyms for information. To be transmitted, information, as difference, depends on the *Er-innerung*, the retention of the trace, and it is not for nothing that re-membering is so essential to the *Phenomenology*." So Derrida-and-Hegel, both together, ought to be interpreted as theoreticians of a quasi-biological *recording*: "The trace the 'organism' leaves on (or in) the 'environment,' and the trace the 'environment' leaves on (or in) the 'organism' is precisely *l'écriture* in Derrida's sense of the gram".

4 - According to such a "biological" restoration of writing in face of speech, it seems necessary to attack, as does Derrida, "the positivistic conception of the 'full origin' . . . Derrida views the 'full origin' as the illusory quest which seeks to rediscover 'being' or 'substance' or 'subject' or 'plenitude' or 'presence' at the origin of life. But 'life must be conceived of as a trace before being is determined as presence.' The 'essence of life' (which is no essence, but rather no-thing) is *différence*." Thus if we come back to the (binary!) opposition between *retrieving* and *recording*, or *speaking* (i.e. *reading*) and *writing*, we find ourselves faced with an opposition between *memory* and *forgetfulness*, but—from the point of view of *memory*. Forgetfulness is only the lack of memory. It is clear from Wilden's diagnosis of the *cool* civilization, grasped as that for which writing as such does not exist, that its "biology" demands that "Everything is designed to minimize the effect of noise on the cultural code"—whereas in the *hot* society, our society, the stability will depend upon the *acceptance* of noise, and the incorporation of this

noise as an information, allowing us to move toward some "new level of organization (evolving)." In the cool society, "the past of the society—its memory, its set of instructions, its sacred text—is literally embodied in every domicile"; "reading" such a society, everybody cannot but *retrieve* the code everywhere—whereas "the hot society records itself in an essential way, on the world outside—on nature, on stone, on wax, on clay, on paper, on film, on tape, in its railway networks, its streets, its freeways"—and, let us add, in its music. Wilden, *loc. cit.*, p. 410.

5 - So far, so good; but as the example of a composer like Nam June Paik easily shows, the general motto (issued from Von Foerster) "order from disorder" or "order from noise," taken as characterizing the hot society which incorporates everything new, hence its complexity and fragility, cannot obtain, since the aim of the composer's activity seems to be the avoidance of any kind of order. A musician becoming a video-tape maker is only contributing to erase difference. And the motto (archaic, primitive, pre-historic, etc. . . .) "order from order," which seems at first sight appropriate to the demand of retrieval, is also a catch phrase, since Nam June Paik's music is *not* "WRITTEN ON ITSELF," and does *not* correspond to the model of the cool society which is supposed to be "both itself and the memory of itself." That does not mean that those models, the hot one and the cool one, are (for any reason) obsolete. On the contrary, they answer very strictly to what we might call (pontifically) the Great Call of Memory, or the Oblivion of Utopia. And their complementarity itself is revealing. The point is that "difference" is, in both, defined as a Trace, i.e. as the active writing of something meaningful—or (even) of meaning itself. Order may well come from order or disorder, it will always be order. But the new music is not so much concerned with order as it is with noise, and with noise as incapable of being redefined as information. Wilden, *loc. cit.*, p. 410.

6 - In Western traditional "great" music, the durations are interpreted as multiples or fractions of real numbers: by a kind of "mirroring" of harmonic

116 Daniel Charles

Frederic Rzewski, "Nonmetrical Rhythm Since 1950," Art. "Rhythm," in John Vinton (Ed.), *Dictionary of Contemporary Music*, New York, Dutton, 1974, p. 622.

theory, they give birth to rational values susceptible to measurement and control. In the "nonmetrical" new music (Cage, Feldman, Wolff), we do not have to *control* durations, but to *listen* to them, thus freeing ourselves from the idea that every sound is related to other sounds by (logical) implications or hierarchy or structural lines concerning what precedes or follows; we have *to get inside the sound* and let it have its own duration. Cage: "One of the things we *don't* need as much as we use it is *memory*".

Cf. C. H. Waddington (Ed.), *Biology and the history of the future*, An *IUBS/UNESCO Symposium*, Edinburgh, Edinburgh University Press, 1972, p. 37.

Frederic Rzewski, *loc. cit.*, p. 623.

John Cage in Waddington, *loc. cit.*, *ibid.*

7 - If each sound is to be viewed as constituting by itself a separate molecular being, then the free-improvisation situation of the performer "represents an attempt, totally modern in its anarchic premise, to create music out of nothing, beginning with a *tabula rasa* uncluttered by any limitations". What reveals this *tabula rasa* is *silence*, i.e. "the multiplicity of activity that constantly surrounds us." *Silence* equals *white noise*—the ground of any possible communications, of any channelization, of any sending/receiving of messages; the point of departure of any adventure in sound, of any soundscape, of any *Klangfarbe*, of any amplification, of any "schizophonia" (Murray Schafer); the *drone* under any periodical or irregular clusters etc. . . . .

8 - In such a "drone" state of "atmospheric" oblivion, any return of any event periodical as well as non-periodic, becomes possible—provided it is not the *return of the same* (which would mean a moving back to the previous controlled situation), but the *coming anew of the different*. Then we *retrieve*, behind

Quoted by C. H. Waddington, *loc. cit.*, p. 38.

what Duchamp called "the curtain of memory," something that we experience *for the first time*, but without any longer having power or domination over it. "Organization in the biological world—and in the physical world too, for that matter—arises not from relations of domination, but from relations of "participation." Everything we give a name to is constituted by its participation with everything else and by everything else's participation with it . . ."

Waddington, *loc. cit.*, *ibid.*

So we may speak, as in physics, of "interaction," or, as in communication theory, of "interface."

9 - How are we to interpret, in music and the performing arts of today, such an "interface" situation? We may describe it as leading to a *stasis*. From a study of Cage's "transcendentalism", or "radical" empiricism," Leonard Meyer thinks it possible to infer that, in the new "experimental" music, "Past and future coexist in an all-encompassing, but fluctuating present." "In short . . . a multiplicity of styles in each of the arts, coexisting in a balanced, yet competitive, cultural environment, is producing a fluctuating stasis in contemporary culture." Experimental music and performing arts are leading toward a static world, without goals or teleology, and precluding even the concept of an avant-garde, since such a concept would imply "goal-directed motion—the conquest of some new territory."

Music, the Arts, and Ideas, Chicago, The University of Chicago Press, 1967, 2nd impression 1969, p. 167. Leonard Meyer, *loc. cit.*, p. 102.

Meyer, *loc. cit.*, p. 169.

10 - Experimental music, according to such a thesis, cannot escape its own neutralization: it negates history, but this ahistoricity, once obtained, negates the negator itself. That situation has been described by Bateson: it is the "degenerative" or "self-corrective" circle, which contains the link "increase in N causes *decrease* in M," and includes a cumulative interaction: the degenerative causal loop functions as a negative feedback, so that the steady state is to be fully regulated. The cumulative interaction which sustains the self-correction here is typical of a "classical" COOL society, taken as that which controls the degenerative loop in order to escape the excessive rise of tensions and climaxes born from the cumulative interaction itself. Meyer's view of the steady state or *stasis* in experimental music treats the situation as if the subjacent conflict between historicity and ahistoricity was of a *schismogenetic* type, i.e. involved some kind of fission and even the breakdown of the system: the "End of Renaissance" is the end of the avant-garde from the point of view of Memory.

Steps to an Ecology of Mind, New York, Ballantine Books, 1972, p. 109, n. 3.

11 - But there is another manner—according to Bateson—to achieve the steady state, another type of system capable of maintaining itself without progressive or irreversible change: the *Balinese* one, where "schismogenetic sequences are rare" and

Bateson, *loc. cit.*, p. 127.

"the contexts which recur in . . . social life preclude cumulative interaction." If some corrective mechanism is required to maintain the steady state, it is *intermittent*, dissimilar from "the continually acting restraints which must be present in all schismogenetic systems." *Balinese* "attitudes based upon bodily balance," for example in music or drama, lead to a "lack of climax," to a music which "does not have the sort of rising intensity and climax structure characteristic of modern Occidental music".

Bateson, *loc. cit.*, ibid.

Bateson, *loc. cit.*, p. 113.

12 - What is specific in such a "lack of climax" is that it prevents any dynamic opposition: in music as in social life, the only maximization concerns stability—a procedure which, "apparently, breaks the cumulative tension by irrelevant interaction." Let us recall here Cage's definition of rhythm as "irrelevance": if war is an affair of mutual avoidance, there is no sense of cumulative time, no crescendo, no continued speech or "stories" or oratory or rhetorical types of social influence; the future is taken as that which is going to have been, but without being distinguished from what has been done—it differs only from the past "as the confused from the clear." Thus no room is left for interiority or subjectivity: the dialectics of recognition may be repeated without producing (in Hegel's terms) any dialectics of work, i.e. any historicity.

Bateson, *loc. cit.*, p. 114.

John Cage, *Pour les oiseaux, Entretiens avec Daniel Charles*, Paris, Belfond, 1977, p. 224.

Claude Lefort, "Société sans histoire et historicité," *Cahiers Internationaux de Sociologie*, vol. XII, 1952, p. 106.

13 - We may notice that such a steady-state or "cooler" society, far from being "WRITTEN ON ITSELF," is *not written at all*. It is not, as Wilden says, "both itself and the memory of itself," but *itself as the oblivion of itself*. Wilden's analysis of communication, consistent with Bateson's descriptions of schismogenesis, cannot but lead to dialectics of work, since it is founded on memory, the *"sine qua non"* of communication, dependent on the TRACE"; but Cage's hope to "leave no traces" (P.S. to *Mureau*) shows a quite different way—non-Occidental, non-schismogenetic, non-violent. And it is consistent with Bateson's analysis of the non-schismogenetic Balinese type of culture. Of course,

Wilden, *loc. cit.*, p. 408.

Loc. cit., ibid.

Wilden, *loc. cit.*, p. 374

Cf. John Cage's presentation of the performance of *Mureau* (simultaneously with David Tudor's *Rainforest*) at the Royal Albert Hall, London, Monday 22 May 1972:

we are not Balinese; but the Balinese model, if understood as modelling Oblivion as a positive, affir-
mative force, precludes any negative interpretation
such as Meyer's avant-garde destroying itself. If
Oblivion is an affirmation, it is not the Other of
Utopia, but the core of utopian practice in music
and performing arts today.

"P.S.
We must
find something else to
do
than art:
we are going to China.
We hope our visit
will leave no traces."
Wilden, *loc. cit.*, p. 374.

Cf. Jean Baudrillard's
definition of poetry
after Saussure's "anag-
rammes" in *L'échange
Symbolique et la mort*,
Paris, Gallimard, 1976,
p.   285-308;   and
Lyotard's formula: *"des
effets, pas de causes,"* in
Economie   libidinale,
Paris, Ed. de Minuit,
1974, p. 306-307.

IV
Traces

The Book or
The Four Phases of a Birth

EDMOND JABÈS

If affirmation is only the negation of a negative, if before it can have the right to cut it must forever negate that which negates it, then all questioning has to pass through systematic rejection of the answers it has called forth. They will serve it as springboards for new interrogations. So that the question of the book which interests us here, today, can only be a permanent challenge of the book, that is of writing, of birth and death, of truth and lie, of presence and absence, of reality and fiction, of what is written and what we read, of what is born in the book, with the birth of the book, and dies of the book's death, of its truth or lie, of its undefinable presence and its infinite absence.

Could it be that man is a book which he can only read *in* the book he will write? And as if the very act of writing made it possible?

My life is in the book, and the book is my life. Life which I learn to read with every moment lived beside the word which fights me for it, for an extraordinary shared adventure.

Does the adventure come before the text or the text before the adventure? And what is this adventure which the text has seized and will force on us until we shall only live *its* adventure which has become, more than any other, our own?

Writing means making an opening in our life through which life becomes text. Words are a stage toward the unknown where the spirit pays for its daring, toward that unknown without which our thoughts would be dead rather than thoughts meant to die in the very quick, the most tortured heart of death.

I

I was born on April 16 of a year which I do not remember. Will this date be my starting point for a long digression around the book? You know that digression is my very method. As if all we are ever led to express, whether with difficulty or in the most spontaneous way, were from the beginning doomed to wandering, an ideal prey for commentaries whose tyrannical

123

grasp we do not suspect. For they insinuate themselves gradually and by approximating known approximations. A parenthesis opened also, and in some way independently, by the word impatient to assert its gagged entirety of which we do not know, once at its mercy, how far it will sweep us away in its wake.

In the book, nothing is said that is not revised in the margins, questioned, cut out, often without our knowing it. Nothing is said that is not a pretext for new expression, other paths, strange and deep ties. So that trying to write anything in all honesty and loyalty would mean trying only to be said by what is said and which this *said* cleverly suppresses, arranges and transforms. This *said* which is itself said, hence manipulated, exploited, liberated in its turn. As if being free meant exactly being exploited by this claimed liberty in whose name we declare ourselves free.

Going back, for an example, to my sentence: "I was born on April 16," I realize as the first phase that it originally forced itself on me by its disclaimer. In fact, in *Elya*, the book which we can now consider the fifth in the cycle of *The Book of Questions*, you can find the following disclosure:

"Although I was born on April 16 in Cairo, my father inadvertently declared to the consul's office making out my birth certificate that I was born on the 14th of that month.

"Is it to this error in calculation I unconsciously owe the feeling that I have always been separated from my life by forty-eight hours? The two days added to mine could only be lived in death.

"As with the book, as with God in the word, the first manifestation of my existence was an absence which bore my name."

I won't insist on the indirect repercussions of this confusion of my father's when about to declare the day and hour of my birth. Confusion all the more astonishing because he was not given to this sort of thing. I won't insist on the repercussions this may have had on my life and certainly had on my books—on my relation to everyday happenings through my books, as if the daily happenings found their authority but in the portion of eternity they assume and by which they are consumed.

I must admit, moreover, that nobody is beyond such an error. At the time, in the Near Eastern country where my family had lived for generations, notices of birth or death could be sent in writing to the local authority, in this case the "gouvernorat," which immediately issued a certificate which alien residents handed on to their respective consuls. Did my father think he was writing April 16 while his pen shaped the figure 14? Still, he always claimed that he made the declaration in person. But as, according to the custom, he had several days, even weeks to discharge his obligation he could have made the error in altogether good faith. Unless it was the fault of a hasty or distracted clerk which is not out of the question.

In any case, this error which I never considered such distressed me so much that I made up my own explanation for it. I saw it as the concrete proof furnished by the unconscious *that we are older than our life*. The Book of Questions has drawn its voice and made its place out of this guaranteed void, this counter-signed outside-of-time: universe of silence and night where there burns the pregnant forgetting of a non-assigned day claimed by no human being. Day which escaped the lies of the light and revives in the distress into which death can plunge us with its refusal to die of a truth which is only a subtle or gross trap set by lies. For all truth passes through lies which so set it off that we might very well deduce that truth speaks through the lies it denounces while really denouncing only itself as the apotheosis of lies buoyed to the height of perfection. And once put into words, once settled in its fictional function, it is with truth as it would be with the journal of an event, the story of a life, the account of a profession of faith in any discourse.

Truth, once put down on paper, is but a word at grips with proofs and counter-proofs which tear it apart. You cannot lay hold of it except through its exemplary experiences as a most prestigious word, exalted, acclaimed, crowned, a word of which we have always demanded much and continue to do so. For a long time, at least since my first texts, I have watched out for its weaknesses as you tremble for a beloved being who accomplishes a dangerous task. For nothing is more vulnerable—or more gratuitous—in its contingent, illusory invulnerability than the truth which presides over the book's fate.

Truth, which is birth, has as opposite the death of a truth. Both are figures of fiction, appearance and disappearance of a story which admits neither prelude nor end, story within a story, like life within non-life, and whose blossoming is for all its triumph also the first announcement of its decline. We are forever the story which recites us and the daring of this story. Being recited without a break, will we ever know who we are? Will we know even at death's threshold which of all the stories words present to us was ours? Story of a life intersected by all the other lives which empty it. The minute trusts only minutes, the word only words. Chance and misfortune of the book's longing for the unattainable book: there is only despair at the foot of which it breaks.

Every word is both a word of lies and a word of truth.

(We live and die of truth as we live and die, not for nothing, but for a sublimated idea of All and Nothing.

Some people claim to know they are lying when they tell the truth; others, most, say they do not know. At any rate it's not they who are at stake, but truth as such.

Clear or obscure writing, polished or dull.
Day and night share the same portion of the
universe
and the same ink.

Not telling the truth is not necessarily lying. We often lie out of ignorance.
The ways of truth go through this.

Truth has no face. Any would fit, but truth rejects all. Still, it always
accosts us with familiar features: the features of evidence.

Truth is by its nature impossible to take.

Evidence, hostile to appearances, has the
void as ally.

As for truth, is all we will glimpse its abyss?)

Seizing the truth, brandishing it like a trophy, gathering around this cherished and fervent word other words, voices, looks (all that digs below the surface of writing, all that speaks and listens in speech, all that sees and reveals in a look)—this means first of all treating with lies, which are lies only because truth passed across them and cleaved them in half. Being lies ourselves means allowing truth to pass clear through us, to recognize itself, to be one day recognized thanks to us, and us, no doubt, with it as its accomplices or, rather, victims. For the truth is such only because lies sacrificed themselves for it and its necessary glory whose reign, alas, is soon cut off. Thus we are a passage of truth in every knowing word and, in the book, a deep opening of written truth onto the light which reads us in what we read. Boon of a proper, reciprocal reading where letters wanted to be seen.

Caught in the game it must play, sometimes to its own disadvantage, the truth which makes us bleed is itself bleeding. It is because of its own torment that every truth torments. Hurt by it, man and the world show the same wounds. There is no innocent truth. Truth is the answer given to the final question. A truth doomed from birth since there is no final question. Only death could ask it and only of itself. It alone owns the answer.

In this case, going toward the truth would mean going toward death, as if death, guardian of the answer, were the truth. A stage on the way toward death, any truth would be but a blinding moment of death, a lie dazzled by its death offered up. The search for truth but an etched path toward the void.

We question only in the hope for an answer which might restart our questioning. Would we therefore refuse to accept an answer given as definitive even if it had the virtue of satisfying us? And would we do so in order to protect our thinking which can only develop through questions?

But how could there be a single answer to the innumerable questions which fluster any one question? The Jew bears witness to this, having for centuries questioned his truth which has become the truth of questioning. God speaks beyond death, at the borders of thought.

> *("A question," he said, "is like a block of cut crystal whose thousand facets strike us all together at the break of day. We must face every single one of them.")*

II

In the second phase, this harmless beginning: "I was born on April 16" leads us, by raising the question of birth, to the idea of biography. I shall come back to this. For the moment, however, I must stress that for nearly twenty years I have not put myself on the stage, have not used the pronoun "I" in my books. Other "I's" with whom I no doubt identify have exploded this "I," "Me," "for My part" as they have exploded the place where I am, the place from which I come, and the place where I am going. Is it surprising then that my works (where so many stories crowd and call to one another) are but the heeded traces of fatal encounters, traces of burned traces, scars of words which we discovered on closer acquaintance? Because every word has its history which is fed by our own. Who could deny that certain obsessive words—in *The Book of Questions*, the words "God," "Jew," "Law," "Eye," "Name," "Book:" God as the extreme name of the abyss. Jew as the figure of exile, wandering, strangeness and separation, which is also the condition of the writer. Book as the impossibility of the book or, rather, as the place and non-place of all possibility of constructing the book. Eye which means law. "In the word *oeil*, 'eye,' there is the word *loi*, 'law.' Every look contains the law." (*Aely*) Name as the unutterable Name, the repeal of all names, the silent Name of God, of the invisible—Who could deny that certain words of our intimate vocabulary turn as if transparent for a story, set off a story which by and by writes itself, story probably truer than the one we pride ourselves on living.

Why be stubborn, I once asked a novelist, why try to invent a story and then make it plausible like a true story when it is enough to question a word charged with the weight of our anxieties, our feasts, our lonely days after, one of those heady key-words for which we are veil and face, sand and horizon, to make stories surface from the bottom of our memory, stories heard, found, or lived? But I was probably wrong. Because writing always means obeying a word which haunts us.

How many dead who we knew, cherished, sometimes detested, are buried in the word "Death." How many loves which marked our lives flower still in the words "Love." Is mentioning them not already speaking of ourselves?

So every book would be autobiographical since the book of my name is but the history of an absent book become the book of my history.

The book would be the biographer of the book whose place it has usurped. Its own biographer.

From the mouth of an anonymous woman, Sarah probably, beloved of Yukel who himself, as hero and narrator of the book, is both a word of flesh and a word of ink, one receiving its life from and losing it with the other—from a woman's mouth we hear the following sentences, we read them in *El, or the Last Book* which closes, without closing anything, the series of *The Book of Questions*:

"...*écrit, récit*, "written," "story:" the same word in a natural inversion of its letter sequence.

"'Any writing suggests its portion of a story,' she said."

Thus a word issued from rearranging the letters of the word under which it lay vegetating allows us, in coming to light, a secret reading of the former. I can perhaps make this clearer farther on. Farther on, that is to say where I have always been unbeknownst to all, and as if this "always" were only the sum of all the instants of a day indefinitely rebegun. But this might suggest that it is a single day formed by all days, past or future, which is not at all the case—although I am not convinced that this perpetual day might not exactly be the day of writing, day within the day or, rather, within the days. A day of such intense light that the lined-up words see only themselves, so does it sear their pupils. Farther on then. But what is far where there is neither coming nor term? Farther could be behind or before me, above or beneath? It could be—and why not—the fixed place where we meet again face to face, but separate? Then everything would happen in this separation which paradoxically moves us apart the moment it brings us together. How? Before answering this we must first ask, I think: what is separation, what does it mean to be separate?

One eye is separate from the other, yet both have a single look. One ear is separate from the other, but they vibrate to the same sound. One hand is separate from the other, and they match in gesture. One leg is separate from the other, but together they make us walk.

Who could ever say the distance which separates the word from the mouth, from the loving fingers which copy it? Yet one is nothing without the other. It is also true that they are nothing with one another, but that is a different story. A different story because with one another they gradually become nothing, whereas without one another they already are. Does life, does a work take shape in the interval between Nothing and Nothing? Does it start from nothing only to be engulfed into Nothing? Our plans, our desires confirm it. Stones are dust. All of life is in breath: a bit of oxygen stolen from the air. Life depends on a heart beat, and the universe on our blinking an eye. With the stream of life, book follows book.

Very far then, here, where distance takes refuge.

In the words *éloignement, lointain,* "distance," "remoteness," there is the word *loi*, "law," as in the word *oeil*, "eye," example I cited above.—Is it not strange, by the way, that we use the expression "above" to refer a reader to something already written when I should normally write "below" since we say "constructing a work" and the only way to build is from the bottom up. But we read pages from top to bottom. Which shows that the top is sometimes the bottom and vice versa. With this settled, let us go back to the text which we never left for all that.—Law is in the eye. Distance is the field of the eye, its law. Law it submits to and imposes. The eye makes the law which made it. It will go out with the last manifestation of this implacable law, along with all that dies of its intransigence. The word *loi*, "law," is also in the words *ploie, déploie, emploie,* "bend," "display," "employ." It governs what is employed or displayed, all that at some time or other bends under the rigor of the law. Texts are subject to law. Some words tell us so: rash, garrulous words which before even saying themselves call out loud: "Law." The law of the text surfaces from its deepest practice with the final word—but did we not follow it, literally, all along by intuition? Likewise, the intimation that he will live an exceptional morning, which exalts the writer glued to his pen all through the night of the word, will only be confirmed at dawn, with the appearance of the sun-law, of the word *soleil*, "sun," which contains, how could we doubt it, in a mysterious order the words *oeil*, "eye," and *Loi*, "law," gigantic pupil, heavenly eye with lashes of fire.

The law is always withdrawing. It is protected by distance. It owes its power and prestige to recoil. In relation to here it is elsewhere, but an else-where-within, as if its measure and menace. So that being here means submitting to the law of remoteness whose here is only an undefined place where it holds sway. Here is never located. It can spread over the whole world. Hence being here means being wherever this here is given as a "here," means acknowledging its dependence on the law which fixes it provisionally and presses on it with all the weight of its alienated space.

The law created a *here* of the law which is accepted as such only through our possible recognition of the law. Hence we are masters of the here, alone to call it so. But if the here of the law, the place where it proclaims and imprints itself, were the book? In that case the book would be both its here and elsewhere. It would be the immeasurable space of law in its written form, the very space of its writing giddy from the base, mixing the

here and elsewhere in their application—the elsewhere no longer showing as altogether elsewhere, or the here as totally here. We are under the
yoke of the law as we are subject to the infinite and the indefinitely finite,
to the habitable and the inhabitable, to eternity and the moment.—The
book would finally be, we might say, the *here* of the *elsewhere* which
rescinds it, the void of the here and the here of the void. For the law of the
book is a law of abysses, and the book which transmits it the abyss of the
law.

If the chief aim of writing were teaching us to read the law without
which there can be no writing, then all writing would be but a reading of
the law which rules it as it rules the universe, a law we could not violate
under penalty of being cut off from the book.

> (*Remoteness is not absence. On the contrary. Assessing the distance which
> separates us from an object, a place, a sorb-apple, gives them back to us in their
> true dimension.*

> "*Could it be that the absence of God is only due to His remoteness? Farther
> than farthest? The mind can conceive of this and the believer's heart suffer
> even though his faith reassures him.*"
> "*But God is without dimension. He is the measure of All.*"

> "*God is the distance of Law and, through the Law, present everywhere,*" he
> said to me.

> "*God,*" I said to myself, "*is perhaps only the distance which separates us
> from any idea of God. The solitude of an Idea.*")

III

Digression is the lonely man's course par excellence. But could we not,
by taking another route, get to the end of our solitude? Tomorrow is linked
to all the swaggering days after. This race is without mercy, that is to say
without pity or thanks. Tomorrow blazes above thousands of exhausted
horses.

Yesterday is our solitude and tomorrow will be likewise. If man is made
in God's image he cannot help being, like Him, eternally alone. Every
book is the book of a solitide, of an absence from the world which the
world inhabits and the word ushers in.

I was born on April 16 . . . If I come back to this sentence in a third phase, it
is to introduce the following. While in fact born on April 16, I could only
bring forward the date of the 14th written in my passport. The triumphant
lie—though nobody lied—not only reduces truth to silence, but supplants
it. The false date of birth, officially recorded, wipes out the true one. On

the 14th, I was still moving in my mother's womb. A warm, red night enveloped me, filled my eyes. I prepared to face my birth as if I were going to be born of myself. Little by little I wrested from the void the face which has become mine. I was a weak creature living the last hours of before-life, a creature without name gloomily waiting for his, a creature outside language, the embryo of a letter, of a word. Ah, was I really born in Cairo, at the dawn of this 16th of April when my mother gave birth to me? My first scream certainly came at that moment, spattered with blood, and stayed engraved in her memory. If being born is simply coming into the world then I was born on April 16th around 4 AM according to my mother. But do we not come into the world as we go to our death, in sacrificed innocence? As if death had opened our eyes onto itself?

At the beginning of the first *Book of Questions*, one of the characters says: "Child, when I wrote my name for the first time I knew I was beginning a book."

If we admit that we exist only in and through the name, that naming gives existence to the named being or thing, allows it to appear as a specific being or thing, to assert itself as such; if we realize also that nothing exists outside the book, that the world is in the book, i.e. that the world is itself the Book through which, through each of whose pages it becomes the world; if, on the other hand, we cannot ignore that, taking a name, we are no more for the book than the letters which determine the word we have become and that this word is fully realized only in the sentence which is the moment it shares with the book, where it gets its true dimension among the words it defies or deals with—then we can claim that we were born on the day we entered the book, the moment we began being written by it. But a book is always the beginning of the unfinished book which is defined by this very non-fulfillment, beginning of an interrupted re-beginning whose sense and key lies in the hands of death. Remains to be seen what the book is. Also, what the lost book of our very first infancy was like. An erased book, no doubt, but whose erasure all books remember.

We enter the book and, right away, are no longer the same. But is this not so whenever we take a risk, even in the most banal situations? It is enough to act violently or shyly to become another person: *the other* who awaited or dreaded his hour—hour which finally embraces even the hours of his waiting or apprehension. For it is true that whole days, months, years sometimes come to a head in a few fateful minutes, happy or unhappy. So a word, a gesture, is enough to make us another: *the other* of surprise or anxiety, of revolt, of desire, of fear, of wonder shaped by death.

Writing would only be a particular kind of action, all the more dangerous for taking place entirely inside us. For us, to be sure, but also against
us, with the studied design of killing us for the benefit of the other us, that
of our hope or misery which will claim our name.

Could the book of our first infancy be the fore-book of which we die?
Could it be the book of death we leaf through along with our books
without ever knowing for sure if it accompanies us and if it is "the book
within the book?"

Thus being named would mean accepting the destiny of life from the
hands of death, would mean for him who is named to rise from dark
toward day. Day, again, within the day, older than that of our birth whose
arrival we mark with the feverish slant of a signature. Nothing comes to
pass, however, which has not been long and carefully prepared as if
outside ourselves, which might make us think that this "outside" is the
rock bottom. For the written body is, like the book, without limits and
would lead us to think that it is writing which explodes limits, that there is
nothing unlimited outside writing which, having the unquestioned
power to limit, assigns new frontiers which will in turn be overrun one
day. The infinite, like the spotless page, is scattered with invisible frontiers which the human mind in its weakness imposed on the word and
which the word in turn imposes on the mind to force it to reject them so
that it may not rest in peace.

If there are only beginnings of the book, the book could never be. And
how do we know if we are in the book when the book is but its own
absence revealed by words, is but the book of an absence maintained
fictitiously through go-between words. Words of an elsewhere judged
accessible, words on which absence would crash, spellbound. An
elsewhere which in turn is delivered to the words as to dogs, torn to pieces
which we gather on and around the corpse of the Word. Do we not know
this (albeit without understanding clearly) because we are ourselves the
breath of an absence whose rhythm our bodies take on and to whose
ambiguity our name adds? Absence present in a sham projection which
our gestures extend beyond their domain, and as if this extension defined
their reach. Absence which is more than real: our actions draw from it
their relative consistency and necessity.

Knowing that we are in the book means having learned that its absence
is our own. We are always on the threshold of an absence about to declare
itself around which crowd words which this intolerable absence stifles. As
if their future depended, from one definite point of the space absence
occupies (and which their dead past denounces) to the infinite of the
other, on this absence itself. For are not word and world, like ourselves,
perpetually becoming? Are they not therefore absence which only wants
to wed its own image? And are images not always ahead?

We must not think absence lacks images. Without them we could not conceive of absence. Images of images rejected by almighty presence and which, O irony, project it. Thus our lightest step encounters the traces our heels could have left on the ground. Non-existent traces, but which alone could have answered to our manyfold movements. Traces in the void where absence get lost at the borders of the unsuspected, like the blue of the sky at the horizon.

The absent book calls the words. The book's voice is toneless, a silent voice which speaks only to the eye at the heart of the law. This call gives away its presence somewhere.—Word: *vocabulum*, from *vocare*, to call. Does the book transform into vocables the called words which, impatient to join it, also called the book, are still calling it? Desire fed by the desire it kindles, desire of a desire fanned by its own echo?—

So the absent book would only be the indefinite space of the book's desire for words and the words' desire for the book. Desire to write which the desirous writing will maintain, having made it the reason for all writing. For the sky is sky only in order to be written with words of desire for the sky. For the earth is earth only in order to be written in the desire for words of earth. For man is man only in order to be written with the insatiable words of his desires: the same words.

The law of the book is law of desire.

The abyss of desire is the fathomless depth of the law, the vertigo of the pact.

The past is not death, but death's chance to change a certain future—its own? ours?—into a fictional time where our history by dint of being exhumed can be rewritten at the pleasure of our pen. Immense story which has conquered oblivion, but which oblivion had already confronted with excess: excess which is itself at the origin of the creation it makes burst forth.

In this sense the past of all writing presents itself as memory of death, memory of the void which keeps it from dying. Words always have a past through which death operates. For there is no language outside death. Creation killed God who from that point has lived only in the life of His Creation, never more his given life, but a life received.

The book is the place of the neutral whose aloofness is always in danger. A place where two contrary, equally strong forces oppose each other in a fight without respite, but also without issue. For as they keep watching each other any lapse would only be temporary. The losing force would immediately double its effort and reestablish the balance for a moment imperiled.

On one side writing: what takes place, writes itself in the book. On the other, facing it, non-writing: what undoes and erases itself in the book. As if it were the very erasing which wrote itself in order to be erased.

The neutrality of the book is matched by the writer.

And what is questioning other than waking these supremely active forces which an answer paralyses and then revives, a showing of the neutral in its refuted negation and whose death—where creative life and destructive life brave each other with indomitable fire, their original indivisible truth—is the highest expression?

The neutrality of book and death lies in the name they escape and which, given back to itself, becomes the name of their absence.

God's life outside the Name is the life of a humble word, life of a life out of His reach and which at the darkest point of the unnamable names Him in His invulnerability.

> (Nom, *"name,"* should be read twice, from left to right and from right to left, because two words compose it: Nom and Mon. My name. The name is mine. All names are personal.
>
> God is the impersonal of a name, the impossibility of uttering the words of all existence.
>
> In God, Evil and Good, Lie and Truth, Dark and Light, Water and Fire, Word and Silence. Thought and the Unthought cancel each other in the Void, le Rien, *where the enclosed imperative* Nie *of the verb* Nier, *"to deny,"* causes problems. For by denying everything the Void is nothing. But by denying itself, *what is it?*
>
> God is the chance of the Void.
>
> God is perhaps only the chance of those three letters which within Rien, the Void, deny this word.)

IV

I was born on April 16. In this fourth phase of my questioning I should perhaps leave it to my body to confirm or deny, after the day and hour, the year of my birth. Because it is the only judge of its age. And our age would be the same as our body's if we did not have thought which in opening the book to lead it to the final word also opens the world to be deciphered down to its last glimmer.

My body was born on April 16, 1912. And I with it.

No matter what I undertake, what I build, how far I advance in the steps of thinking, the time of my life will never be more than that of my flesh and bones. As if the body were really, in its unlimited closure, the readable limit of the book.

All that we are given to feel, understand, contemplate: this world which subjects us, this half-tamed infinite where words get lost that are giddy with their loss because they can reach us only across the silence of their vanishing—all that captures, releases, carries, destroys us is bound to the body and the space it bestows, to the body in which alone lies their future.

Without body we would be a breath in the wind, silence within silence. Without body there would be no book. As if the absence of books were a suppression of the body.

But could we, without body even distinguish presence from absence, waking from sleep, dawn from dusk? And what is a breath for the wind, a silence for silence when it is the body which speaks or is quiet, breathes or expires? When it is the body which names and comes to terms with names? And what is the book except the body's long preparation for the hidden words of its absence?

Is the body's age the age of the text? If I write a text in three days can I say that the text is three days old? This would also mean that the age of the book of which this text is part would correspond to the sum of hours of its pages. Now, we know that the pages of a book do not add up, but cut down. Out of the book's incalculable number of spotless pages we keep those we cover with words. It is unimaginable to cover them all. Numbering the pages of a book means numbering the pages taken out of the book. Each one sends us back to a virgin page.

Multitudinous body, justified! Do we owe it to the words of our five senses that we have a body ready to give body—its own—to all that seeks existence: vegetal, animal, human body, body of a scent, a sound, a presence of an absence? All along the book death scatters our bodies pell-mell. There will always be a body which makes us die its death.

The dejection, even prostration, which usually precedes the act of writing or follows it closely—to what should we trace it unless perhaps to our body's failure to resist a death which it recovers quickly, so strong is its vitality and so unquenched its thirst for the unknown.

Dying through language a death other than our own, to which our own death finally submits, and surviving this death which will abandon us to its void—does this not mean realizing that we are ourselves creatures of the void to which the words pledge us?

If my body bred the precarious bodies I inhabit then it is the oldest of all. And the lives of all those bodies will never go beyond that of my flesh and bones, my life, that which I feel the right to call my life although I do not know at which moment it began or when it will end, as if, albeit mine, I were in no way master of it.

So what is the use of making a big deal of any date of birth? Saying "I was born on . . ." is as absurd as declaring "I shall die on . . ." because there are no frontiers between life and death and because the body which has felt this tangle knows it will die of it. Being born is already suicide.

I used to think writing led to suicide. I was wrong. It is death which uses writing to tempt us. Blindfolded we play, as in blind man's bluff, at recognizing it: Death, this word which reduces its own signs to ashes.

The question of the book has been for nearly twenty years *my* question.

To approach the book directly would mean cutting short the questioning which is its very reason. It would mean turning our back on the unease, anxiety, torment to which it (often unknowingly) bears witness.

For us as for the book, lie and truth, presence and absence, completeness and incompleteness are at the heart of our interrogations along with the questions of origin and death.

Besides, I do not think there is a valid theory of writing which did not come out of practice.

I have tried to show this practice which for me is always linked to life. And I cannot say to what degree this fuses with the life of every word, so inseparable, so solidary are they in the face of risk.

If all the books which are in the book are to fit within its pages, our multiple, successive lives cannot have any other duration than the single, unforeseeable one of the life of the body.

The body opens like a book. And the word consumed with thoughts, rushes off to conquer the unknown. But the unthought makes it die.

If we do not die of our words it is no doubt because they carry our thoughts, and we are incapable of thinking the unthought.

Flesh can only have a future of flesh.

Translated from the French by Rosmarie Waldrop

Mythotherapy and Postmodern Fictions:
Magic is Afoot

CAMPBELL TATHAM

> *O nobly-born, if thou dost not now recognize*
> *thine own thought-forms, whatever of meditation*
> *or of devotion thou mayst have performed while*
> *in the human world--if thou hast not met with*
> *this present teaching--the lights will daunt*
> *thee, the sounds will awe thee, and the rays*
> *will terrify thee. Shouldst thou not know this*
> *all-important key to the teachings--not being*
> *able to recognize the sounds, lights, and rays*
> *--thou wilt have to wander in the Sangsara.*
>
> Bardo Thödol

Let's see: let's say that certain postmodern fictions resonate a particularly
sensitive chord in our individual and collective psyches; they not only reflect
our deep yearning for (and memory of, in the soul) freedom, they suggest ways of
enacting it in our everyday lives. (*All my speeches were preface to this, all my*
exercises but a clearing of my throat.) Emptiness replaces nothingness, a highly
significant shift of perception. If all seems uncertain, if one day my landscape
wavers to reveal itself as stage scenery, if I sit down before my mirrors in order
to remove my make-up only to discover yet another layer of powder beneath the surface and endless others beneath that with emptiness at the presumed core, if we
come to survey emptiness without and emptiness within -- I need not despair: we
can always create a new role, initiate a new performance, conduct a renewed transformance, amid the endless series. The weary existential *angst* of the modern is
transformed/performed by the spirited free play of the postmodern. I can't go on,
fatigue and disgust prevent me, the roads lead nowhere drearily, I am a voice
without substance, less than nothing, lessness barely personified -- so whimpers
the Old Vision, one we have been well-trained to live comfortably with: down,
Sam. Shift your focus, imagine the funny edge of the world, whispers the New Vision,
assume nothing precisely in particular, open to all and all is possible, imagine.

137

The play is far from over, perhaps only just begun; change is the director, our (multiple) selves infolding and outfolding dazzling perspectives, leaving the merest trace of a script which in turn can be implied only as it edges the trail of our movements. *(Old friend, you may kneel as you read this, for now I come to the sweet burden of my argument.)* We were never able to distinguish the dancer from the dance; now we start to sense we may not need to: the two are one, aspects of reciprocity shimmering in a limitless spectrum. I am, the line of crests along waves of possibilities. Unfixed, without goals, each stroke a vital deflection. We shift to play and find ourselves between. Such at least is the vision, abstract in its seeming. High-altitude projections? But more, or less. For now it may be told.

I lose track of the track. As usual. Hoping to learn to spread myself in every direction. At once. Old habits dog my steps. How to obliterate one's trail as one advances? He asks. Oh. How you do go on. She laughs. Ron stands up. As if to say something. I want to write a book like a cloud that changes as it goes. I want to erase all books. My ambition is to unlearn everything I can't read or write that's a start. I want to unlearn and unlearn till I get to the place where the ocean of the unknown begins where my fathers live. Then I want to go back and bring my people to live beside the ocean where they can be whole again as they were before the Wasichus came.[1] Enough! Ron. You're making this all up. It does not make a bit of sense. It's not a promising beginning. What will your friends say? They'll say. "Ron, cut it out, you're making it all up, you're fucking around with the boredom in our heads." Which may be the point. But not my point. Of course. Look it up in Steve Katz if you really want to know.[2] Or ask my paredros. Who? Who mounts his platform. "I want to tell a story that cancels itself as it goes."[3] Which is inevitable. Or may yet be. All stories cancel themselves progressively. That is. If they go at all. (I confess I tortured you but only to draw your attention to this.)

The viability of Supreme Fictions is what we're seeking. If we improvise our

novels as we improvise our lives, and if the didactic job of the modern novel is
to teach people to invent themselves and the world,[4] then we may hope to find ourselves (in) increasingly richer fictions for all concerned. As Clarence Major shows:
"In fiction we are all swimmers in a collective unconscious where language continually segments us and we keep trying to rediscover the sense of wholeness we
suspect we once possessed. At the right moment we are given the reality we imagine
to be ourselves."[5] Is it that easy? Yes and no. We must be present, at the *right*
moment, in the *right* space, at precisely the *right* turn of the path. Control and
abandon, then, are involved. It's a new discipline, for us; we must patiently learn
new moves if we are to achieve the balance of letting-go, as a matter of form.

We do have gurus. Those who would diagram the intricate forms and speculate
on the energy-flows. √Ihab Hassan, PARACRITICISMS, 1975

√Raymond Federman, SURFICTION, 1975

√Jerome Klinkowitz, THE LIFE OF FICTION, 1977. And we have
those who show the form in action, the energy flowing. √Ron Sukenick

√Steve Katz

√Raymond Federman

√Clarence Major

√William Gass

√Madeline Gins

√Tom Robbins

√Rhoda Lerman

√Richard Grossinger

√Pat Knudsen

Playing, they teach us to play; dancing, they teach us to dance. They hold before
us a mirror of our possibilities. Dare we ponder such reflections? What might we
be/hold? Our selves, varied, split, and split again? Doubled or nothing, in particular?

Yet
again
there i
s in ever
y act of im
agination a d
isdain of utili
ty, and a gloriou
s, free show of hum
an strength; for the
man of imagination dare
s to make things for no b
etter reason than they plea
se him--because he lives. And
everywhere, again, he seeks out
unity; in the word he unifies bot
h sound and sense; among many meani
ngs, he discovers similarities, and c
reates new and singular organizations;
between words and things he further makes
a bond so that symbols seem to contain thei
r objects [...]; while in the other direction
(and at the same time), he experiences his spee
ch as he does himself when he's most fit, when he
is One--and moving smoothly as a stream. Imaginatio
n is, as Sam said, the unifying power, and the acts o
f the imagination are our most free and natural; they r
epresent us at ou
r best.[6] *All fic*
titious work form
s a block: nothin
g can be taken aw
ay from it nor ca
n a single word be changed. That is what makes of the n
ovel a lure. We think we are going to find in it the
expression of our unity, whereas in fact it only ma
nifests the desire of it. We believe, as we are r
elating ourself, that we are going to discover,
to find, that being that we are already. But
that being, that somebody, exists in the wo
rk only, it is the product of it and not
the source. And this is because the ess
ence of a literary discourse is to fi
nd its own point of reference, its
own rules of organization in itse
lf, and not in the real or imag
inary experience, on which it
rests. Through all the deto
urs that one wishes the s
ubject who writes will
never seize himself i
n the novel; he wil
l only seize a no
vel which, by d
efinition, ex
cludes him.[7]
This we k
now now
again
yes

[Of course, some aspects of these fictions absolutely refuse to find their own points of reference and tend to distrust their own rules of organization. They move along the lines of their discontent. They rather suspect they'd rather be something else, somewhere else. Since they can't, evidently, they do their best to obscure themselves, deface all signs of their furtive passages. They demonstrate continual disrespect for their condition. They are willfully difficult. That much may be admitted, certainly.

[Meanwhile, I want you to imagine the difficulties involved under these conditions, holding the various threads of this narrative together, the subplots, the counterplots. In this environment any surprise is possible, and as much as I try to avoid chaos, chaos too often waits for me at the end of a story line, squatting there, wiping his lips on his wrist. Despite these gloomy predictions, I'm going to try to demonstrate that I'm a novelist in good faith. At this point, I'm going to attempt to tie in one of the ends that was left quite loose some pages back. I'm doing

it because I know you need some sense of continuity, and so do I, and getting this done now will save my having to tuck in this strand with all the others at the final denouement.[8] But perhaps you failed to notice that slender line which waggled slyly and trailed off? Really, you must learn to be less careless. It was where I likened this performance to a long, interrupted tenor solo. Only it occurs to me that it's more like something Milt Jackson might play. Words like notes jumping out of Bag's groove, occasionally sharp, more often slurred slightly, electric echoes. Okay, I admit I'm hardly of Milt's stature, but I can dream, can't I? I'd like to think of myself with Milt's tense concentration, his eyes not quite balanced but his touch steady and sure. I saw him the other night on t.v., he was playing with Dizzy Gillespie, James Moody, Al Haig, Ray Brown, and Kenny Clark, it was quite a show. Diz talked about the original impulse of bop, how such music could be understood only insofar as the audience could give up traditional expectations and truly listen. The dazzling dissonance of bop, Diz said, worked from "the same fundamental spiritual basis" as all the ancient religions. Is this a parallel to fiction-making, each a metaphor for the other? I'm not sure why I'm telling you all this. I think there are connections, can you sense them? You

see what's happening here you take a few things that interest you and you begin
to make connections. The connections are the important thing they don't exist before you make them. This is THE ENDLESS FICTION. (*This I mean to whisper to my
mind. This I mean to laugh with in my mind.*) It doesn't matter where you start.
You must have faith. Life is whole and continuous whatever the appearances.[9] Can
you believe that? I can try. I connect this and that, provisionally; you must do
the same, and you do anyway. Now real-ize it. Take it apart; de-, con-, and refuse the elements; add your own aspects, probable and/or possible; (re)assemble
a whole, more and/or less; pass it on. Imagine: chain-letters, in which the point
is to compose increasingly fantastic variants of whatever texts are delivered to
you, the only prize (but what a fine one!) the compositions shared. The texts?
Our lives, offered to and by ourSelves. The process is endlessly alchemical.

      Or: connect with the following: Husserl's use of the notorious εποχή, "this
universal depriving of acceptance, this 'inhibiting' or 'putting out of play'
of all positions taken toward the already-given Objective world and, in the first
place, all existential positions (those concerning being, illusion, possible
being, being likely, probable, etc.),--or, as it is also called, this 'phenomenological epoché' and 'parenthesizing' of the Objective world."[10] The purpose
of bracketing the assumed *reality of the Ob-jective world* is to reveal the operations of *pure Consciousness* and, ultimately, an *eidetic grounding of the Transcendental Ego.* There is, in this introductory step toward a phenomenological
philosophy, an implied dualism between consciousness and the presupposed life-
world: the philosopher temporarily *inhibits* all speculation concerning the
nature of brute existence, which is nonetheless accepted as being-actually-
there (*vorhanden*), in order to return to that world at some later (unspecified)
time with renewed clarity. But is such a suspension possible, much less desirable?
Husserl's tactic tempts, especially as an ontological basis for ... mythotherapy,
but must finally be rejected as little more than a *pensée de survol.* I find

myself, in a state of wild surprise, intricately hooked to the world, the presence of my body reflecting that of all existence. The world (incorporating my
selves, probable and possible) presents itself as a question -- a question which
I extend endlessly without answering. Merleau-Ponty: "The effective, present, ultimate and primary being, the thing itself, are in principle apprehended in trans-
parency through their perspectives and offer themselves therefore only to someone
who wishes not to have them but to see them, not to hold them as with forceps, or
to immobilize them as under the objective of a microscope, but to let them be and
to witness their continued being."[11] Situating himself at the *chiasm* of the visible
an invisible aspects of Being, the writer (you and/or I) engages himself in an un-
ending interrogation of his situation; he speaks to the world, even as the world
speaks through him; if he has a thought which "has a future in every possible reader, this can only be that thought that leaves me with my hunger and leaves them
with their hunger, that betokens a generalized buckling of my landscape and opens
it to the universal, precisely because it is rather an *unthought*. [...] Whether in
discussion or in monologue, the essence in the living and active state is always a
certain vanishing point indicated by the arrangement of the words, their 'other'
side, inaccessible, save for him who accepts to live first and always in them."[12]
The fiction-maker need not, indeed cannot bracket himself nor his world; we encounter him along the fluid horizons of his perception, where we discover ourselves unfolding. Fiction is not the product of a consciousness divorced from a reality
"out there"; fiction highlights the interwoven strands of possible-beings which
form the (invisible) structure of our world; fiction speaks *of* and *through* the
shimmering web along which we dance and have our beings. (*This I mean my mind to
serve till service is but Magic moving through the world, and mind itself is Magic
coursing through the flesh, and flesh itself is Magic dancing on a clock, and time
itself the Magic Length of God.*)

Phew! So much for ontology. I considered describing the world-as-text, bringing in Heidegger and Derrida and saying more about Merleau-Ponty's view of

hyperdialectic (a mode of questioning which resolutely avoids synthesis and contin

ally glides between affirmation and negation) as a paradigm for the intersubjectiv

con-textuality of fiction and so on -- but I reflected, then blinked, then yawned

and fell into a fit of ambiguity where I remain to this very word. Having lost the

thread of phenomenology, I assure you I shall avoid any attempt to unravel struc-

turalism and its attendant schools of exoteric intellection. After all, "reality"

is whatever you and I agree to say/see it as, its probabilities outreaching any

particular version. If you feel the need of arriving somewhere, and then of being

able to describe precisely where you've been, you may perhaps require a map of

some sort. But if, like me, you prefer to wander, receptive to any mystery willing

to disclose itself, then you will choose to abandon all maps and say of what you

see in the holy dark. (*God is alive. Magic is afoot.*) The Fool, green and golden,

with eye of Horus and singled rose, the first and the last, surpasses the frozen

peaks and dances creation into Being. We dog his heels to learn of that joy which

spans the abyss.

I doubt that a person normally develops a coherent sense of identity, and to the extent that he does, he may experience severe emotional stress. [...] If playing a role does in fact lead to real changes in one's self-concept, we should learn to play more roles, to adopt any role that seems enjoyable--a baron, a princess, a secret agent, an Italian merchant--and, if the other is willing to play, a storehouse of novel self-images emerges. The mask may be not the symbol of superficiality that we have thought it was, but the means of realizing our potential.[13]

Human freedom includes freedom to create the metaphors by which we live, then to choose whether these metaphors limit or extend. All ideas can be tools or weapons. It is the choice that makes the difference.[14]

Now, not only are we the heroes of our own life-stories--we're the ones who conceive the story, and give other people the essences of minor characters. This is generally true. If any man displays almost the same character day in and day out, all day long, it's either because he has no imagination, like an actor who can play only one role, or because he has an imagination so comprehensive that he sees each particular situation of his life as an episode in some grand over-all plot, and can so distort the situations that the same type of hero can deal with them all. But this is most unusual.

This kind of role-assigning is myth-making, and when it's done consciously or unconsciously for the purpose of aggrandizing or protecting your ego--and it's probably done for this pur pose all the time--it becomes Mythothera

Here's an exercise you might do right now: imagine yourself sitting in a relaxed posture, totally relaxed, perhaps naked, before a large mirror, with a candle flickering to your left. Settle deeply into yourself, each muscle progressively relaxed, each pore open, each inner sense alert; breathe deeply and regularly, without effort. Find yourself inducing a trance state as you contemplate your reflected otherself. Let go of any expectations, any assumptions that what you might see must correspond to remembered images of yourself. Notice only what can be, only the possible. As you focus on your reflection, permit the flowing lines and colors to blur, thereby liberating your imaged self from supposed identity and leaving you utterly free to follow whatever transformations occur. You will be able to 'tune in' to past selves, future selves, alternate possible 'realities.' Do not fear, you will 'lose' only a rigid, restricted notion that you must be a single, cohesive, unified persona. The "general expansion" you will experience "must expand the entire reality consensus --making the whole human reality deeper, broader, much more multidimensional, and richer, until we will one day look back astounded at the impoverished world of consciousness we once shared, and supposed to be the real world--our officially defined and defended 'reality.'"[16] As you develop your narrative skills, accepting that you are the subtle author of your own life-story, you will explore wondrous sub-plots beyond your present imaginings, dazzling digressions, truly marvelous characters. Time is but the current you swim in; there are rapid channels, inward spiralling eddies, still pools. And strange creatures curling beneath the surfaces, darting among the shadows. And all at once you realize that you are but returning (and mind itself is Magic) to your most natural element to see it as if for the first time (and time itself the Magic Length of God). The worlds we see are those we create, the 'original' situations from which we come, through which we move, toward which we journey. To comprehend this in-sight, we must wake ourselves to dream anew. This I mean to whisper to your mind. Magic is the hinge, open the crack between the the world we read and the world we write. All fiction is magic, all is fiction.

IMAGINE: WHATEVER CAN BE IMAGINED IS FUNDAMENTALLY TRUE, WITHIN
CERTAIN LIMITS, WHICH ARE THEMSELVES ONLY THE CONFIGURATIONS OF
             this transformance, like any other, works on th
             e principle of collage. i simply take various t
             exts and contexts, blend them with my own thoug
             hts, feelings & phantasies, then scatter them i
             n the space before us (that is, right here).i d
             ecline to indicate, generally, which of these a
             spects is mine and which is not mine, for all t
             hat filters through me is 'mine' and 'me' in th
             e only way that finally matters. call it playgi
             arism, it works. everything has been said alrea
             dy in all probable combinations; originality is
             the hobgoblin of rigid egos. what i assume is w
             hat you shall assume, that is, very little. you
             must further blend the elements provided and im
             plied with your own thoughts, feelings & phanta
             sies, scattering as you go (call it sowing), ex
             tending the area of our contextual freeplay. ea
             ch page is a field on which is inscribed the tr
             ace of every conceivable page recorded in the p
             ast or anticipated in the future; the traces ar
             e the elements which await our response; we act
             ivate them through rearrangement. and each aspe
             ct of life, once activated, generates another p
             age. to read is to write, to write is to inscri
             be the ground of each (re)reading. the self is
             a collage in a state of perpetual transformance
AN IMAGINATION AND ARE THEREFORE ABLE TO BE TRANSFORMED THROUGH
OPEN POSSIBILITY, FOR BEYOND THE LIMIT OF THE IMAGINED LIES THE
UNIMAGINED, AND BEYOND THAT, PERHAPS, THE UNIMAGINABLE: IMAGINE

Connections continue. If the self-as-text transforms itself through the
world-as-text, then growth and expansion of consciousness becomes a function
of inter- and con-textuality. When he reads, each reader is the reader of
himself. The writer's work is only a kind of optical instrument which he offers the reader to permit him to discern what he might not have seen in himself without the book. Thus, Philippe Sollers adds, the reader is put in the
position of becoming the deciphering act which can never be definitive and
global but which manifests itself as a circular metamorphosis and sliding.[17]
Our critical stance reflects our most inward assumptions about the positionings
of consciousness. If we insist upon definitive certitude in matters of interpretation, then it is likely that we shall value a fixed identity and be
uneasy, if not actually hostile, when offered a vision of free play. We loud-
ly demand clarity, even as anxieties and ego-defenses most effectively cloud
our vision. Our vehicular consciousness, to borrow Carl Levett's provocative
term, distrusts metamorphosis and sliding; we cling obstinately to a pre-
programmed internal dialogue (which we naively assume takes its authority
from the inherited standard version of the world-text) and block any openings
to the spirit flow.[18] Only the diligent practice of *wu wei*, of radical letting-
go, can overcome what C. G. Jung has called our veritable cramp of consciousness.[19] The way of wholeness and individuation (which in no way conflict with
digressive multiplicity) demands a disciplined receptivity, an art of control
and abandon. Jung recommended active imagining as a means of establishing
fruitful connections, open channels, between the conscious and the unconscious:
choose a dream or some fantasy-image, and con-
centrate on it simply by catching hold of it
and looking at it. [...] Usually it will alter,
as the mere fact of contemplating it animates
it. The alterations must be carefully noted
down all the time, for they reflect the psychic processes in the unconscious

*Is this life becoming art? Or
is it art becoming life? Does
it matter? The only thing that
matters is to keep going from
moment to moment, as quick and
fluid and surprising as one moment flowing continuously into
the next.*[20]

background, which appear in the form of images consisting of conscious memory

material. In this way conscious and unconscious are united, just as a water-

fall connects above and below. A chain of fantasy ideas develops and gradually

takes on a dramatic character: the passive process becomes an action. [...] In

other words you dream with open eyes.[21] When we dream in such a fashion outward,

that is when we dream the world as well as ourselves, we hook into powerful

lines of connection between the reciprocal energies of 'inner' and 'outer.' The

self that dreams is the dream itself. James Hillman calls this soul-making:

What a bore is the everlasting question: By 'soul' I mean the imaginative pos-
What did you mean by [----------]? Come,
come, be more sensuous, less cerebral, sibility in our natures, the experienc-
start dancing with the book instead of
asking for meanings. Why take so much ing through reflective speculation,
interest in the skeleton if it's got
a body? See whether it is capable of dream, image, and fantasy--that mode
pleasing and is not devoid of grace and
passion.[22]   which recognizes all realities as pri-

marily symbolic or metaphorical.[23] To behold our worlds in all their emerging,

always new and wonder-filled varieties, we must assent to the natures of our in-

trinsic inner multiplicity -- that is, in Hillman's view, we must grow to see

through ourselves and live in polytheistic senses, for the house the psyche

actually inhabits is a compound of connecting corridors, multi-leveled, with

windows everywhere and with large ongoing extensions 'under construction,' and

sudden dead ends and holes in the floorboards; and this house is already filled

with occupants, other voices in other rooms, reflecting nature alive, echoing

again the Great God Pan alive, a pantheism rekindled by the psyche's belief in

its personified images.[24] The house of the psyche bears a remarkable resemblance

to the houses of our postmodern fictions. Each a metaphor for the other, and

both metaphors for and metaphored by all that is. To enter such houses we need

only to open the door and follow our dream-guides -- is it not strange that so

many prefer to stop outside and hold themselves tightly as if to keep off the

cold? Yet inner and outer are but different beats of the same rhythm, so that

we are all 'inside' together -- if we could but real-ize such a dream.

STOP IF YOU FIND THE FOLLOWING PAGE DIFFICULT OR IMPOSSIBLE TO READ, YOU MAY
CUT OUT THIS SPECIAL SKELETON-KEY AND APPLY IT TO THE PHOTOGRAPH. DO NOT BE
AFRAID THAT YOU WILL DAMAGE THIS BOOK, IT IS YOUR BOOK ... AND NO ONE IS WATCH-
ING.*

```
                        ell if e
                     less each        raws
                    t call arc       s and wh
     us to t        e and keep      off the re
    that we so      assume tha      ee play wi
     and anarc      only force     t holds us        force
    hy not imag     possibiliti   of everyon      co-author
    text instead    oiled artist   competing      that don'
    ut life is a      more compl ated than        gine and
    e is bound to     inadequate o our exis       ere is no
    ginings the w..ld is neither more nor       han what w
      s a metafiction and its author or au     prefer th
       t to care for if I'm going to be a fictional char
want     g good yarn as they say not some piece of avan
precious     nge the style there is no 'Master Author' nor
some fiendis     playing at being a lord of karma and waiting to
cancel your scri    Well what about standards tell me that you mus
   ood fictions and bad fictions. I admit that while heartfelt ine
   peal so does heartless skill but what we want is passionate vi
   not beyond us imagine that. That's still pretty hypothetica
    n whose personal fiction comes up against a competing
     re or rewrite he might become schizophrenic or simp
      herapy doesn't cure anything except the mind a
       ould be hard to overestimate the importa
         ld I say creating the world in w
```

*But why not make up your own story, fill in the blanks yourself? You must learn
to trust your own abilities, your own sense of proportion. You are the only writer
here, it is your hand which holds down the words, you have but to lift it to
grasp this vision.

Hey wait hold on STOP you're going too fast this soul-making or mythotherapy
isn't as simple as that. Yes? Well, if everyone went around telling his own
story then we'd have chaos. Unless each of us draws upon a more or less common
source of images which we might call archetypes and which generate the energy
that hooks onto the collective and keeps us off the reef of solipsism and
why is it that we so typically assume that free play will necessarily lead to
destruction and anarchy is the assumption that holds together the force of
convention which determine the possibles and one's being a creature
of the world-theater of sport and contests and for prizes that don't
exist anyway? But there's always the comedic illusion we can imagine so
any play we write has to be imminent to our existence. There is no life
outside of our imagined world and there never less than the dream.
Then what if there is some supreme and final author and the kind
of story we happen not to ... I'm going ... character I
want to be in a roaring ... they say now some play ... avant-garde
... ness. Then characters ... here is no Master Author's note is there
... h editor ... and waiting to revise or
... ipt.[25] ... that you must admit there
are ... le heartfelt ... titude has
its ap ... t is passionate virtuosity[26]
which is ... imagine that ... still pretty hypothetical what
about a person ... personal fiction comes up against a competing fiction too
powerful to ignore rewrite he might become schizophrenic or totally shattered.[27]
You're right mythotherapy doesn't cure anything except the mind and the mind
cures through acts it ... to overestimate the importance of the imagination in confronting or should ... which we live.[28]
Enough Ron you're making this all up it doesn't make a bit of sense you're fucking around with the boredom in our heads.[29] I am only the medium for a voice in
your own head you bore yourself. I distrust the story we're in then. And you too?

[Here's a partial outline of the next section. Go on, fill in the blanks your-self, you're ready for the practice and you must learn to depend more on your-self. Remember, it is far easier and no doubt healthier to write your own book than it is to read someone else's.]

III. APPLICATIONS & IMPLICATIONS
  A. The Principle of Endless Digressions: *"But that's silly, when there's no plot line there are no di-gressions"* [Ron Sukenick, "The Death of the Novel"]
  B. The Principle of Leapfrogue [Raymond Federman, *Take It or Leave It*]
  C. The Principle of Simultaneous Multiplicity: *"What we have to become is master jugglers, perfect a balancing act"* [Ron Sukenick, "The Death of the Novel"]
  D. Don Juan on Personal History: *"Little by little you must create a fog around yourself; you must erase everything around you until nothing can be taken for granted, until nothing is any longer for sure, or real. Your problem now is that you're too real. Your endeavors are too real; your moods are too real. Don't take things so for granted. You must begin to erase yourself"* [Carlos Castaneda, *Journey to Ixtlan*]
  E. The Critical Act
    1. Critic-as-everyman & everyman-as-critic?
    2. Paracriticism v. Critifiction
    3. Beyond criticism
  F. Psychic Politics: *"The Book of the Gods—I'd like to write that, and* The Book of the Universe, *in which people-gods or god-people rise from nonphysical to phys-ical life because they want to; because they dreamed in their solitary godhoods of green grasses and soft flesh and yearned to be born as men and women; flinging their godness into bodies joyfully, recklessly, come what may. And maybe, in between lives, they wander on the shores of inner rivers, planning their 'future' lives with great excitement, creating them as a writer does his book, plotting crises and achievements, challenges and glories—then, once on earth again, changing the stories, making surprise endings, each character alive, remaking the plot; with each life forming a new dimension of ac-tuality, providing greater knowledge of honor and love, and a new marriage of the soul with the seasons"* [Jane Roberts, *Psychic Politics*]

IV. BEYOND MYTHOTHERAPY

(All my speeches were a preface to this, all my exercises but a clearing
of my throat. . . . God is alive. Magic is afoot. . . . This I mean to whisper to my mind. This I mean to laugh with in my mind. This I mean my mind to
serve till service is but Magic moving through the world. . . .) I believe I
should tell you, at this point, that our discussion of mythotherapy was little
more than bait. Or rather, its practice is the first step toward Seeing, which
is itself the start of a path of Power. You see, I believe in powers meaning
(as Ron puts it) the extension of the ordinary to the point of the incredible.[30]
I would add that only the incredible is truly ordinary. What is extraordinary
is what most people accept as credible. Which brings me to a consideration of
negative hallucinations. This is what Ron has to say: A negative hallucination
is when you don't see something that's really there. [...] He believes that to
get rid of negative hallucinations you have to be enchanted. He believes that
all people need to enchant their lives but that only those succeed who neither
search nor close their minds (and mind itself is Magic) but simply remain open
to the unknown. [...] People also have the power to enchant one another and
when this happens they are what he refers to as in touch. When people are not
in touch it's dull and sometimes painful. It's even possible for people to be
out of touch with themselves and he now believes that when this occurs on a
mass scale as he thinks it has the only resort is to The Ancien Caja. But he
doesn't even know what The Ancien Caja is. Exactly.[31] But I'm not sure I can
trust Ron, he's trying to learn to speak Bjorsq a language no one can understand. Sometimes he imagines himself as Cloud who feels that life is a lot like
a novel you have to make it up. That's the point of psychosynthesis in his opin-
ion to pick up the pieces and make something of them.[32] Or call it mythotherapy
or active imagining or positive hallucination or psychic politics or seeing or
magic. And magic, according to Leonard Cohen, is definitely afoot.[33]

Old friend------------kneel-----------------now------------------------
-------------------I---------------------------tell-------------------know

```
-----------------------------proclaim-------------------sure--------------
-----preface-----------------------------clearing-------------------confess-
---------------------------attention----------------------------------------
----------tap-----------------------------our------------------------ancient-
--------------whisper.
      God----------Magic----------------------------whisper--------------mind
----------laugh----------mind-------------------mind---serve----------------
-------Magic-------------------world-------mind-------------Magic-----------
-------flesh------flesh----------Magic----------------------------------time
---------Magic Length of God.
```

But there is another kind of seeing that involves a letting go. When I see this way I sway transfixed and emptied. The difference between the two ways of seeing is the difference between walking with and without a camera. When I walk with a camera, I walk from shot to shot, reading the light on a calibrated meter. When I walk without a camera, my own shutter opens, and the moment's light prints on my own silver gut. When I see this second way I am above all an unscrupulous observer.[34]

"My benefactor was a sorceror of great powers," he went on. "He was a warrior through and through. His will was indeed his most magnificent accomplishment. But a man can go still further than that; a man can learn to *see*. Upon learning to *see* he no longer needs to live like a warrior, nor be a sorceror. Upon learning to *see* a man becomes everything by becoming nothing. He, so to speak, vanishes and yet he's there. I would say that this is the time when a man can be or can get anything he desires. But he desires nothing, and instead of playing with his fellow men like they were toys, he meets them in the midst of their folly. The only difference between them is that a man who *sees* controls his folly, while his fellow men can't.[35]

Many postmodern fictions serve as 'esoteric writing' waiting to be deciphered, as if in terms of an initiatory rite: to read them, we must have mastered Seeing, which in turn enables us to transcribe our reading on to the world-text. Seth reminds us that THE PRESENT IS THE POINT OF POWER, the hinge between multiple realities, to which we may apply our will in order to revise the past, enlarge the present, extend the possibilities of the future.[36] That we so rarely recognize our personal power is hardly surprising. Many find themselves in a kind of in-between, or intermediate zone, in which we begin to sense the death of certain outworn modes of perception, even as we apparently fear to transcend Seeing and seek a continually reintegrated psyche within an ongoing vision. Those familiar with *The Tibetan Book of the Dead*, that ancient postmodern masterpiece, will note the parallels with the Bardo state, specifically the Chönyid Bardo.[37] For it is in the Chönyid Bardo that we are provided with the opportunity to achieve illumination and possible liberation through a confrontation with archetypal apparitions, both personal and collective.[38] The Seven Peaceful Deities, comprising projections of emotional states, and the Seven Wrathful Deities, projections of the intellect, all play out before us versions and variations of our life-story. It is of vital importance, we are told, that we give free play to these visionary experiences; to flee or repress them is to invite constricted karma and premature submergence in the Sangsara. Even more important is to recognize that these archetypal seeds, from which we harvest so much wisdom, are nonetheless aspects of ourselves, our "own thought-forms" -- this is the "all important key to the teachings."[39] Discipline, practice, and perseverance are required if we are to develop precisely the right balance between control and abandon. Mythotherapy is a game designed to tap these innate skills, postmodern fictions provide the pieces of the game and the field in which it may be played. And the stakes may be higher than we have yet imagined.

AREAS FOR FURTHER RECREATION:

1. Connect the works of Carlos Castaneda with Ron Sukenick's OUT (1973). Re-view Mircea Eliade's SHAMANISM (1964).

2. Connect the myth of The Return with Sufism and Doris Lessing's BRIEFING FOR A DESCENT INTO HELL (1970)

3. Imagine the possible significance of humanistic astrology as envisioned in the fictions of Dane Rudhyar.

4. Connect attitudes toward dreaming in Saul Bellow's HUMBOLDT'S GIFT (1975) with Rudolf Steiner's AN OUTLINE OF

OCCULT SCIENCE {1972} and W. Y. Evans-Wentz's TI-
BETAN YOGA AND SECRET DOCTRINES {1935, 1974}.

5. Connect the techniques of alchemy as outlined in
   Israel Regardie's THE PHILOSOPHER'S STONE {1970}
   and C. G. Jung's ALCHEMICAL STUDIES {1967} with
   Richard Grossinger's THE SLAG OF CREATION {1975}.

6. Connect the teachings of Qabalah, as outlined in
   Dion Fortune's THE MYSTICAL QABALAH {1935}, with
   Pat Knudsen's TASHTEGO {1977}.

7. Imagine the structure of Annie Dillard's PILGRIM
   AT TINKER CREEK {1975} in terms of the Tarot. Review Paul Foster Case's THE TAROT {1947}.

8. Imagine the connections between Ceremonial Magic,
   as outlined in Israel Regardie's THE GOLDEN DAWN
   {1971}, and Robert Kelly's THE SCORPIONS {1967}.

9. Imagine connecting any or all of these con-texts
   and pre-texts with your own Life-Story.

It all becomes a matter of myth, myths for our times. I share with Jung the
view that "myth is more individual and expresses life more precisely than does
science." And, as with Jung, active imagining is central to my personal myth:
I can "only 'tell stories.' Whether or not the stories are 'true' is not the
problem. The only question is whether what I tell is *my* fable, *my* truth."[40] And
my stories intersect with yours, and theirs, on various levels through various
versions, for the connections have not been broken. How could they? They endure
as we endure. And now it may be told: I read to write and learn by writing what
I have to tell: we are the telling: may the story be endless....

> *God is alive. Magic is afoot. . . . This I mean to whisper
> to my mind. This I mean to laugh with in my mind. This I mean
> my mind to serve till service is but Magic moving through the
> world, and mind itself is Magic coursing through the flesh, and
> flesh itself is Magic dancing on a clock, and time itself the
> Magic Length of God.*
> **Leonard Cohen**

[1]Ron Sukenick, *Out* (Chicago, 1973), p. 136.

[2]Steve Katz, *The Exagggerations of Peter Prince* (New York, 1968), p. 3.

[3]Raymond Federman, *Take It or Leave It* (New York, 1976), Ch. VII.

[4]Ron Sukenick, *The·Death of the Novel and Other Stories* (New York, 1969), p. 47.

[5]Clarence Major, "Making Up Reality," *Fiction International*, 2/3, p. 151.

[6]William Gass, *Willie Masters' Lonesome Wife, Tri-Quarterly Supplement Nº Two* (1968), no page numbers.

[7]Raymond Federman, *Double or Nothing* (Chicago, 1971), p. 146.5.

[8]Steve Katz, p. 62.

[9]Ron Sukenick, "The Endless Short Story: Verticles and Horizontals," *Statements: New Fiction from the Fiction Collective* (New York, 1975), p. 187.

[10]Edmund Husserl, *Cartesian Meditations*, trans. Dorian Cairns (The Hague, 1970), p. 20.

[11]Maurice Merleau-Ponty, *The Visible and The Invisible*, trans. Alphonso Linguis (Evanston, 1968), p. 101.

[12]Merleau-Ponty, pp. 118-119.

[13]Kenneth Gergen, "The Happy Healthy Human Being Wears Many Masks," *Psychology Today* (May 1972), p. 66.

[14]Bob Samples, *The Metaphoric Mind* (Reading, Mass., 1976), p. 164.

[15]John Barth, *The End of the Road,* Revised Edition (Garden City, 1967), pp. 82-83.

[16]Robert Masters and Jean Houston, *Mind Games: The Guide to Inner Space* (New York, 1972), p. 230.

[17]Philippe Sollers, "The Novel and the Experience of Limits," in *Surfiction: Fiction Now and Tomorrow*, ed. Raymond Federman (Chicago, 1975), p. 70.

[18]Carl Levett, *Crossings: A Transpersonal Approach* (Ridgefield, Conn., 1974), no page numbers.

[19]C. G. Jung, "Commentary," *The Secret of the Golden Flower*, trans. Cary F. Baynes (New York, 1962), pp. 93, 95.

[20]Ron Sukenick, "The Death of the Novel," *The Death of the Novel and Other Stories,* p. 7.

[21]C. G. Jung, *Mysterium Coniunctionis*, trans. R. F. C. Hull, The Collected Works of C. G. Jung, Vol. 14 (Princeton, 1970), pp. 495-496.

[22]Witold Gombrowicz, *Ferdydurke*, trans. Eric Mosbacher (New York, 1968), p. 9.

[23]James Hillman, *Re-Visioning Psychology* (New York, 1975), p. x.

[24]Hillman, p. 42.

[25]John Barth, "Life-Story," *Lost in the Funhouse* (Garden City, 1968), pp. 119, 120.

[26]John Barth, *Chimera* (New York, 1972), p. 24.

[27]John Barth, *The End of the Road*, p. 84.

[28]Ron Sukenick, *UP* (New York, 1968), p. 308.

[29]Cam Tatham, "Mythotherapy and Postmodern Fictions: Magic Is Afoot," *Correspondances* (New York, 1987), p. 77.

[30]Ron Sukenick, *98.6* (New York, 1975), p. 11.

[31]Sukenick, *98.6*, pp. 11-12.

[32]Sukenick, *98.6*, p. 122.

[33]Leonard Cohen, *Beautiful Losers* (New York, 1966, 1967), pp. 197-198.

[34]Annie Dillard, *Pilgrim at Tinker Creek* (New York, 1975), p. 33.

[35]Carlos Castaneda, *A Separate Reality* (New York, 1972), p. 153.

[36]Jane Roberts, *The Nature of Personal Reality: A Seth Book* (Englewood Cliffs, 1974), pp. 344 ff.

[37]*The Tibetan Book of the Dead*, ed. W. Y. Evans-Wentz, trans. Lama Kazi Dawa-Samdup (New York, 1927, 1960), esp. pp. 28-35.

[38]José A. Argüelles, *The Transformative Vision* (Berkeley, 1975), p. 227.

[39]*The Tibetan Book of the Dead*, p. 104.

[40]C. G. Jung, *Memories, Dreams, Reflections,* trans. Richard and Clara Winston (New York, 1961), p. 3.

Federman: Voices within Voices

Process of displacement: to take written texts -- poems/fictions --
already fixed set printed in one place. Author-ized by a name: in
this case Federman. Finished? Temporarily finished (even printed,
words refuse totalization). To relocate these into other spaces:
oral/visual.

> *The possibility of displacement is found in the very*
> *nature of language, in the fact that language is se-*
> *mantic, that is, in the vibration or movement that*
> *surrounds the words and that no dictionary will ever*
> *succeed in rendering. The possibility of displacement*
> *is found in the play of meaning.*

Process of cancellation: to annul written texts -- poems/fictions --
pregnant with signification. To remove by superimposition by double
exposure (bilingual and multilingual) the established meaning of words:
the something-to-be-said that always pretends to be there even before
texts are written. Blur meaning by mixing voices. The single voice
multiplied by itself: in this case Federman's voice speaking within
itself.

> *More and more we have come to recognize that art cancels*
> *itself. The Tinguely machine works to destroy itself.*
> *The blank page and the white canvas pretend to deny*
> *their existence. Modern music abolishes itself*
> *into silence or discordance. Fiction/poetry*
> *writes itself into non-sense or lessnessness. Radical*
> *irony implicit in the statement of the old Cretan who*
> *affirms that all Cretans are liars thus canceling both*
> *the truth and the lie of his perfect rhetorical statement.*

Process of pulverization: to decompose written texts -- poems/fictions --
already organized into a form a structure a syntax. Stylized by a name:
in this case Federman. To destructure words in their syntactical unity by
dissemination. Oral/visual dislocation: echoes of echoes that designify
language.   Here

   the design-word

  · and the design-syntax   independent of one another

   are set against one another!

   Syntax, traditionally, is the unity, the continuity of
   words, the law which dominates them. It reduces their
   multiplicity, controls their violence. It fixes them
   into a place, a space, prescribes an order to them.
   It prevents them from wandering. Even if it is
   hidden, it reigns always on the horizon of
   words which buckle under its mute exigency.

Process of repetition: to repeat written texts -- poems/fictions -- by
overlapping (orally but also visually) with slight variations distortions
(ironies?) in an attempt to prevent unity of presence.

   The author (in this case Federman) is (perhaps) that
   which gives the disquieting language of poetry/fiction
   its unities its knot of coherence its insertion into the
   real.

   We listen only for the pleasure of repeating. And yet,
   we write under the illusion that we are not repeating
   what has already been written.

   To tell or retell, to make or remake works on the prin-
   ciple of duplication and repetition. Memory does not
   separate itself from imagination, or if it does it is
   only through a slight displacement of facts.

Process of revision: to rewrite (collectively) texts seemingly static
in their written form. Speaking, reading words of others -- in this
case Federman's poems/fictions -- is to rewrite. To listen to words,
to look at words already frozen on the page is to rewrite.

> The writer is no longer to be considered a prophet a
> philosopher or even a sociologist who predicts teaches
> reveals absolute truths nor is he to be looked upon
> (admiringly/romantically) as the omnipotent omniscient
> omnipresent creator but must stand on equal footing
> with the reader/listener in an effort _to make sense_
> out of the language common to both of them.

> To write, in this sense (orally/visually), is always
> to rewrite, and to rewrite does not mean to revert to
> a previous form of writing, no more than to an anterio-
> rity of speech, or of presence, or of meaning. To re-
> write: undoubling which always precedes unity, or sus-
> pends it while plagiarizing it. To rewrite is performed
> apart from all productive initiative and does not pretend
> to produce _anything_, not even the past, or the future, or
> the present of writing. To rewrite while repeating what
> does not, will not, did not take place, inscribes itself
> in a non-unified system of relations which intersect
> without having any point of intersection affirm the co-
> incidence, thus inscribing itself under the exigency of
> return by which we are pulled away from the modes of
> temporality which are always measured by a unity of
> presence.

Process of self-pla(y)giarization: to replay texts by inserting them
into other texts. Intertextualization: in this case Federman's imagination plagiarizing itself. To pla(y)giarize one's life: voices
within voices.

> Libère-toi de la trop longue parole/free yourself of the
> never ending utterance.

162

to demystify the sacrosanct name of the author	and not vice versa
to allow the text to invent (re-invent?) the author	and not vice versa
to let the words become meaning unpredictably	and not vice versa
to desacralize the origin of the text	and not vice versa
to unglorify the name of the author	and not vice versa
to relocate the author's consciousness in the text	and not vice versa
to remove the authorial voice from the center of the text	and not vice versa
to perform on the text a syntactical deconstruction	and not vice versa
to allow words to wander into other spaces other places	and not vice versa
to liberate language from its discursiveness	and not vice versa
to suspend the will of economic communication	and not vice versa
to make of nonsense a positive quality	and not vice versa
to affirm the intrinsic value of nonsense	and not vice versa
to perturb the logic of ratiocination	and not vice versa
to refuse the desire of influence upon the real	and not vice versa
to reject all formulas	and not vice versa
to use one's imagination lest others use it for us	and not vice versa
to be indifferent towards efficacity	and not vice versa
to place attentiveness on the form of the message	and not vice versa
to prevent the text from being something other than itself	and not vice versa
to assume the risk that language takes when it speaks	and not vice versa
to release impetuousness language has for dissoluteness	and not vice versa
to lead language into the chaos of indifference	and not vice versa
to demonstrate that imagination is exercised in vacuo	and not vice versa
to prove imagination cannot tolerate the limits of the real	and not vice versa
to accept confusion/disorder as an intrinsic part of art	and not vice versa
to dismember the unity of presence in the text	and not vice versa

The intrinsic value of a discourse does not depend on the importance of its subject, for then theologians would have it by far, but in fact in the way we approach the accidental and the meaningless, in the way of mastering what is insignificant. The essential never requires, as far as I know, the least talent.

A work is finished when one can no longer improve it even though one knows it to be insufficient and incomplete. One is so worn out, that one no longer has the courage to add a single comma, even if indispensable. What determines the degree of completion of a work is not at all the exigencies of art or of truth, it is fatigue, and even more so, disgust. There is no true art without a strong dosage of banality.

FACTS ABOUT THE POST-MODERN PERFORMANCE

THE PERFORMANCE -- presented on November 18, 1976, as part of an "International Symposium on Post-Modern Performance" at the Center for 20th Century Studies, University of Wisconsin-Milwaukee.

THE TAPE -- (36 minutes & 34 seconds) was recorded in the studios of WXXI-FM in Rochester, New York, on June 1-7, 1976, under a grant from the New York State Arts Council as part of the INTERGALACTIC POETRY CIRCUS. Eleven texts (poems/fictions) by Federman were recorded in multi-voice on four track tape, the voice being that of Federman multiplied by itself, at times superimposed upon itself (within itself) up to ten times, either in English or bilingually in English and French simultaneously.

THE SLIDES -- (84 of them) were made by Federman at the State University of New York at Buffalo with the equipment available in the Photography Department. In color, the slides reproduce the manuscripts of the texts recorded on tape but by pulverizing these with collages and montages, superimpositions and double exposures.

THE TEXTS -- (in the order in which they are recorded on tape):
IN THE BEGINNING (a concrete poem)
WALLS / LES MURS (a bilingual poem)
ME TOO (a schizophrenic poem)
NOW THEN / ET MAINTENANT (a bilingual poem)
THE VOICE IN THE CLOSET (fiction -- excerpt from a work in progress)
WORDS OUT OF A BAD DREAM / MAUVAIS MOTS D'UN REVE (a bilingual poem)
HISTORY OF THE BALLOON / HISTOIRE DU BALLON (bilingual fiction)
THE OTHER COUNTRY / L'AUTRE PAYS (a poem in two languages)
THREE BILINGUAL POEMS: OLD SKIN / VIEILLE PEAU
                          THE GAME / LE JEU
                          THE HAND / LA MAIN

IN THE BEGINNING (a concrete poem)

TAPE

time: 2 minutes & 6 seconds

the text recorded eight times, each time with a slight staggering
of the voice thus creating a verbal overlapping of the voice with
the text beginning eight times upon itself.

SLIDES (6)

1. manuscript of the text
2. collage pulverization of the text
3. text photographed upside down with photo of new born baby in
    lower right corner (probably photo of Federman at birth)
4. double exposure of text
5. text upside down pulverized by cutting and folding
6. manuscript of the text

in the beginning
before the alpha
bet was invented
to make words it
was impossible t
o name things si
nce they were no
t yet in existen
ce because there
were no words to
name them in the
beginning before
numbers were ass
embled one after
another from one
to infinity it w
as impossible to
count the things
that had not ye
t been named bec
ause there was n
o alphabet to ma
ke words to name
things therefore
it was impossibl
e then to design
ate in a convent
ional manner thi
ngs and events f
rom A to Z or fr
om 0 to 10 for i
n fact nothing c
ould be distingu
ished from nothi
ng nor was it po
ssible to establ
ish some kind of
order or some so
rt of series num
erical or alphab
etical in the be
ginning since ob
viously it was i
mpossible for an
yone to begin an
ywhere nor to pr
oceed forward or
backward or in a
ny direction tha
t made sense whe
ther or not a co
herent series of
letters words sentences or numbers

IN THE BEGINNING

count the things
e indeed to name
it was impossibl
assembled before
ore numbers were
was invented bef
ore the alphabet
he beginning bef
n existence in t
at was not yet i
what was from wh
d have been from
parate what coul
impossible to se
ngs since it was
nd counting thi
o begin naming a
ds and numbers t
le to invent wor
t exist to be ab
d numbers did no
epts of words an
matter even conc
ence or for that
not yet in exist
and numbers were
arly since words
nything particul
ssible to know a
fore it was impo
was formed there

WALLS / LES MURS (a bilingual poem)

TAPE

time: 1 minute & 40 seconds

the text recorded four times in English and four times in French
on eight different tracks then synthesized into a superimposition
of voices (Federman's voice multiplied by eight speaking simultaneously in English and in French) against the background of the
rhythmic pattern of the single word WALLS and the single word MURS
recorded on separate tracks.

SLIDES (4)

1. manuscript of the text (English version)
2. photo of Federman's face against a brick wall
3. photo of wall structures
4. manuscript of the text (French version)

```
WALLS   WALLS  WALLS  WALLS  WALLS  WALLS  WALLS  WALLS  WALLS  WALLS

WALLS       I'M FED UP WITH WALLS                          WALLS
            THEY'RE EVERYWHERE
WALLS       TALL ONES       SMALL ONES                     WALLS
            THICK ONES        HIGH ONES
WALLS       ROUND AND SQUARE AND HUGE AND DARK             WALLS
            HOLLOW WALLS WITH HIDING PLACES INSIDE OF THEM
WALLS       EVERYWHERE                          WALLS      WALLS
            INSIDE           OUTSIDE          ALL AROUND
WALLS       METAL    STONE PLASTER MUD    WOOD     ADOBE    WALLS
            WITH RATS CRAWLING INSIDE  AND UGLY BUGS   TOO
WALLS       AND THEY HAVE ALL KINDS OF BAD ATROCIOUS NAMES WALLS

WALLS                                    PARTITIONS        WALLS
                                         PARAPETS
WALLS                                    RAMPARTS          WALLS
                                         FENCES
WALLS                                    CURBS             WALLS
                                         FRAMES
WALLS                                    RAILINGS          WALLS
                                         BALUSTRADES
WALLS                                    BATTLEMENTS       WALLS
                                         BREASTWORKS
WALLS                                    BARRICADES        WALLS
                                         BULWARKS
WALLS       DIVIDING WALLS               ENCLOSURES        WALLS
            DEFENSIVE WALLS
WALLS       CELL WALLS    TOWN WALLS    SURROUNDING WALLS  WALLS
            GREAT WALLS       PAPER WALLS    CHINA WALLS
WALLS       INNER WALLS               OUTER WALLS          WALLS

WALLS       ENOUGH TO DRIVE YOU MAD     NUTS      CRAZY    WALLS
            OUT OF YOUR MIND   UP THE WALL  SCHIZOPHRENIC
WALLS       AND YOU FEEL CORNERED LOCKED IN ENCLOSED STUCK WALLS
            IN THERE                      WALLED IN
WALLS       PRISONER                ALIENATED             WALLS
            AND YOU FEEL SICK SAD LONELY COMPRESSED MORBID
WALLS       CLAUSTROPHOBIC                     IN THERE   WALLS
            AND YOU'RE FED UP  UP TO HERE   ABOVE THE HEAD
WALLS       AND YOU WANT TO GET THE HELL OUT TAKE OFF GONE WALLS

WALLS       AND SO YOU JUMP OVER THE FIRST WALL HEAD FIRST WALLS
            OR ELSE YOU GO RIGHT THROUGH IT   STRAIGHT ON
WALLS       SIDEWAYS       FLAT ON YOUR BACK      SIDEWAYS WALLS
            ON ALL FOURS                    EYES CLOSED
WALLS       BUT ON THE OTHER SIDE ANOTHER WALL  AND ON THE WALLS
            OTHER SIDE OF THE OTHER SIDE ANOTHER WALL   AND
WALLS       ANOTHER ONE AND ANOTHER ONE AND ANOTHER AND AN WALLS
            AN INFINITY OF WALLS      AN INFINITY OF WALLS
WALLS       AN ETERNITY OF WALLS      AN ETERNITY OF WALLS WALLS
            EVERYWHERE EVERYWHERE EVERYWHERE EVERYWHERE EV
WALLS       WALSWALLSWALLLLLSSWALLSWALLSWALLSWALLSWALLSWAL  WALLS

WALLS   WALLS  WALLS  WALLS  WALLS  WALLS  WALLS  WALLS  WALLS  WALLS
```

```
LES MURS LES MURS LES MURS LES MURS LES MURS LES MURS LES MURS LES MURS

LES MURS                                                            LES MURS

LES MURS      j'en ai marre des murs                               LES MURS
              y en a partout des murs
LES MURS      des grands    des hauts    des petits                LES MURS
LES MURS      des épais       des sombres      des ronds           LES MURS
              des immenses                     des sombres
LES MURS      des creux avec des cachettes dedans                  LES MURS
LES MURS      y en a partout      dedans et dehors                 LES MURS
              des murs          tout autour        de la pierre
LES MURS      du bois   aussi   du fer  du plâtre   du carton      LES MURS
LES MURS      avec des rats                   des cafards          LES MURS
              et ça s'appelle des tas de choses affreuses
LES MURS                                                            LES MURS

LES MURS      parois                                               LES MURS
              cloisons
LES MURS      murailles                                            LES MURS
LES MURS      murets                                               LES MURS
              muretins
LES MURS      remparts                                             LES MURS
LES MURS      pans                                                 LES MURS
              parapets
LES MURS      enceintes                                            LES MURS
LES MURS      garde-fous                                           LES MURS

LES MURS      y a de quoi devenir fou  cinglé  dingue             LES MURS
LES MURS      et on se sent emmuré  cloîtré  coincé                LES MURS
              cloisonné          là-dedans        prisonnier
LES MURS      et on en a la claustrophobie                         LES MURS
LES MURS      et on en a marre   plein le dos    par-dessus        LES MURS
              la tête             et on veut se tirer
LES MURS      foutre le camps       se barrer     sortir           LES MURS
LES MURS      mettre les bouts    s'en sortir      partir          LES MURS

LES MURS                                                            LES MURS
              alors on saute par-dessu un mur
LES MURS      le premier qui se trouve là devant soi               LES MURS
              ou bien on passe à travers
LES MURS      à quatre pattes            à plat ventre             LES MURS
LES MURS                  en douce                                 LES MURS
              mais de l'autre côté              encore un mur
LES MURS      et encore un et encore un et encore un autre         LES MURS
LES MURS      que des murs que des murs que des murs que           LES MURS
              des murs des murs des murs des murs des murs
LES MURS      une infinité de murs    une éternité de murs         LES MURS
              partout partout partout partout partout partout
LES MURS      que des murs                   que des murs          LES MURS
              des murs des murs des murs des murs des murs et
LES MURS      encore des murs encore des murs encore des murs      LES MURS
LES MURS                                                            LES MURS

LES MURS LES MURS LES MURS LES MURS LES MURS LES MURS LES MURS LES MURS
```

ME TOO (a schizophrenic poem)

TAPE

time: 55 seconds

text recorded on a single track against the background of seven
synthesized voices (Federman's voice multiplied by itself) in
echoes as though the single voice is speaking in the hollow of
its own sound.

SLIDES (7)

1. title page of book (ME TOO) in which text is published illus-
    trated by graphic computer figures
2. title of poem and name of author
3. manuscript of text (first version)
4. double exposure of two different photos of Federman (one being
    a photo of a photo)
5. second version of the text playing on repetition of certain words
6. double exposure of text superimposed on itself
7. text with drawing of two grotesque (human?) figures surrounding
    the text as published in ETHOS (a literary magazine, Buffalo)

ME TOO

I undouble
I multiply
I play hide and seek with myself
I subdivide
I cry and decry in two languages
I disappear
I see me seen
I use the THOU form with myself
I cut and recut me
I remend myself with red thread
I disperse
I am moved
I put me in myself
I me WE
I unknot
I me US
I me too
I singularize
I pluralize too
I decenter
I play ping pong alone from both sides
I schizophrenize
I split in several
I mask my mask
I metwice
I me we am I are
I decentralize
I concentrate towards the open side
I add up
I metooize
I meusize
I double up and undouble again
I redouble
I multiply by two and demultiply by four
I me me I

ME TOO

I undouble undouble
I multiply multiply
I play hide and seek play hide and seek with myself
I subdivide subdivide
I cry and decry cry and decry in two languages
I disappear disappear disappear
I see me seen see me seen
I use the THOU the THOU form with myself
I cut and recut and cut and recut me
I remend myself remend myself with red thread
I disperse disperse disperse disperse
I am moved moved moved
I put me in myself myself myself
I me WE me WE me WE me
I unknot unknot
I me US me US me US me
I me too me too twice
I singularize
I pluralize pluralize
I decenter decenter decenter decenter decenter
I play ping pong ping pong pong ping alone from both sides
I schizophrenize phrenize phrenize schizophrenize
I split in several several
I mask my mask my mask my mask
I metwicemetwice
I me we am I are
I decentralize decentralize
I concentrate concentrate towards the open side the open side
I add up add up add up add up
I metooize
I meusize
I double up and undouble again and double up and undouble again
I redouble redouble
I multiply by two and demultiply by four
I me me I me me I me me I me me I me me I me me I

NOW THEN / ET MAINTENANT (a bilingual poem)

TAPE

time: 3 minutes & 5 seconds

text recorded on two different tracks, one in English and one in
French and synthesized so that the English and the French alternate so that Federman's bilingual voice answers itself.

The French/English poem is spoken against the background of a
transcribed piece of electronic music.

SLIDES (7)

1. manuscript of the text (English version)
2. double exposure of a landscape
3. photo of a man with arm raised (probably Federman)
4. photo of a man with arm raised (probably Federman), different position
5. manuscript of poem entitled YOU TOO with superimposition of young girl
   with a doll (possibly Federman's sister, age 4)
6. young girl with a doll (possibly Federman's daughter, age 4)
7. manuscript of the text (French version)

NOW THEN   raymond   federman   ET MAINTENAI

I forever been --- where to now --- moi pour toujours --- avoir été --- où maintena
don't even say why --- ne jamais dire pourquoi ---
but --- you --- you ask how --- mais --- toi --- toi tu demandes --- comment ---
I skip --- je passe ---
never before spoken --- jamais avant redit ---
yet --- what --- for me --- no --- et pourtant --- quoi --- pour moi --- non ---
I repeat --- I repeat --- je répète --- je répète ---
moments of surprise --- moments de surprise ---
when --- without --- quand --- sans vouloir ---
I want to speak --- je veux parler ---
there --- now --- voilà --- maintenant ---
you too --- toi aussi ---
speech of moon --- langue de lune ---
silent pieces of words --- silencieux morceaux de mots ---
memorized hearts --- or hands --- violence à la mémoire --- coeurs --- ou mains ---
down to this --- réduit à ça ---
I resume --- voices to try --- now --- je résume --- voix à essayer --- maintenant -
how --- the beast speaks --- comment --- remarque la bête ---
whether they came --- dying --- même s'ils viennent --- mourants ---
never before --- jamais avant ---
I wait --- I wait --- j'attends --- j'attends ---
soft lies --- moribunds --- mensonges doux --- moribonds ---
faces to words --- figures aux mots ---
now then ---   et maintenant ---

THE VOICE IN THE CLOSET (fiction -- excerpt from a work in progress)

TAPE

time: 17 minutes & 25 seconds

text read into six different microphones as technician displaced
the voice (in this case Federman's voice reading his own text) into
six different spaces -- oral spaces: close, far, remote, hollow,
echo, distant -- corresponding to six different moments in time.
A sound montage (sound of selectric typewriter, glass breaking,
laughter, jazz, and various other noises) was superimposed on the
voices while the entire recording is played against a background of
metallic electronic music.

SLIDES (33)

1. title of text (THE VOICE IN THE CLOSET) with photo of a group of
    soldiers (Federman possibly present among them)
2. manuscript of page 1 of the text (small print) with photo of Sam
    (obviously Samuel Beckett)
3. manuscript of page 1 of the text (enlarged)
4. manuscript of page 2 of the text (small print) superimposed on
    photo of lush landscape
5. manuscript of page 2 of the text (enlarged)
6. Pleasurism (a page of typographical designs)
7. manuscript of page 3 of the text (small print) with photo of woman
    repeated six times (perhaps photo of Federman's mother)
8. photo of man against a fence in double exposure (probably Federman)
9. manuscript of page 3 of the text (enlarged)
10. typographically pulverized page of the text
11. manuscript of page 4 of the text (small print) with double exposure
    of a man (probably a snapshot of Federman)
12. photo of a bird flying out of a tree

13. manuscript of page 4 of the text (enlarged)
14. photo of a bird (same as 12) flying back into a tree
15. manuscript of page 5 of the text (small print) superimposed on photo of winter landscape
16. manuscript of page 5 of the text (enlarged)
17. typographically pulverized page of the text with letters enlarged
18. manuscript of page 6 of the text (small print) superimposed on picture of a cat and garbage cans
19. photo of monuments (possibly the Trocadero in Paris)
20. manuscript of page 6 of the text (enlarged) with hardly visible superimposed human figures
21. manuscript of page 7 of the text (small print)
22. photo of a man playing tennis (certainly Federman)
23. Federman playing tennis superimposed on poem which typographically writes the word MOON
24. manuscript of page 7 of the text (enlarged)
25. manuscript of page 8 of the text (small print) with double exposure of photo of two young girls (perhaps Federman's daughters, age 4 and 8)
26. manuscript of page 8 of the text (enlarged)
27. manuscript of page 9 of the text (small print) with double exposure of photo of young boy (probably Federman, age 12)
28. manuscript of page 9 of the text (enlarged)
29. WEATHER REPORT (a concrete poem)
30. manuscript of page 10 of the text (small print) with double exposure of photo of garbage cans (and perhaps Federman's cat)
31. manuscript of page 10 of the text (enlarged)
32. manuscript of page 11 of the text (small print) with superimposed figures against background of giant icicles (Niagara Falls?)
33. manuscript of page 11 of the text (enlarged) with double exposure of recent photo of Federman pulverized

here now again *selectricstud makes me speak with its balls all balls
foutaise* sam says in his closet upstairs but this time it's going *to*
be serious no more masturbating on the third floor escaping into *the
trees* no the trees were cut down liar it's winter now delays no *more
false* starts yesterday a rock flew through the windowpane voices *and
all* I see him from the corner of my eye no more playing dumb boys *in
the* street laughing up and down the pages en fourire goofing my *life
it*'s a sign almost hit him in the face scared the hell out of him *as*
he waits for me to unfold upstairs perhaps the signal of a *departure
in* my own voice at last a beginning after so many detours *relentless
false* justifications in the margins more to come in my own words *now
that* I may speak say I the real story from the other side *extricated
from* inside roles reversed without further delay they pushed me *into
the* closet on the third floor I am speaking of us into a box beat *me
black* and blue question of perspective how it should have started *in
my* little boy's shorts I am speaking of me sssh it's summertime *lies
again* we must hide the boy sssh mother whispering in her tears *hurts
to lose all the time in the courtyard bird blowing his brains out on*

alto guts squeaking lover man can you hear *it* now *yellow feather cam
sent it to* me at *his fingertips plagiarizing my life boys passing in
the s*treet they threw sand in his eyes it begins downstairs sol*diers
calli*ng our names his too federman all wrong don't let him escape *no
not t*his time must save the boy full circle from his fingers in*to my
voice* back to him on the machine just heard the first echo tiol*i how
idioti*c what did he expect callow it says after twenty years ban*ging
his* head against the wall rattling the old stories ah what's the *use
watch* him search in his dictionary callow unfledged youth almos*t hit
him i*n the face federman featherless little boy dammit in our *closet
after* so many false names foisted upon me evading the truth he *wrote
all t*he doors opened to stare at my nakedness a metaphor I suppos*e a
twis*ted laugh wrong again writing himself into a corner inside *where
they* kept old newspapers delirious strokes of typographiphobia *fatal
however* only on occasions his fingers on the machine make me book *of
flig*hts speak traps evasions question of patience determination *take
it or leave it of all places hundred years of solitary work* down the
drain through the windowpane something about the futility of telling

experimenting with the peripatetic search for love sex self or is it real people america aside from what is said there is nothing silence sam again what takes place in the closet is not said irrelevant here if it were to be known one would know it my life began in a *closet a symbolic* rebirth in retrospect as he shoves me in his *stories whines his radical* laughter up and down pulverized pages with his *balls mad fizzling* punctuation question of changing one's perspective *view the self from* the inside from the point of view of its capacity *its will power federman* achieve the vocation of your name beyond all *forms of anthropologism* a positive child anthropomorphism rather than *the sad off-spring* of a family giggling they pushed me into the clo*set among empty skins* and dusty hats my mother my father the soldiers *they cut little* boys' hands old wife's tale send him into his life cut *me now from your* voice not that I be what I was machines but what I *will be mother father* quick downstairs already the boots same old *problem he tried oh how he tried of course imagining that the self must be made remade caught from some retroactive present apprehended reinstated I presume looking back how naive into the past my life began not again*

whereas in fact my mother was crying softly as the door closes on me
I'm beginning to see my shape only from the past from the reverse of
farness looking to the present can one possibly into the future even
create the true me invent you federman with your noodles gambling my
life away double or nothing in your verbal delirium don't let anyone
interfere with our project cancel our journey in my own words inside
the real story again my father too coughing his tuberculosis as they
locked him into the closet they cut little boys' hands alone waiting
on his third floor crapping me on his paper what a joke the soldiers
quick sssh and all the doors slammed shut the boots in the staircase
where it should have started but not him no instead calmly he shoves
the statue of liberty at us very symbolic over the girl's shoulder I
tremble in his lies nothing he says about the past but I see it from
the corner of my eye even tried to protest while the outside goes in
then smiles among the beasts and writes one morning a bird flew into
my head ah what insolence what about the yellow star on my chest yes
what about it federman the truth to say where they kept old wrinkled
clothes empty skins dusty hats and behind the newspapers stolen bags

of sugar cubes how I crouched like a sphinx falling for his wordshit moinous but where were you tell me dancing when it all started where were you when the door closed on me shouting I ask you when I needed you the most letting me be erased in the dark at random in his words scattered nakedly telling me where to go how many times yes how many times must he foist his old voice on me his detours cancellations ah that's a good one lies lies me to tell now procrastinations I warned him deep into my designs refusing to say millions of words wasted to say the same old thing mere competence never getting it straight his repetitions what really happened ways to cancel my life digressively each space relating to nothing other than itself me inside his hands progress quickly discouraged saying that it was mad laughter to pass the time two boxes correspondence of space the right aggregate while he inflicts false names on me distorts our beginning but now I stoop on the newspapers groping to the walls for the dimensions of my body while he stares at his selectricstud humping paper each space within itself becoming the figure of our unreality scratched from words the designs twirl just enough for me to speak and I fall for his crap to

become puppet believing he is me or vice versa born voiceless I wait
in the dark now down the staircase with their bundles moaning yellow
stars to the furnace the boots my father mother sisters too to their
final solution when I needed him the most last image of my beginning
to the trains to be remade unmade to shade the light and he calls me
boris when I stood on the threshold boris my first false name but he
erased that too in a stroke of impatience made me anonymous nameless
choose for yourself he mutters a name among infinite possibilities I
tried to protest gives us blank spaces instead while he hides inside
his own decomposition homme de plume hombre della pluma reverses his
real name namredef between the lines in the corners featherman sings
his signs anticipating his vocation leaps over the precipice cancels
the real story with exaggerations I watched him long ago make images
among the beasts how many false starts for me to go but where if the
door had opened by mid-afternoon the world would be alive dust burnt
pains in the guts squeaking pretending to be dead I replay the scene
down the staircase perhaps I slept the whole time and a bird flew in
my head past his face through the windowpane scared him face to face

with myself I threw sand in his eyes struck his back with a stick in
his delirium whining like a wounded animal I squat on the newspapers
unfolded here by shame to defecate my fear as he continues to scream
multiplying voices within voices to silence me holding my penis away
not to piss on my legs clumsily continues to fabricate his design in
circles doodles *me up and down his pages of insolence* two closets on
the third floor *separate correspondence of birth in time* seeking the
right connection *meaning of all meanings but from this* angle never a
primary phenome*non to end again reducible to nonsense* excrement of a
beginning in the *dark I folded the paper into a neat* package for the
birds smelling *my hands by reflex or to disintegrate* years later but
he ignores that *too obsessed by fake images while* sucking the pieces
of stolen sugar *on the roof by the ladder outside the* glass door the
moon tiptoed across the clouds curiosity drove me down the staircase
but I stumbled on the twelfth step and fell and all the doors opened
dumb eyes to stare at my nakedness among the beasts still hoping for
survival my mother father sisters but already the trains are rolling
in the night as I ran beneath the sky a yellow star struck my breast

and all the eyes turned away I told him tried to explain how it must
have started upstairs they grabbed me and locked me in a box dragged
me a hundred times over the earth in metaphorical disgrace while the
soldiers chased each other with stones in their hands and burned all
the stars in a *furnace my survival a mistake he cannot* accept forces
him to begin *conditionally by another form of sequestra*tion pretends
to lock hims*elf in a room with the if of my existence the* story told
in laughter *but it resists and recites first the displace*ment of its
displacement*s leaving me on the threshold staring dumbf*ounded at the
statue of liberty *over the girl's shoulder question of* selecting the
proper begin*ning he claims then drags me into the subway* to stare in
guilt again *between a woman's legs at the triangular* cunt of america
leads me down *the corridor to masturbate his substitutio*n instead of
giving me an *original experience to deceive the absence* of a woman's
hand makes believe that I am dead twelve years old when they left me
in the primordial closet moment upstairs on the third floor with the
old newspapers empty skins seeking unknown pleasure which is only an
amorphous substitution thinking that memory is innocent always tells

the truth while cheating the original experience the first gesture a
hand reaching for the walls to find its proper place since he failed
to generate the real story in vain situates me in the wrong abode as
I turn in a *void in his obligation to assign a beginning* however sad
it may be *to my residence here before memory had a source* so that it
may unfold *according to a temporal order a spatial displace*ment made
of words *inside his noodling complexities of plagiaristic* form I was
dead he *thinks skips* me but *I am being given birth into* death beyond
the open *door such is my condition the feet are clear al*ready of the
great cunt *of existence backward my head will be last to* come out on
the paper *spread your arms voices shout behind the walls* I can't but
the teller *rants my story again and I am alive promising* situation I
am my *beginning in this strange gestation I say I for the* first time
as he *gesticulates in his room surrounded gy his madness* having once
more *succeeded in assembling single-handedly the carbon* design of my
life as I remember the first sound heard in this place when I said I
to invent an origin for myself before crumbling into his nonsense on
the edge of the precipice leaning against the wind after I placed my

filthy package on the roof its warmth still on my hands far away the
empty skins already remade into lampshades past moments old dreams I
am back again *in the actuality of my fragile predicament* backtracked
into false *ambiguities smelling my hands by reflex out of* the closet
now to af*firm the certainty of how it was annul the hypo*thesis of my
excessiveness on which he postulates his babblings his unqualifiable
design as I *register the final absence of my mother crying* softly in
the night *my father coughing his blood down the staircase* they threw
sand in *their eyes struck their back kicked them to exterminate* them
his *calculations yes explanations yes the whole story crossed* out my
whole *family parenthetically exed into typographical symbols* while I
endure my *survival from its implausible beginning to its* unthinkable
end yes *false balls all balls ejaculating on his machine reducing* my
real life *to the verbal rehearsals of a little boy half* naked trying
to extricate *himself as he goes on formulating yet another* paradox I
witness to *substitute a guilty gesture for my innocent pleasure* call
that cleverness indeed to impose on my predicament his false notions
of order truth plausibility down the corridor tiptoes now listens to

voices murmuring behind the doors refusing that which negates itself
as it creates itself both recipient and dispatcher of a story teller
told creature on my hands the smell of the package up on the roof to
disintegrate in laughter divided I who speaks both the truth and the
lie of my condition at the same time from the corner of its mouth to
enclose the enunciation and denunciation of what he says in semantic
fraudulence because I am untraceable in the dark again as I move now
toward my birth out of the closet unable to become the correspondent
of his illusions in his room where everything happens by duplication
and repetition displacing the object he wants to apprehend with fake
metaphors which bring together on the same level the incongruous the
incompatible whereas in my paradox a split exists between the actual
me wandering voiceless in temporary landscapes and the virtual being
federman pretends to invent in his excremental packages of delusions
a survivor who dissolves in verbal articulations unable to do what I
had to do admit that his fictions can no longer match the reality of
my past me blushing sphinx defecating the riddle of my birth instead
he invents me playmates in his chaotic progress for his deficiencies

WORDS OUT OF A BAD DREAM / MAUVAIS MOTS D'UN REVE (a bilingual poem)

TAPE

time: 2 minutes & 8 seconds

text recorded in English and in French on two different tracks each
line of the poem being spoken alternatively against a background of
sound effects: women talking, then giggling, then laughing, the sound
of laughter growing louder and decreasing as the text is read. The
sound effect (collective mumbling, giggling, and laughing) meant to
desentimentalize the poem.

SLIDES (5)

1. manuscript of text (English version) with collage of photo of a
   MAN with the word MAN (probably Federman as portrayed on a green
   poster with only the last syllable of his name appearing with the
   face)
2. crowd of women laughing in a semi-darkness (the figure in the fore-
   ground possibly Federman's mother-in-law)
3. a drawing of circles surrounding the French words LA MORT
4. two young girls dressed in black as though for a funeral
5. manuscript of the text (French version)

WORDS OUT OF A BAD DREAM

MAUVAIS MOTS D'UN REVE

and if we were to die *(hahahahahahaha)* et si nous devions mourir

unexpectedly while waiting *(hahahahahahahahahahahaha)* comme ça tout à coup en attendant

before the moment came *(hahahahahahahahahahahahahahahaha)* avant que le moment ne vienne

desire wasted in words *(hahahahahahahahahahahahahahahahahahahaha)* le désir gaspillé en mots

hands barely touching *(hahahahahahahahahahahahahahahaha)* les mains se touchant à peine

and if we were to die *(hahahahahahahahahahahaha)* et si nous devions mourir

one morning in the midst of a dream *(hahahahahahaha)* un matin au milieu d'un rêve

an unfinished nightmare *(hahahahahahahahahahahahahahahahahahahahahaha)* un cauchemar inachevé

leaving our body cold *(hahahahahahahahahahahahaha)* laissant notre corps froid

at the edge of an afternoon *(hahahahahahahahahahaha)* au bord d'un après-midi

would they stare at our empty eyes *(hahahahahahahaha)* oseraient-ils regarder dans nos yeux vides

would they whisper among the stones *(hahahahahahaha)* murmureraient-ils parmi les cailloux

invent reasons for our absence *(hahahahaha)* inventeraient-ils des raisons pour notre départ

follow our memory while questioning the sky suivraient-ils notre souvenir tout en interrogeant le ciel

their steps disturbed by the fallen leaves *(hahahahaha)* leurs pas dérangés par les feuilles fanées

or a cloud hiding the sun *(hahahahahaha)* ou un nuage qui cache le soleil

would they fumble for umbrellas *(hahahahahahahaha)* s'embarrasseraient-ils de leurs parapluies

and what of the dull horse *(hahahahahahahahahahahahahahahahahaha)* et que dire du vieux cheval

dragging us to our place *(ahahahahahahahahahah)* qui nous traînerait vers notre place

among millions of unfinished moments *(hahahahahahahahahahahahahahahah)* parmi ces millions de moments inachevés

HISTORY OF THE BALLOON / HISTOIRE DU BALLON (bilingual fiction)

TAPE

time: 5 minutes & 6 seconds

the English text is recorded four times and the French text also
four times on eight different tracks then the two languages are
synthesized but remaining distinct from one another so that the
two voices (Federman's English voice multiplied by itself and
Federman's French voice multiplied by itself) speak within themselves in a bilingual duet. On two other tracks the words BALLOON
(in English) and BALLON (in French) are recorded to create a rhythmic pattern while the entire recording is superimposed on a piece
of electronic music for four trombones.

SLIDES (10)

1. manuscript of the text (English version)
2. first in a series of drawings: idée du ballon
3. jeux du ballon
4. amour du ballon
5. matin du ballon
6. nuit du ballon
7. connaissance du ballon
8. pensées du ballon (superimposed on title of the text)
9. photo of metallic spheres
10. manuscript of the text (French version)

H I S T O R Y   O F   T H E   B A L L O O N

why this image every night this word BALLOON in my head yes word
at night I must especially explain sometimes until morning dream
this BALLOON image of the word probably understand before dying!

first sphere rounded form hollow of air circle convex rather yes
concave from the inside giant fruit apple orange moon bottomless
sun extinguished other possibilities circular in depth hole void
BALLOON ball bowl hollow globe cycle dream transformed word of a
secondary image BALLOON word probably image to see before dying!

second color without certainly blue yes sometimes red often blue
atrocious leaning towards dragging violet without fear of course
even at night never seen towards yellow too colorless disturbing
at night BALLOON dream if the color not unseen false BALLOON the
spectrum to touch probably measure once soon alone before dying!

third dimensions unknown not too big too wide even dimensions of
the dream to discover measure even unknown impossibilities forms
of a specific infinity but finished all circles finished or else
false data of a BALLOON round against itself circle sphere globe
unfinished BALLOON closing probably in space above before dying!

fourth weight no doubt heavy it falls does not rise no never the
dream above immobile with a slight displacement in time of a not
too distant past of course time of dream quick without space the
temporary movement BALLOON awakening between two airs flat falls
hollow BALLOON probably impossible to define alone before dying!

fifth function vague certainly sensitivity reacting only to word
image BALLOON in the hollow sleep dream here not all yet specify
function even remote from thought of the thought of this form of
the true BALLOON memory image above the dream in a whirlwind now
sensible to decipher probably to hold soon perhaps before dying!

sixth the true BALLOON the BALLOON not dream and not image of an
infinite word comparison to be made understandably of the sphere
circle round rounded form but hollow colorless its form its data
weight and the function probably respective to the word image of
realization of the true BALLOON probably never saw before dying!

conclusion of the BALLOON without story in a dream transposed by
a very slight bursting rather in a word image which themselves a
deflation leaning again towards the true BALLOON the real sphere
word image of the concrete form of the BALLOON word image yes of
dream hollow at last to explain one day once again before dying!

H I S T O I R E   D U   B A L L O N

pourquoi cette image tous les soirs ce mot BALLON dans ma tête la
nuit surtout la nuit il faut parfois jusqu'au matin expliquer oui
ce BALLON image mot probablement comprendre vite avant de mourir!

premièrement sphère forme arrondie creux de l'air cerceau convexe
concave plutôt de l'intérieur fruit géant pomme orange lune ronde
sans fond soleil éteint autres possibilités circulaires profondes
BALLON balle boule creuse bille cercle rêve devenu mot image d'un
BALLON mot image probablement signe à voir image avant de mourir!

deuxièmement sans couleur c'est certain si bleu parfois mais trop
souvent rouge affreux rouge gênant qui penche sans peur même vers
le violet sans tache bien entendu jaune aussi sans couleur ici le
noir ne se voit pas tire vers la nuit du BALLON rêve spectre faux
à toucher probablement mesurer une fois l'espace avant de mourir!

troisièmement dimensions inconnues pas trop grand pas trop étroit
dimensions du rêve à découvrir mêmes inconnues les impossibilités
infinies sont finies tout cercle est fini sinon données fausses à
refaire d'un BALLON rond en lui-même cercle sphère fini finie les
deux se refermant probablement de haut en bas en avant de mourir!

quatrièmement pesanteur lourd sans doute mais il tombe non jamais
ne s'élève non plus au-dessus du rêve immobile avec un léger bien
sûr déplacement dans le temps rapide du rêve sans espace avant le
réveil mouvement provisoire le plus souvent entre deux airs tombe
dans le creux probablement impossible à démettre avant de mourir!

cinquièmement fonction vague certainement sensibilité réagissante
seulement au sommeil mais le mot image du BALLON dans le rêve ici
aucunement fonctionnel même éloigné de la pensée de la pensée des
formes du véritable BALLON souvenir image au-dessus du rêve remou
à déchiffrer probablement saisir lentement un os avant de mourir!

sixièmement le vrai ballonnement du BALLON non rêve et non mot de
l'image comparaison à faire bien entendu du possible de la sphère
cercle rond forme arrondie mais creuse sans couleur sa forme même
sans dimensions le poids et la fonction probables étant bientôt à
mesure de sa réalisation probablement inconnue au sens de mourir!

conclusion de BALLON sans histoire dans un rêve se transpose s'il
le faut par un léger dégonflement en mot image qui eux-mêmes vers
le BALLON réel du BALLON penchent au-delà du vrai mot image de la
forme concrète du BALLON mot image mot BALLON certainement devenu
le rêve ici probablement sans l'avoir vu compris avant de mourir!

THE OTHER COUNTRY / L'AUTRE PAYS (a poem in two languages)

Dedicated to Samuel Beckett

TAPE

time: 1 minute & 35 seconds

text is recorded on two different tracks in English and in French
with the French version echoing the English as though spoken from
a distant place.

SLIDES (7)

1. photo of the Eiffel Tower superimposed on title of poem
2. typographical montage of the text (in English and French) with
    small photo of Samuel Beckett at center of text
3. photo of man in Tokyo (probably Federman in his youth)
4. manuscript of the text (English version)
5. large photo of Samuel Beckett (face only)
6. manuscript of the text (bilingual version)
7. large photo of Samuel Beckett (face only, same as 5)

THE OTHER COUNTRY   (for samuel beckett)

there are no doors
no windows here
you enter from the wings
where living hurts
you croutch
you kneel
you drag yourself to the center
and you wait
you wait under a gray canvas sky
near a dead tree
until they come to beat you blue
to stone you dead
then you crawl inside a wooden box
to sleep it off
your bones dry of marrow
dust in your mouth
sometimes you hear voices in your head
or the croaking of frogs
in the morning before the pale sun
you perform the gymnastics of the mind
split like a centaur
and you wait
you wait for the shy moon
to roll into a ball before you
movement a heresy
but one day another man comes
who carries his life on his hands
he too must perform
and the day is saved
even though the moon never returns
and laughing is a painful process

L'AUTRE PAYS

il n'y a pas de portes
pas de fenêtres ici
on entre par les coulisses
où vivre fait mal
on s'accroupit
on se met à genoux
on se traîne vers le centre
et on attend
on attend sous un ciel toile grise
à côté d'un arbre mort
jusqu'à ce qu'ils viennent nous matraquer
nous caillouter à mort
alors on rampe dans une boîte
pour cuver sa douleur
les os desséchés de moelle
de la poussière dans la bouche
parfois on entend des voix dans sa tête
ou le coassement des grapauds
le matin devant le soleil albinos
on fait sa gymnastique mentale
coupé en deux comme un centaure
et puis on attend
on attend que la lune timide
roule sa balle devant nous
le mouvement une hérésie
mais un jour un autre homme vient
qui porte sa vie dans ses mains
lui aussi doit jouer
et la journée est sauvée
même si la lune ne revient pas
et le rire est aussi une douleur

THREE BILINGUAL POEMS -- OLD SKIN / VIEILLE PEAU
                         THE GAME / LE JEU
                         THE HAND / LA MAIN

dedicated to Campbell Tatham

TAPE

time: 1 minute & 20 seconds

texts of the three poems are recorded four times in English and four
times in French on eight different tracks the French voices echoing
the English with a slight overlapping of the voices so that the French
voices seem to interrupt the flow of the English voices or rather take
over in the middle of words.

SLIDES (6)

1. manuscript of text (OLD SKIN / VIEILLE PEAU) typographically brin-
    ging French and English versions together
2. hand closed into a fist superimposed on manuscript of OLD SKIN /
    VIEILLE PEAU
3. manuscript of text (THE GAME / LE JEU) typographically bringing
    French and English versions together
4. back of hand fingers spread out superimposed on manuscript of THE
    GAME / LE JEU
5. manuscript of text (THE HAND / LA MAIN) typographically bringing
    French and English versions together
6. hand facing up showing life line superimposed on manuscript of
    THE HAND / LA MAIN (probably Federman's hand in all three shots)

raymond   federman

a

bilingual poem

OLD SKIN   VIEILLE PEAU

forty almost and not a word	quarante ans presque pas un mot
mumbling like a jerk	balbutier comme un con
at best	au plus
one two three	un deux trois
that's about all	et voilà c'est tout
quaquaqua how it is	quaquaqua comment c'est
with bubbles in the skull	avec des bulles dans le crâne
dragging yourself in verbal mud	et je me traîne dans la boue verbale
looking for	en attendant
the first word	le premier mot
a noun	un nom
an imperative	un impératif
perhaps	peut-être

raymond   federman

a

bilingual poem

THE GAME LE JEU

trembling false voice	tremblement fausse voix
a path	un chemin
the train no longer comes	le train qui n'arrive plus
merry-go-round	dans ce manège
a child far away	enfant lointain
behind me	derrière moi
in this doubly deceiving mirror	dans ce miroir doublement menteur
look now	regarde
I surpass myself	je me dépasse

raymond federman

a

bilingual poem

THE HAND   LA MAIN

handful of words	poignée de mots
clutched	serrés
inside the life line	dans la ligne de ma vie
nonsense	non-sens
of spread fingers	des doigts écartés
suddenly	tout à coup
mute speech	langage muet
sign of my presence	signe de ma présence

V
Projections

Prometheus as Performer:
Toward a Posthumanist Culture?

A University Masque in Five Scenes

IHAB HASSAN

—For Anima

He goes from death to death, who sees the many here.

The Vedanta.

*

The eternal body of man is the Imagination, that is, God himself.

Blake.

*

The mystery of the world is its comprehensibility.

Einstein.

*

Our mission, unfinished, may take a thousand years.

Mao.

*

From women's eyes this doctrine I derive:
They sparkle with the right Promethean fire....

Shakespeare.

THE CHARACTERS IN ORDER OF THEIR APPEARANCE:

PRETEXT: who opens and presumably explains the nonaction.
MYTHOTEXT: *who is obsessed with the story of Prometheus.*
TEXT: who carries the burden of the intellectual narrative.
HETEROTEXT: who speaks only to quote from various authorities.
CONTEXT: who pretends to be a historian.
METATEXT: who enjoys commenting on Text and criticizing colleagues.
POSTEXT: who vainly attempts to conclude the nonaction.
PARATEXT (inaudible in print): who breaks the frame now and then with his comments, and who has already appeared as a version of the speaker.

201

PRETEXT

(appearing from nowhere, speaking rather superciliously)

Good ladies and gentle men:

This masque attempts to place the subject of postmodern performance in a wide and speculative context. About performance as such, little will be said, about postmodernism, even less. (Certain academics on this campus have already turned postmodernism into a tedious travesty.) This masque would rather reflect upon the lineaments of an emergent culture. Call it posthumanist culture—or call it nothing at all. It remains the matrix of all our performances. And it remains (blessings on great Tom Eliot) undefined.

One or two words more. If posthumanist culture is the matrix of contemporary performance, there is a matrix larger still: the universe itself, everything that was, is, and will become. What a performance! But who can speak for the universe? No one—no, not even the Titan Prometheus. Still, linking Cosmos and Culture, Divine Space and Human Time, Sky and Earth, the Universal and the Concrete, Prometheus may prove himself to be a figure of flawed and evolving consciousness, an emblem of human destiny.

No more pretexts; the masque follows in five scenes.

SCENE ONE

from Myth to Politics: the Question of the One and the Many

MYTHOTEXT

(in a voice resonant with the archetypes)

Prometheus, son of Iapetus, Titan turncoat and trickster. There are many versions of his story, but the main outlines are familiar. He sided with the new Olympian gods (Zeus & Co.) against his own chthonic kind. Yet Prometheus, that forethinker, could never leave well enough alone.

Some say he created men out of clay and water; some say he only gave them fire. The fire was stolen from the smith-god Hephaestus—or was it taken from Apollo's sun? It was stolen, in any event, and hidden in a fennel stalk. But this fire was no simple element: it was knowledge and imagination, the alphabet, medicine, and all the arts. Stolen fire, red forbidden fruit. We owe everything to a crime. "Prometheus's double nature is always acknowledged; as by Coleridge who said that he was the Redeemer and the Devil jumbled into one" (Denis Donoghue, Thieves of Fire*).*

Ah, but the doubleness of this trickster is not merely theological; it is political and epistemological as well. And it is a doubleness that wants to become one again. Socrates here is our authority: "There is a gift of the gods. . .which they let fall

from their abode, and it was through Prometheus, or one like him, that it reached
mankind [no emphasis on theft here], together with a fire exceeding bright." This
gift, Socrates goes on to say in the "Philebus," is a perception that "all things
. . . consist of a one and a many, and have in their nature a conjunction of limit
and unlimitedness."
Thus the One and the Many enter Western thought.

TEXT

(forcefully)

Thank you, Mythotext, you have led us from myth to politics through philosophy. Your image of Prometheus mirrors our own present, in which the one and the
many, the ecumenical will of mankind and its will to secession, hold their bloody
play under the twin aspects of totalitarianism (torture) and anarchy (terrorism).
Convergences and divergences, conjunctions and disjunctions, are visible
everywhere; on the one hand various myths of totality, on the other, diverse
ideologies of fracture. Thus, the more Marshall McLuhan proclaims "the global
village," or Buckminster Fuller "spaceship earth," or Norman O. Brown "the
mystic body of mankind," the more Jacques Derrida and his *confreres* insist upon
différance and the metaphysics of fragments.

The news, alas, seems to favor Derrida. Our planet continually splinters, breaks
according to ideology, religion, class, race, language, sex, and age. The earth
splits into blocks, blocks into nations, nations into provinces, provinces into
tribes, tribes into families, families into feuding individuals—and individuals,
soon enough, alas, into random atoms. Can it be fortuitous that atoms themselves
have been split into the tiniest, the shiest particles, particles that seem a mathematical whisper, a mere breath? Whose breath? The breath of the universe?

No doubt, convergence and divergence are but two aspects of the same reality,
the same process. Totalitarianism and anarchy summon each the other. And the
more communication threatens to become global, the more individuals, insisting
on their quiddity, will discover the deep and obscure need for misunderstanding.
But is this all we can expect from our earth and sky, our brief moment of sodality?

There are poets and philosophers, scientists and mystics, who lead us to expect
more. They believe in some richer relation between the one and the many, the
universal and the concrete. Like Blake, in his prophecy called "America," they
envision a movement "beyond struggling afflictions," toward "another portion of
the infinite." Like Whitman, they sing of an "orbic vision," in which the inner
divisions of consciousness and the external divisions of humankind are healed and
made whole—made whole but *not* homogeneous, healed but *not* rendered uni-
form.

> Have you thought there could be but a single supreme?
> There can be any number of supremes...
> All is eligible to all.

Is this the project of the Promethean consciousness? The project is more problematic than we can imagine or foretell.

HETEROTEXT

(chiming in)

Text and Mythotext listen to some other voices of the "orbic vision," speaking variously of the concrete and the universal:

Hegel in *The Phenomenology of Mind*:
This simple force [concrete spirit in government] allows, indeed, the community to unfold and expand into its component members, and to give each part subsistence and self-existence of its own. Spirit finds in this way its realization or its objective existence. . . . But spirit is at the same time the force of the whole, combining these parts again within the unity which negates them . . . and keeping them aware that their life only lies in the whole.

*

Marx in *The Economic and Philosophic Manuscripts of 1844*:
Man, much as he may therefore be a *particular* individual. . . is just as much the *totality*—the ideal totality—the subjective existence of thought and experienced society present for itself....

*

Teilhard de Chardin in *The Future of Man*:
If there is any characteristic clearly observable in the progress of Nature towards higher consciousness, it is that this is achieved by increasing differentiation, which in itself causes ever stronger individualities to emerge.... In other words, in a converging Universe, each element achieves completeness, not directly in a separate consummation, but by incorporation in a higher pole of consciousness in which alone it can enter into contact with all the others.

*

Jacques Monod in *Chance and Necessity*:
The weight of an allosteric enzyme molecule capable of the same performances is of the order of 10^{-17} of a gram. Which is a million billion times less than an electronic relay. That astronomical figure affords some idea of the "cybernetic" (i.e. teleonomic) power at the disposal of a cell equipped with hundreds or thousands of these microscopic entities, all far more clever than the Maxwell-Szilard-Brillouin demon.

Hegel and Marx, Teilhard and Monod, a motley crew. But do they not all sing, each in his key, the same song of singleness in variousness?

TEXT.

(severely)

Heterotext, do be sensible. Your voices are a little too obscure and worse: mystical. There is nothing supernatural in the process leading us to a posthumanist culture. That process depends mainly on the growing intrusion of the human mind into nature and history, on the dematerialization of life and the conceptualization of existence. In that sense, we need not wait for the end of History, as Hegel thought, to witness the synthesis of the Concrete and the Universal, Slave and Master, Individual and State. Each of us, by virtue of Dream, Hope, and Language, provides some awkward version of the Concrete Universal. For what is the human animal, as Monod himself says, but the most distinctive organism on earth, and at the same time the most self-transcendent—I mean the most capable of abstracting itself through language, and rising equivocally through layers of consciousness?

As for you, Mythotext, I must tell you this. Prometheus may be a vague metaphor of a mind struggling with the One and the Many. Yet, I prefer to view his struggle in narrower perspective. His mind is where Imagination and Science, Myth and Technology, Language and Number sometimes meet. Or put it both prophetically and archetypically: Prometheus presages the marriage of Earth and Sky. Only then, perhaps, will posthumanism see the dubious light of a new day.

(No one answers Text; the scene closes.)

SCENE TWO

From Lascaux to Henry Adams: A Historical Collage

CONTEXT

(entering ponderously; gravid with history)

Allow me to have my turn, young texts: this matter you so ardently discuss requires a less hurried perspective. Posthumanism seems to you a sudden mutation of the times; in fact, the conjunctions of imagination and science, myth and technology, have begun by firelight in the caves of Lascaux. But unlike Mythotext here, I am less concerned with myth than with history. From the Pythagoreans, through medieval alchemists, to the European Renaissance, a rich hermetic tradition has opened itself to both science and mystery.

MYTHOTEXT

(interrupting)

So much hermetic knowledge throughout history–and so little wisdom! Why then did the Promethean fire fail humankind? Is it merely because it was stolen, a power unearned, exceeding the reach of human piety? Or is it rather because the gift itself lacked an essential element: civic wisdom. In Plato's dialogue, Protagoras tells how Epimetheus, having squandered all the divine gifts on animals, found nothing more to give mankind. While Epimetheus sat puzzling about this, "Prometheus came to inspect the work, and found the other animals well off for everything, but man naked, unshod, unbedded, and unarmed.... Prometheus, therefore, being at a loss to provide any means of salvation for man, stole from Hephaestus and Athene the gift of skill in the arts together with fire.... In this way, man acquired sufficient resources to keep himself alive, but had no political wisdom. This was in the keeping of Zeus, and Prometheus no longer had the right of entry to the citadel where Zeus dwelt. . . [emphasis mine]."

CONTEXT

(ponders the interruption, then decides to ignore it)

The European hermetic tradition included Albertus Magnus, Paracelsus, Giordano Bruno—authors whom that "New Prometheus," Dr. Victor Frankenstein, studied profoundly before turning to shallower things. Surprisingly, this same hermetic tradition affected some eminent scientists, not in fiction but in history. Kepler, we know, wrote the horoscope of Wallenstein in 1609; and stated in *De Stella Nova* (quoted in Koestler's *Roots of Coincidence*):

> Nothing exists nor happens in the visible sky that is not sensed in some hidden manner by the faculties of Earth and Nature.... The natural soul of man is not larger in size than a single point, and on this point the form and character of the entire sky is potentially engraved, as if it were a hundred times larger.

Even the great Newton spent much of his earlier life in alchemical and Faust-like pursuits. "His deepest instincts," wrote Lord Keynes, "were occult, esoteric, semantic." Of this darker Newton, George B. Leonard has also said in *The Transformation*:

> More than a million words of. . .[his] occult writing has survived. Much of the summaries have to do with an elixir or Philosopher's Stone that not only will aid in the transmutation of metals but will also invest the owner with magical powers—seeing at a great distance, forcing others to bow to one's will, gaining eternal youth.

But the outstanding example of the conjunctions between science and imagination, technology and art, remains Leonardo da Vinci, who has haunted so many minds since the Renaissance. Both Freud and Valéry saw in Leonardo more than a total and meditative curiosity; they also saw in him something approaching a unified consciousness, perhaps even the radical process of consciousness itself, made incarnate. This has led Roger Shattuck to say:

> At the very moment when. . .Western consciousness was hardening into a division between reason and feeling, two of the greatest contemporary minds were saying precisely the opposite in terms that recapitulate the history of modern European thought. They assert, in effect, that the experience of four hundred years tells us urgently and insistently not to divide up the mind.

At that same turning point of the twentieth century, Henry Adams recorded his own intuition of the undivided mind. Dating his words exactly in the year 1900, Adams wrote in a famous passage of his *Education*:

> Copernicus and Galileo had broken many professional necks about 1600; Columbus had stood the world on its head toward 1500; but the nearest approach to the revolution of 1900 was that of 310, when Constantine set up the Cross. The rays that Langley disowned, as well as those which he fathered, were occult, supersensual, irrational; they were a revelation of a mysterious energy like that of the Cross....

METATEXT

(clipped, logical, almost prissy)

Myth, philosophy, and history are all very nice. But this collage—shall we say of significant moments?—must leave the audience nonplussed. Permit me, therefore, to summarize the inactions of this masque. Insofar as I can understand my learned and loquacious colleagues, they wish to maintain that:

1. the cosmos is performance, posthumanist culture is a performance in progress, and their symbolic nexus is Prometheus;
2. Prometheus is himself the figure of a flawed consciousness struggling to transcend such divisions as the One and the Many, Cosmos and Culture, the Universal and the Concrete;
3. with regard to posthumanism itself, the most relevant aspect of the Promethean dialectic concerns Imagination and Science, Myth and Technology, Earth and Sky, two realms tending to one:
4. this dialectic, however, has a hoary history; the languages of imagination and the languages of science have often mingled and crossed in certain epochs and certain great minds of the past;

5.because both imagination and science are agents of change, crucibles of values, modes not only of representation but also of transformation, their interplay may now be the vital performing principle in culture and consciousness—a key to posthumanism?

(Text, Mythotext, Context coldly nod their approval; the scene ends.)

SCENE THREE

Contemporary Culture

TEXT

(delighted to hold forth again)

Humanists are a little Epimethean, I fear; the astonishing convergences of imagination and science, myth and technology, in contemporary culture have tended to elude them. Nor have the great modern minds which currently command the greatest authority—I mean Marx, Nietzsche, and Freud, Sartre and Lévi-Strauss, Heidegger and Husserl—illuminated particularly this question. (William James may prove a curious exception.) Yet, more and more, the evidence suggests that the "two cultures" of C. P. Snow and F. R. Leavis, of abstract, sky-haunted technophiles dominated by the male principle, and moist, earth-bound arcadians ruled by the female principle, are slowly becoming obsolete as consciousness evolves, through many setbacks and contradictions, to include them both.

Evidence of these problematic convergences centers on four regions of contemporary culture:

a. the creative process in science and art.
b. the new twilight zone of experimental science.
c. The incorporation of technology into the arts, both as theme and form.
d. the existential search for a unified sensibility.

A recent article, entitled "Beyond Arcadians and Technophiles" (which appeared in the Spring, 1976, number of the *Massachusetts Review*) deals superficially with these issues. Perhaps I can call on Heterotext, whose penchants are bibliographic, to summarize *briefly* its argument.

HETEROTEXT

(with alacrity)

I will first quote, then query, then cite a few bibliographic references.

A. On the Creative Process:

— **Quotation:**

Max Planck: "The pioneer scientist must have a vivid intuitive imagination for new ideas, ideas not generated by deduction, but by artistically creative imagination."

Jacques Monod: "I am sure every scientist must have noticed how his mental reflection, at the deeper level, is not verbal: to be absorbed in thought is to be embarked upon an *imagined experience*, an experience simulated with the aid of forms, of forces, of interactions which together only barely compose an 'image' in the visual sense of the term."

— **Queries:**

What, then, are the roles of dream, play, imagination, and aesthetic sensibility in scientific, mathematical, and artistic creation? Which traits do creative personalities share, regardless of their fields? What indeed do we mean by creativity? Do certain mental structures constitute the languages and methods of various disciplines? Can neurological research on the one hand and phenomenological theory on the other move toward a unified concept of brain and mind?

— **References:**

Frank Barron, *Creativity and Personal Freedom*
Brewster Ghiselin, ed., *The Creative Process*
Arthur Koestler, *The Act of Creation*
Rollo May, *The Courage to Create*
Wilder Penfield, *The Mystery of Mind*
Jean Piaget, *Biology and Knowledge*
Hans Seyle, *From Dream to Discovery*
A. M. Taylor, *Imagination and the Growth of Science*
Paul Valéry, *The Art of Poetry*

B. The Twilight Zone of Science:

— **Quotation:**

Carl Friedrich von Weizsäcker: "the [yoga] concept of *Prana* is not necessarily incompatible with our physics. *Prana* is spatially extended and vitalizing. Hence above all it is moving potency. The quantum theory designates something not entirely remote from this by the term 'probability amplitude.' "

Gunther Stent: "Since John Cage had pointed out to me the analogy between the genetic code and the *I-Ching*, I have looked into this matter a little more. To my amazement I found that the 'natural' order of the *I-Ching* hexagrams generates a table of nucleotide triplet codons which shows the same inter-codon generic relations as Cricks' table!"

Lyall Watson: "All the best science has soft edges, limits that are still obscure and extend without interruption into areas that are wholly inexplicable."

— Queries:

What changes in the logos (the rationality) of the sciences may be expected as their frontiers expand? What are the epistemological as well as social implications of current scientific experiments with transcendental meditation, bio-feedback, parapsychology, alien and artificial intelligence, or cosmic consciousness?

— References:

Ludwig von Bertalanffy, *Robots, Men, and Minds*
Fritjof Capra, *The Tao of Physics*
Gerald Feinberg, *The Prometheus Project*
C. G. Jung & Wolfgang Pauli, *Naturerklärung und Psyche*
Arthur Koestler & J. R. Smythies, eds., *Beyond Reductionism*
Lawrence LeShan, *The Medium, the Mystic, and the Physicist*
Raymond Ruyer, *La gnose de Princeton*
R. G. H. Siu, *The Tao of Science*
C. H. Waddington, *Beyond Appearance*
Lyall Watson, *Supernature*
Norbert Wiener, *God and Golem, Inc.*

C. The Interpenetration of Techonology and Art (with acknowledgement to Kathy Woodward):

— Quotation:

Marcel Duchamp to Stieglitz: "You know exactly how I feel about photography. I would like to see it make people despise painting until something else will make photography unbearable."

Andy Warhol: "Machines have less problems. I'd like to be a machine."

Douglas Davis: "Art, technology, and even science seem to me three veils for the same face, three metaphors that cover, then dissolve, into a single reality."

— Queries:

To what extent are various technologies integrating themselves into our art forms? Has technology begun to affect not only particular genres—cybernetic or op art, electronic music, video art, contemporary dance—but also the very definition of art? Indeed, is it possible that technology may be transforming human consciousness itself, so as to make art as we have known it gradually obsolete? In short, where will Marinetti's Futurism finally lead us?

— References:

Jonathan Benthall, *Science and Technology in Art Today*

Jack Burnham, *Beyond Modern Sculpture*
John Cage, *Silence* and *A Year From Monday*
Douglas Davis, *Art and the Future*
Marcel Duchamp, *Complete Works*
Harrold Harris, ed., *Astride the Two Cultures: Arthur Koestler at 70*
Gyorgy Kepes, ed., *Structure in Art and Science*
Marshall McLuhan, *Understanding Media*
Thomas Pynchon, *Gravity's Rainbow*
Jasia Reichardt, *The Computer in Art*
Wylie Sypher, *Technology and Literature*
Calvin Tomkins, *The Bride and the Bachelors*
Robert Wilson, *Einstein on the Beach*

D. The Existential Search for a Unified Sensibility

— Quotation:

Charles Lindbergh: "Decades spent in contact with science and its vehicles have directed my mind and senses to areas beyond their reach. I now see scientific accomplishments as a path, not an end; a path leading to and disappearing in mystery."

Robert Pirsig: "The Buddha, the Godhead, resides quite as comfortably in the circuits of a digital computer or the gears of a cycle transmission as he does at the top of a mountain or in the petals of a flower."

Jimi Hendrix: "It's music.... It's electricity. . .that will take us all to that spiritual high I call the electric church...."

Margaret Mead: "We need a religious system with science at its very core, in which the traditional opposition between science and religion, reflected in grisly truth by our technologically desecrated countryside, can again be resolved, but in terms of the future instead of the past."

— Queries:

To what extent do the diverse careers of an astronaut like Michael Collins, a writer like Thomas Pynchon or Norman Mailer, a musician like John Cage or Jimi Hendrix, a historian like William Irwin Thompson, an anthropologist like Margaret Mead, and a Zen cyclist like Robert Pirsig reflect an authentic quest in our post-industrial society for an infinitely optative yet unified sensibility? And again, what are the personal, political, and philosophical implications of such a quest?

— References:

Michael Collins, *Carrying the Fire*
Norman Mailer, *Of a Fire on the Moon*
Margaret Mead, *Twentieth Century Faith*
Joseph Chilton Pearce, *The Crack in the Cosmic Egg*

Robert M. Pirsig, *Zen and the Art of Motorcycle Maintenance*
William Irwin Thompson, *Passages About Earth*

(Having over-extended its mind with queries, Heterotext suddenly stops; thus ends
Scene Three.)

SCENE FOUR

The Future of Vitruvian Man

TEXT

(now determined to quote almost as much as Heterotext)

At present, posthumanism may appear variously as a dubious neologism, the
latest slogan, or simply another image of man's recurrent self-hate. Yet posthumanism may also hint at a potential in our culture, hint at a tendency struggling
to become more than a trend. The Promethean myth, after all, contains an
enigmatic prophecy. How, then, shall we understand posthumanism?

We need first to understand that the human form—including human desire and
all its external representations—may be changing radically, and thus must be
re-visioned. We need to understand that five hundred years of humanism may be
coming to an end, as humanism transforms itself into something that we must
helplessly call posthumanism. The figure of Vitruvian Man, arms and legs defin-
ing the measure of things, so marvellously drawn by Leonardo, has broken through
its enclosing circle and square, and spread across the cosmos. "Stands he not
thereby in the center of Immensities, in the conflux of Eternities?" Carlyle
ominously asked. Less than a century after, Pioneer 10 carries the human form and
the human sign beyond the solar system into the intergalactic spaces; and Carl
Sagan wryly speculates, in *The Cosmic Connection*, about the future of human
intelligence, babbling its childhood to the universe.

This expansion of human consciousness into the cosmos, this implication of
mind into farthest matter, becomes awesome when astrophysicists reflect upon the
"origin" of the universe. As Sir Bernard Lovell, Professor of Radio Astronomy at
the University of Manchester, put it:

> The transference from the infinities of density and size at time zero
> [when the universe began] to the finite quantities encompassed by the
> laws of the physical world may lie beyond scientific comprehension.
> Does man face this difficulty because he has externalized the object of
> his investigation? Is there reality in these externalized procedures?
> What is man's connection with the universe of atoms, stars, and
> galaxies?. . . Indeed, I am inclined to accept contemporary scientific
> evidence as indicative of a far greater degree of man's total involve-
> ment with the universe. . . . A remarkable and intimate relationship

between man, the fundamental constants of nature, and the initial moments of space and time seems to be an inescapable condition of existence.

New York Times Magazine, November 16, 1975

This cosmological view, I think, requires from us a genuine alteration in our modes of feeling and thought and performance, an alteration that must go beyond, say, Albert Schweitzer's "reverence before life," and beyond the *participation mystique* attributed to primitive man.

But this cosmological extension of human consciousness (which both Teilhard de Chardin and Marshall McLuhan have long, if differently, perceived) is not the only force tending toward posthumanism. Indeed, the re-vision of man is currently promoted by certain prescient humanists as well as by most scientists. Thus, for instance, Claude Lévi-Strauss, both humanist and scientist, speaks darkly at the end of *A World on the Wane*:

> The world began without the human race and it will end without it. The institutions, manners, and customs which I shall have spent my life in cataloguing and trying to understand are an ephemeral efflorescence of a creative process in relation to which they are meaningless.

And thus, again Michel Foucault in *The Order of Things*:

> One thing in any case is certain: man is neither the oldest nor the most constant problem that has been posed for human knowledge.... As the archaeology of our thought easily shows, man is an invention of recent date. And one perhaps nearing its end.

Yet both Foucault and Lévi-Strauss, I am convinced, mean not the literal end of man but the end of a particular image of us, shaped as much by Descartes, say, as by Thomas More or Erasmus or Montaigne. That is why contemporary structuralist thought emphasizes so much the dissolution of the "subject," the annihilation of that hard Cartesian ego or consciousness which distinguished itself from the world by turning the world into an object. The self, structuralists and poststructuralists insist, following the intuition of Nietzsche, is really an empty "place" where many selves come to mingle and depart.

A similar perception, deriving from biology more than psychology or philosophy, persuades Elizabeth Mann Borghese that human nature is still evolving:

> One might even say that whether postmodern man is still *Homo sapiens* remains to be seen. A species that can fly is different from one that cannot. A species that can transport itself out of earth's biosphere to other planets is different from an earthbound species. A species that can transplant vital organs from one member to another, blurring the boundaries between this individual and that individual and between life and death, is different from a species whose members cannot do this.

Center Magazine, March/April, 1973

Projected out of this world and into the universe, the physical and mental possibilities of evolution become even more staggering. "Only a minute fraction, an inconceivably small fraction of all possible forms of life have existed on earth," writes James F. Danielli, Director of the Center for Theoretical Biology at SUNY-Buffalo. "It is inconceivable that the terrestrial organisms we now have are representative samples of the organisms which can exist." (*Center Magazine*, October, 1972). Concretely, this means that the re-vision of human destiny must ultimately consider that destiny in a vast evolutionary scheme.

More soberly, more immediately perhaps, a posthuman philosophy must address the complex issue of artificial intelligence, which most of us know only by the familiar name of HAL (the supercomputer in Kubrick's "2001," so strangely human, that is, at once so sinister and pathetic in every circuit and bit). But artificial intelligence is not merely a figment of science fiction; it almost lives in our midst. There is an anecdote about Alan Turing, the young mathematical genius who died in 1954, on whose work John von Neumann built modern computer theory—a sombre anecdote that we do well to ponder. It is told by the wife of one of Turing's closest colleagues:

> I remember sitting in our garden at Bowdon about 1949 while Alan and my husband discussed the machine and its future activities. I couldn't take part in the discussion. . .but suddenly my ear picked up a remark which sent a shiver down my back. Alan said reflectively, "I suppose, when it gets to that stage, we shan't know how it does it."
> *New York Times Magazine*, February 15, 1976

So much for the chilling obsolescence of the human brain.

Yet the human brain itself does not really know whether it will become obsolete—or simply need to revise its self-conception. The argument explored by Arthur Koestler, in *The Ghost in the Machine*, that the human brain may be radically flawed—may be, that is, an organ inadequate to its task, a "mistake" among countless other "mistakes" of evolution—remains a hypothesis, perhaps itself more mistaken than the brain which conceived it. Will artificial intelligences supersede the human brain, rectify it, or simply extend its powers? We do not know. But this we do know: artificial intelligences, from the humblest calculator to the most immanent computer, help to transform the image of man, the concept of the human. They are agents of a new posthumanism, even if they do no more than the IBM 360-196 which "performs in a few hours all the arithmetic estimated ever to have been done by hand by all mankind" (Henry J. Taylor, in *Dimensions of the Future*).

All these visions finally boggle the minds of poor humanists like ourselves. Yet they are not the visions of science fictionists and future shockers, intended to amuse and terrify us—even as they make the best seller lists. These visions are immediate and concrete. Technology and the pharmaceutical industry have already altered most performances in the Olympic Games; and those Bionic Women from the German Democratic Republic may point to a future more golden than all their medals. And when the figure of Leonardo's Vitruvian Man appears on the cover of our *TV Guide* nowadays, under it runs the caption: "Compared with the real bionic people we expect in the not-too-distant future. . . . The Six Million Dollar Man is Just a Tin Lizzie" (August 28, 1976).

What then will the future, in its middle distances, bring to us?

(Long pause as Text tries to penetrate Time; the scene slowly fades and ends.)

SCENE FIVE

The Warnings of the Earth

MYTHOTEXT

(speaks in outrage)

This optimism is more kitsch than vision. You forget: Prometheus was a trickster and thief. In the end, Text here seems to side more with Goethe, Percy Shelley, and Gide, in their romantic interpretation of the myth, than with wise Aeschylus, Mary Shelley, or Kafka. But to open oneself with hope to the Promethean endeavor is also to recognize its error and terror, its madness within.

Consider for a moment. We know that Iapetus was father to Prometheus. But, pray, who was his mother? Was it Asia, or Themis, or perhaps Clymene, "shapely daughter of Ocean"? Accounts differ. Yet their differences do not obscure a certain point: the shameless mysogyny of the myth. Epimetheus, we know, takes Pandora to wife. Fashioned exquisitely by Hephaestus, she is sent as the cunning revenge of Zeus. Hesiod put it brutally: "Gods and men were speechless when they saw how deadly and how irresistible was the trick with which Zeus was going to catch mankind. This was the origin of the damnable race of women.... They have no place where the curse of poverty is; they belong with luxury" (Theogony). But the curse is not simply economic; Epimetheus, against the advice of his brother, opens Pandora's box, and all the ills of mankind ensue.

From the start, great writers have sensed that Prometheus must do more than overthrow patriarchic Zeus; he must also recover the female principle within his own consciousness. Thus Aeschylus included in his work both Themis and the watery nymph Io; and Percy Shelley gave Asia a creative role. Indeed, Shelley tried to place love at the heart of his work. And Dick Higgins went farther: he made Prometheus a sexy woman.

The Earth must be heard. Yes, Earth must be heard, else Consciousness turn the Sky into fire.

TEXT

(placatingly)

Calm yourself, Mythotext, I concur, I freely concede the point. Obviously, the marriage of Earth and Sky may never find a happy consummation. It may also beget monsters and mutants. We know all too well the litany of our failures: pollution, population, power that serves only to suppress—in short, man's deadly exploitation of nature and himself. Some, for instance, say that the technological capacities bungled in Watergate would make the "Miracle, Mystery, and Authority" of the Grand Inquisitor seem like childish play. Others caution of present and "future shock"; of cloning, parthenogenesis, transplants, prosthesis; of the alteration of memory, intelligence, and behavior; of the creation of chimeras, androids, and cyborgs. Others, still, simply prophesy of famine and global war. From D. H. Lawrence and Friedrich Juenger to Lewis Mumford, Rachel Carson, Jacques Ellul, and the Club of Rome, men and women of vision have warned against dehumanization, and challenged rampant technology—and Marx preceded them with his famous doctrine of alienation. I know all this.

Even Heidegger, despite his postmodern turn in philosophy (see the work of Richard Palmer), even Heidegger is full of foreboding on the subject. In an interview (taped in 1966 but published only this year in *Der Spiegel*) he warns that technology is no longer empowered by human reality (*"Die Technik in ihrem Wesen ist etwas, was der Mensch von sich aus nicht bewaltigt"*), warns that it no longer corresponds to the human measure or way (*"wir haben noch keinen Weg, der dem Wesen der Technik entspricht"*). How, then, can the human race "spare the earth, receive the sky, expect the gods, and have a capacity for death," Heidegger might well wonder?

Yet even Heidegger sensed that "Not only is man by nature more daring than plant and beast. Man is at times more daring even 'than Life itself is'." Will this daring take us to "where all ground breaks off—into the abyss"? Or will the transhumanization of the human mean our "childhood's end" (Arthur Clarke)?

HETEROTEXT

(quietly)

I wish to quote from Arthur Clarke's *Profiles of the Future*. Speaking of the future races, Clarke says:

> They will have time enough, in those endless aeons, to attempt all things, and to gather all knowledge. They will not be like gods, because no gods imagined by our minds have ever possessed the powers they will command. But for all that, they may envy us, basking in the bright after glow of Creation; for we knew the universe when it was young.

MYTHOTEXT

(who will not be assuaged)

Text mentions the capacity for death; Heterotext speaks of the future. Prometheus is connected with both. In the "Gorgias", Socrates claims that Prometheus had also given men exact foreknowledge of their death. But Hades, god of the underworld, complained to Zeus, and the gift was revoked. Could it be that for once Zeus acted with tact? Robbed of human mortality, how can Earth give continual birth? Without death, how can there be surprise or generation?

Yet the motives of Zeus were seldom pure. We know that after aeons of pain, Heracles delivered Prometheus from his bondage on Tartarus; for Prometheus knew a secret vital to the rule of Zeus. Some say Zeus was finally toppled, others maintain a reconciliation ensued, and a few still whisper that the sick centaur, Chiron, offered to resign his gift of immortality, and take the place of Prometheus under the vulture. Or perhaps Kafka, after all, puts it best: "everyone grew weary of the meaningless affair. The gods grew weary, the eagles grew weary, the wound closed wearily.

There remained the inexplicable mass of rock.—The legend tried to explain the inexplicable. As it came out of a substratum of truth it had in turn to end in the inexplicable."

(Hush; last scene ends.)

POSTEXT

I come at the end, though there are no ends; I come only after. And what I must say has already been said, and will be said many times thereafter.

Is it not finally plain? Prometheus, prophet, Titan transgressor and trickster, giver of fire, maker of culture—Prometheus is our performer. He performs Space and Time; he performs Desire. He suffers.

We are ourselves that performance; we perform and are performed every moment. We are the pain or play of the Human, which will not remain human. We are both Earth and Sky, Water and Fire. We are the changing form of Desire. Everything changes, and nothing, not even Death, can tire.

(Here ends the Masque.)

Postface

On Styles of Postmodern Writing

CHARLES CARAMELLO

(1)

> (Stoop) if you are abcedminded, to this
> claybook, what curios of signs (please stoop), in
> this allaphbed! Can you rede (since We and Thou
> had it out already) its world?
>
> *Finnegans Wake*

When commentary abandons its margins, the interrogative can become its voice. Commentary and text can couple in a playful exchange of strategies, a mutual probing that causes distinctions between them to vanish. Many of the essays in this collection are discursive—well-formed, classical, *readerly*—and superbly so. But some—those of Hassan, Tatham, Jabès, and Federman—essay the language of commentary itself. Not only *about* postmodern performance, they *are* postmodern performance.

Finnegans Wake, as pre-text, becomes an obvious choice. Beckett explained the matter perfectly when the *Wake* was still *Work in Progress*:

> Here form *is* content, content *is* form. You complain that this stuff is not written in English. It is not written at all. It is not to be read—or rather it is not only to be read. It is to be looked at and listened to. His writing is not *about* something; *it is that something itself*.[1]

Autocritical literature—the *Wake* and fiction "in the wake of the *Wake*," as a recent *TriQuarterly* has it—now finds its complement in literary criticism—"paracriticism" or "critifiction" to mention two modes in this volume. Having echoed through a half century of criticism, Beckett's comment inevitably re-sounds with variations in *critique de la critique*. Here, for example, is Geoffrey Hartman on Derrida:

> . . . *Glas*, like *Finnegans Wake*, introduces our consciousness to a dimension it will not forget, and perhaps not forgive. It is not only hard to say whether *Glas* is "criticism" or "philosophy" or "literature," it is hard to affirm that it is a book. *Glas* raises the specter of texts so tangled, contaminated, displaced, deceptive that the idea of a single or original author fades, like virginity itself, into the charged Joycean phrase: "Jungfraud's messonge book."[2]

The ubiquity of the *Wake* in current criticism doubles its suitability as
pretext. Having chosen a particular *Wake* quote, that is, I discover that
Jonathan Culler had already used it as a chapter epigraph in his *Structuralist Poetics*. The chapter begins: "'Today the essential question is no
longer that of the *writer* and the *work*,' writes Philippe Sollers, 'but that of
writing and *reading*.'"[3] Since I would also sub-scribe to this, I begin as a
decentered reader ("This 'I' which approaches the text is already itself a
plurality of other texts. . . ,"[4] Barthes writes) enmeshed in intertextuality
("Which is what the inter-text is: the impossibility of living outside the
infinite text. . . ,"[5] Barthes also writes). "I," that is, begin as an intersection
of Joyce, Culler, Sollers, and Barthes, among others. Whether "I" or I,
prior to this writing, did (does) so, and whether it is "I" or I who makes
that determination, remain moot. These questions, however, are germane
to the attitudes toward postmodern performance that these essays take,
and to the essays themselves as writings.

*

Finnegans Wake intentionally opens itself to the free play of language.
The above citation, for example, suggests most questions raised by current literary theory. Confronted with the book of death and life—the
clay-book, which, through typographical gapping, is also the day-book
(cl = d)—does the reader stop or stoop? Do we give up? Do we attempt to
stop, or fix, the proliferating signifiers in a unified signification? Do we
stoop in deference: To Allah: God, Father, Sky, authority, meaning? To
ALP's bed: Myth, Mother, Earth, sensuality, fecundity of plural meanings? To the alphabet: system and denial of system, sequence and the
endless recombinations of its elements? Or do we stoop in defer-ence:
alpha-betting, or wagering against origin? Can we really make these
decisions? How will we read this curios(ity shop) of signs that is also a
museyroom, a public house, a dreamspace? If, after all, we prefer the
linear and continuous (are abc-minded), we must nonetheless acknowledge the polyvalent and discontinuous (must be abced-minded); however strong our desire for presence, we must be playful (absent-minded)
as well. And what is *it* that We and Thou had out? That meaning is
dialogic? That first- and second-person, text and reader, dissolve—as
Shem and Shaun into HCE, Issy into ALP, and ALP finally into HCE—
into one intersubjectivity reading itself endlessly, or into one intertextuality expanding perpetually: into all-read-I? Do we read the world?
or speak the word? or read the word? or speak the world? (cf. Martha
Clifford to Bloom: "I do not like that other world.") Do we speak the word
as world, as a phenomenologist might? or read the world as word(s), as a
structuralist might? or, inhabiting a post-structuralist epoch, do we speak
and read *in writing*, recognizing *the infinite hesitation between presence and
playfulness*?

(2)

> A book is not shut in by its contours, is not
> walled-up as in a fortress. It asks nothing better
> than to exist outside itself, or to let you exist in it.
> In short, the extraordinary fact in the case of a
> book is the falling away of the barriers between
> you and it. You are inside it; it is inside you; there
> is no longer either outside or inside.
>
> Georges Poulet
> "Phenomenology of Reading"[6]

> On the stage of the text, no footlights: there is
> not, behind the text, someone active (the writer)
> and out front someone passive (the reader);
> there is not a subject and an object.
>
> Roland Barthes
> *The Pleasure of the Text*[7]

Dispersing the problematics of the text into the categories of text production and text reception poses a false dichotomy: we should understand text reception, dialectically, *as* text production. Yet I must speak
provisionally of "authors" and "readers" here, for the problematics inherent in all writing are exacerbated by the particular contours of a collection
such as this. Consider:

1) Several persons are asked to *speak* on postmodern performance.
These speakings are performances and, as Richard Palmer reminds us,
performative. Much, consequently, is unrecoverable. A reader loses the
act(or)'s presence of a Blau or a Hassan. We lose the complexity of the
video feedback system that fractured Palmer's presence into a multiplicity
of perspectives and, perhaps, reintegrated it at another register of perception. We evade the fissures of so-called instantaneous translation.
Jabès and Lyotard spoke their texts in French while accomplices broadcast
English versions over a network of headsets. Those plugged-in watched a
speaker while listening to "his" words anticipated, delayed, and
superimposed in another voice and another language: a vertigo of the
out-of-synch and dubbed film multiplied by the ontological confound-
ings of the theatre.

These persons then proffer *written* statements. Ihab Hassan's is prescriptive to its performance: he preforms a verbal masque that he later
performs in vocal masks; Raymond Federman's is post-scriptive to its
performance: he reforms in the media of typography and page what he
had performed in slides, tapes, live voice; Campbell Tatham's is scriptive

as performance (and only that): he performs in writing what he had only indicated in presentation. Some of these fourteen texts, in short, were written to be spoken and heard; others were written to be printed and read; others still were written to be spoken and heard, then rewritten to be printed and read. Could we, if we wanted to, sort out authority at even this level?

2) Now they confront the reader *as texts*, and insofar as several are not discursive, we must decide how to read them. Whether we adopt a "criticism of consciousness" or a semiotic approach, we are faced with our involvement in text production (*i.e.* actualization). Will we, as Poulet does, take the text as a conscious subjectivity that invades and speaks through us? Or will we adopt Wolfgang Iser's revision of Poulet's thesis and say that the literary work has an "artistic" pole created by the author and an "esthetic" pole realized by the reader: that it "exists" only in this "virtual convergence" of text and imagination; that this convergence is itself subjectivized as an "alien 'me'" engaging dialectically "the real, virtual 'me'."[8] Should we, in other words, speak of intersubjective reading. Or, as Barthes suggests, will we understand these *writings* as "stereographic space[s] where [x] codes, [x] voices, intersect"?[9] Will we, that is, take a semiotic approach? Will we turn toward distinctions between readerly (*lisible*) and writerly (*scriptible*) texts (*S/Z*), and toward a playful erotics of reading (*The Pleasure of the Text*)? Should we, in other words, speak of intertextuality, agreeing with Julia Kristeva that "every text takes shape as a mosaic of citations, every text is the absorption and transformation of other texts. The notion of intertextuality comes to take the place of the notion of intersubjectivity."[10]

*

My intention, in fact, is not to provide either phenomenological or semiotic readings of these essays; it is simply to point out that the questions many of them raise about postmodern performance are also self-referential. At whatever level we take the shorthand notation "presence-play" (*e.g.* speech/writing, intentionality/code restraint, intersubjectivity/intertextuality), it slices vertically through the production-reception sequence.

As American critics, we can no longer evade even arcane Being-*différance* debates; nearly any issue of *Sub-stance, boundary 2,* or *diacritics* proves that they are no longer in-house squabbles behind the thresholds of *Tel Quel*. The recent Heidegger issue of *boundary 2* is exemplary. In it, William Spanos argues that "'Modernism' in Western literature—and the New Critical and, more recently, Structuralist hermeneutics it has given rise to—is grounded in a strategy that spatializes the temporal process of existence."[11] For him, what is "post-Modern and thus postmodern" is a "new literary hermeneutics of dis-closure"[12] that revises Heidegger through Kierkegaard. As Palmer does here, Spanos proposes a hermeneutic circle that "is, paradoxically, *a liberating movement, an opening towards being*."[13] Turning this toward post-structuralism, Joseph Riddel writes in the same issue that in the optics of *écriture* and *différance* "the limitlessness of 'literature' is not the concealed fullness of language, but its disruptive and temporalizing function. 'Literature' is neither a full text nor an empty text, neither a presence nor an absence."[14] This "neither" returns us to these essays, to their particular post-structuralist and postmodern attitudes: to *the infinite hesitation between presence and playfulness* that Michel Benamou has identified as their thematic and stylistic leitmotif.

(3)

> Silence may be an element of postmodernism, if by "silence" we intend a metaphor for many languages which place themselves in radical doubt.
>
> Ihab Hassan,
Paracriticisms.[15]

Let us take the range of postmodern performance activities—non-matrixed theatre events, the new music, intermedia fiction, the various permutational, concrete, and sound poetries, experimental cinema and video—as analogical strivings toward the hypothetical *writerly text* that Barthes posits.

> [It] is not a thing, we would have a hard time finding it in a bookstore. Further, its model being a productive (and no longer a representative) one, it demolishes any criticism which, once produced, would mix with it: to rewrite the writerly text would consist only in disseminating it, in dispersing it within the field of infinite difference. The writerly text is a perpetual present, upon which no *consequent* language (which would inevitably make it past) can be superimposed; the writerly text is *ourselves writing*, before the infinite play of the world (the world as function) is traversed, intersected, stopped, plasticized by some singular system (Ideology, Genius, Criticism) which reduces the plurality of entrances, the opening of networks, the infinity of languages.[16]

As I say, postmodern performances may be striving toward this condition; similarly, the more radical essays here may be striving toward discourse that is necessarily beyond the interpretative, becoming the postmodern performances of which they speak. Barthes asks: "Why is the writerly our value?" He answers: "Because the goal of literary work (of literature as work) is to make the reader no longer a consumer, but a producer of the text."[17] This is Benamou's meaning when he writes in his Introduction that postmodern poems or artworks *no longer aspire to mean or to "be," but literally to "work."* "To work" (as in, "to perform"): this is what these essays demand of their subjects, of themselves, and of their readers.

Discursive in style, some do not raise, self-reflexively, such problematics of reading and writing. Yet the questions inhere, nonetheless. Herbert Blau, for example, eloquently and sharply dissents from the playful ethic that pervades these essays. Trusting language, Blau speaks with authority. Barthes's conception of *writing aloud* (*l'écriture à haute voix*), however, may be pertinent. What Barthes means by this (Durand quotes the entire passage) is "a text where we can hear the grain of the throat, the patina of consonants, the voluptuousness of vowels, a whole carnal stereophony: the articulation of the body, of the tongue, not that of meaning, of language.[18] Now Blau's language does *mean*; even the perversity of textual bliss cannot deny that. As Durand says, however, "the voice is inextricably bound up with bodies: the body of language, the body of the speaker. 'Between body and language'." Something, clearly, *attracts* in this essay: is its charisma in the body of the man who directs KRAKEN and practices T'ai Chi, in the incarnate consciousness of the text, or in the body of language within which it so stylishly plays?

The essays of Cheryl Bernstein, Régis Durand, and Daniel Charles drift more clearly toward playful conceptions of textuality. Apparently straightforward, Bernstein's essay conflates text and parody of text. It moves away from the *readerly* by becoming parody *that does not advertise itself as such* (see *S/Z*).[19] It cannot. And we must engage it in the same art/un-art dialectic with which it engages the SLA, with which the SLA perhaps engaged politics and media. The essays of Durand and Charles, conversely, are straightforward as discourse, but cunning in appearance. More than a convention of European format, their sidenotes are *"where the garment gapes."* As Barthes says, "it is this flash itself which seduces, or rather: the staging of an appearance-as-disappearance" (see *The Pleasure of the Text*).[20] In short, they adumbrate (no more) the infiltration of text by margin, the erasure of text and margin as discrete rhetorical spaces. As Joyce demonstrates in the homelesson section of *Finnegans Wake*, the typographical body of a text can play against its scholarly paraphernalia, causing indeterminate meaning to vibrate in the gaps. Michael Wood, elsewhere, asks a pertinent question: "When Hegel and Genet divide a page of *Glas* equally between them, does the margin disappear, or conversely does everything become a margin?"[21]

The writings of Edmond Jabès, Ihab Hassan, Campbell Tatham, and Raymond Federman remain the most radical examples of interrogative language in this collection. What they *are* is impossible to ascertain. "Impossible to classify these books," Rosmarie Waldrop writes of Jabès's *Le Livre des Questions*. "They have the texture of poetry, but are mostly prose."[22] The comment applies to his meditation here. Hassan's masque is a poetry infused with paradox, tenaciously prophetic despite the probable absence of ground on which prophecy must stand. Hassan defines "paracriticism," punningly, as "an attempt to recover the art of multivocation":[23] to recover *and* re-cover the play of voices *and* the vocation of presence. Tatham's "critifiction" assumes that every text participates in perpetual intertextualism, that every text is a pre-text demanding extension. Revoicing pre-texts, Tatham uses their words to create a critifiction that becomes itself a pre-text. For Tatham, however, this is more mystical than semiotic. Federman is temperamentally closer to current French theory. He has discussed his central concept of "pla(y)giarism" (the premise of critifiction) in "Imagination as Plagiarism [an unfinished paper. . .]." Writing and reading alike, he argues, are pla(y)giaristic because of the inherent free play of language. Pla(y)giarizing Jacques Ehrmann, Federman explains: "Poetry (or fiction) [or criticism, I add] is therefore not to be found *within* texts of a given (conventional) type, but virtual and diffuse within language itself, that is, in the relationship between writer and reading, reading and reader, and even more generally, in the play of all communication."[24] Yet Federman too meets his body's ghost in the jolly corners of the text.

These essays would seem to validate Edward Said's comment:

> Writing without genre, with obsessive textuality, moves inexorably to the silence of differance, to the loss of quotes as well as of the comforting ontology of presence. (. . .) Away from naming, language plays; it is a trace bringing together an economy of here and there, of inscription and effacement, or of cancellation and recognition as aspects of the play of differences.[25]

Yet they do so with *infinite hesitation*, disturbed that the unmoored drifting of words in differential space renders truth, vision, and will extremely problematic. As they assert the metaphoric silence of play, they also affirm the meaningful silence of the interstice—and retain a dread that it may have no meaning. An edge in Tatham and Federman, whose intertextual *jouissance* is considerable, this ambivalence incarnates as pain in Jabès and desire in Hassan. In their essays, recognition of play cannot obviate— rather, *necessitates*—nostalgia for a presence that perhaps has never been and hope for one that perhaps may never become. The styles of these four essays, moreover, are functions of their degrees of hesitation. Tatham and Federman, more attuned to what language can do, tend toward prolixity and humor, toward playfully extravagant textuality. Jabès and Hassan, more attuned to what language cannot do, tend toward a peculiar verbal parsimony, toward rhetorical flourishes (the paradox of their virtuosity) that constantly undermine themselves. All four reveal the fissures that open when the plates of language slide across one another.

Written *from*, as well as *in*, the margins of critical discourse, these essays demonstrate what Michel Benamou has said elsewhere of ethnopoetics—that when everything is marginal, there will be no margins. These writers too are "reaching back to primitive graphism; beyond justified margins and typographical conformities, to a non-alignment of voice and writing which is a dialectic essential to marginality: recovering the voice *and* the sign."[26] When Benamou writes in his Introduction here that criticism is "no longer content to gesticulate in the margins of texts," he is suggesting that from a decentered perspective margins *are* centers. He is also suggesting that to *write about* is to *write* . . . but that it is also to *rede*.

*

> *Magic, after all, is the hinge, the crack between the world we read and the world we write. All fiction is magic, or should be.*

Wholly comfortable with intertextuality and the performance possibilities of the IBM Selectric, with the shift from "modern *angst*" to "postmodern free play," Campbell Tatham extolls imagination, dream, dance, and play as the components of postmodern verbal performance. "The self that dreams is the dream itself," he seems to recall the *Wake*; "we were never able to distinguish the dancer from the dance," he echoes Yeats; "The key to the treasure is the treasure," he might have quoted John Barth, whose notion of mythotherapy centers this essay. Tatham's refrain, *"God is alive. Magic is afoot,"* however, deflects play from an erotics of the text: again, his concerns are mystic, not semiotic.

Sympathetic to phenomenology—"fiction speaks *of* and *through* the shimmering web along which we dance and have our Being"—Tatham nevertheless displaces it toward mythotherapy, toward an intertext of collective fictions: a dash of Barthes with a dose of Jung. What Sukenick calls THE ENDLESS FICTION, the intertextuality of postmodern writing, resembles James Hillman's house of the psyche more than Heidegger's house of Being, and certainly more than Henry James's house of fiction. Realism and point of view are evicted; dream and play take up residence.

"We are the telling: may the story be endless . . . ," Tatham concludes, suggesting that, for him, a magical presence does not subtend play but is co-extensive with it. Consequently, critifiction and postmodern fiction alike must balance control and abandon. Distrustful of fixity, of "definitive certitude in matters of interpretation," the critifictionist juggles view-points; contemptuous of author-ity, he pla(y)giarizes in a criticism of collage transformance. "I simply take various texts and contexts," Tatham explains, "blend them with my own thoughts, feelings and phantasies, then scatter them in the space before us (that is, *right here*)."

The page, *right here*, is the stage of this performance, evident not only in the double-pointed concretism that abandons justified margins to impose an even more rigid control on the typist-as-performer, but especially in the two hands that turn physical book into mythotherapeutic exercise. A dismembered text follows Gombrowitz's warning against obsession with textual skeletons. Re-membering it, pasting it over the ambiguous hand on the following page, we remember our presence in the book. Control and abandon: we attack the medium to complete the message; we violate the book to understand the book; *but* attack and violation of the book fetish precede wholeness. We can, on the other hand, choose to create our own fictions: cover the hand and dis-cover ourselves as readers. The black hand—announcing death before rebirth?—is at once the left hand of whomever is behind the page and the right hand of whomever is in front of it. Two times two, its paradoxical messages multiply: go on, stop; cut, paste; dismember, remember; drop dead, wake up. But left and right, Shem and Shaun, are reconciled *on* and *as* this page without footlights—this page which conflates inner and outer in the playful performance of the book.

> *Process of self-pla(y)giarism: to replay texts by insert-ing them into other texts. Intertextualization: in this case Federman's imagination plagiarizing itself. To pla(y)giarize one's life: voices within voices.*

Raymond Federman writes in his cover letter to the editors: "Nowhere should the name RAYMOND FEDERMAN appear with the text." There it is. When Raymond Federman performed, he did so not as *metteur en scène*, but as *comédien*: his physical presence both himself and sign of himself, one duplicitous medium among three (tapes, slides, Federman), each one already a multiplicity of superimpositions. Having displaced print to performance, as the prologue to his post-script explains, Feder-man must now replace performance on the page. What results is a paginal performance that consumes Raymond Federman and spews him out as FEDERMAN, polyglot featherman-penman, Daedalian (or Icarian) homme de plume hombre della pluma, who spins out an all balls selec-tricstud pla(y)giarism of himself and, notably, Samuel Beckett.

As a post-scriptor, Federman faces the problems of an Allan Kaprow or a Robert Whitman. As a novelist, a teller of tales, however, he resolves them by turning post-script into pre-text for the performance of fiction.

The processes are disclosed at the outset—displacement, cancellation, pulverization, repetition, and revision—followed by a page of WHY's that speaks the litany of a positive atheology of play. The nine texts are introduced by "facts" (as each, in turn will be). No play here? One should note that after the conversion of Raymond Federman into Federman, photos can only be "possibly" or "probably" what they are said to represent. In this complex performance of voices, languages, syntaxes, genres, and media, *all* fixity is called into question. There is nothing here that is not differential, that does not play.

Nowhere, however, does the rhetoric of play deny seriousness. A man "must perform" (*doit jouer*), Federman writes, but "laughing is a painful process" (*le rire est aussi une douleur*). Discontinuity abounds, to be sure; but crisis and craft also obtain in this spiraling interrogation of voices that play between the silences of origin and end. Division is everywhere: Raymond Federman/Federman; French/English; pre-texts/texts/post-texts. Federman's walls are perhaps more Barthesean than Sartrean: the walls of Antithesis that Moinous constantly transgresses but cannot unify. More than a rhetorician's game, however, this performance rolls shut on "mute speech/sign of my presence" (*langage muet/signe de ma présence*). Ultimately, it is not the play of signs that is the sign of presence: it is the absence behind them, the void which they defy.

The excerpt from "The Voice in the Closet," the most compelling verbal performance here, is also the purgatory of the performance as a whole. (I have in mind Beckett's comment that *Finnegans Wake* is "a continuous purgatorial process"[27] and Raymond Federman's application of it to Beckett's work.) Purging itself with ceaseless duplicity, this voice, this "divided I," exists only *as the text* whose margins are perfectly justified. Not only does each block of type *suggest* a closet, but the eleven pages together, justified in depth, *form* a closet. No matter how many pages we turn, how many doors we open, we can never dis-cover Federman's "nakedness." The closet exists only *as* a sequence of doors, as Federman exists only *as* the voice of discourse. We can extend the voice intertextually, but we can never find the door to its origin. And it can never find the door to its end.

> *For us as for the book, lie and truth, presence and absence, completeness and incompleteness are at the heart of our interrogations along with the questions of origin and death.*

How can I comment on the dense, elusive essay which conducts that interrogation, and which does so in reference to the seven-volume *Le Livre des Questions*? How can I quote from an aphoristic essay whose every sentence demands quotation? What can I say about an essay that speaks not of presence and play, but of any pretense, any grasping, at presence as being gnawed by absence from within and without?

"You know that digression is my very method," Jabès writes, disclosing in that digression a metaphysic as well as a style. This essay's constant circling—structurally and syntactically—is precisely its theme. In her lucid essay, "Edmond Jabès and the Impossible Circle," Rosmarie Waldrop writes that "Jabès's books are about the word, because it is through the word that man both questions and defines himself"; that, for him, the book intends "towards a totality which, however, remains transcendent"; that "The writer searches for words, but the word needs the writer to come into being. The periphery wants the center, but the center is in search of the periphery."[28] Unknowable, without and within search for one another in the house of the book that is itself a search: "Book as the impossibility of the book, or rather, as the place and non-place of all possibility of constructing the book." Not a house of Being, this book is the writer—rather the *absence between* writer and book—the absence between *body* and *name* that refers always to the final absence, the final interrogative: death. This text about a book about the Book both asserts and defies decentering by turning the Book into an impossible nomadic center (see Durand's essay). As Waldrop, referring to Jabès's poems, expresses it: "The writer, like the Jew, on the margin of society, has no home other than his book: in writing 'je bâtis ma demeure.'"[29]

Jabès's performance is postmodern in its very rejection of postmodern joy. Jabès understands play: he remains marginal; he knows that texts are pre-texts; that books are revised in unknowable margins; that language lies; that one *must* invent, create, will, in the face of what is Not. *But,* marginality, pla(y)giarism, intertextuality, chance, cabalism, are all turned toward origin and death: toward the "erased book . . . whose erasure all books remember," and toward the death which may, or may not, disclose which book has been ours. Jabès plays, but the rules of his game are as enigmatic as the blank page on which he moves—and which defies those moves. His questions are as primordial as they are postmodern, his performance as elegant as the silence to which it returns.

> Ah, but the doubleness of this trickster is not merely
> theological; it is political and epistemological as well.
> And it is a doubleness that wants to become one again.

A kind of matter to Jabès's anti-matter, Ihab Hassan's masque prophetically asserts presence in the face of absence, cosmic order in the face of play. Hassan consistently distances himself from what he calls philosophies of "unmaking" (see Text's first speech),[30] though he remains edgy about this. Profoundly antinomian, he is also profoundly aware of the antinomies inherent in a postmodern profession of faith. "[A]n Existentialist, a Utopian, and an Orphist" quarrel in his temperament, he says in *Paracriticisms*;[31] the correlative quarrel in his sensibility pits *homo faber* against *homo ludens*.

Thus, Hassan performs a masque, a play of "multivocation" present-ed by a body outside the frame. The masque as format calls attention to masking as a strategy: the decentered, multi-perspectival voices are also one voice, fragmented discourse also dramatic structure. In *Paracriticisms*, he writes that "Criticism should learn about playful discontinuity and become itself less than the sum of its parts."[32] Here, as there, Hassan plays, but his play is governed by "the whole conduct of the shaping presence."[33] When he performed this masque, the presence was "Myself: who breaks the frame, interrupts various speakers as the spirit moves him, and has already appeared." In written form, "Myself" becomes "Paratext . . . (inaudible in print)," not only paracritic, but paracritic-*in-text*. The shift is both more and less significant than it appears: the gesture is toward a play of voices, but Paratext, *who does not speak*, evades the intertext by acting as context—*as shaping presence*. The discontinuities can never be schematized, however, because the schema is beyond our, and Hassan's, ken. Doubleness seeks oneness, but presence, Hassan silently affirms, cannot be presented. The postmodern performer must play on, striving for the "orbic vision" of which Text speaks, singing "of singleness in variousness."

Like Jabès, Hassan interrogates the largest performance, the *cosmic* performance. Its star is Prometheus, "an emblem of human destiny," whose method is *will* and whose current role is posthumanist culture. Posthumanism: not only a prophetic future of "the expansion of human consciousness into the cosmos," but also the playful present of the post-structuralist Self as "an empty 'place' where many selves come to mingle and depart." In both conceptions, however, the body fades: and like Jabès, Hassan always returns to the body.

Exemplary of the volume as a whole, Hassan's masque hesitates between play and presence, between Prometheus and the Earth that he denies, the female principle that he must rediscover in himself—the Earth that "must be heard, else Consciousness turn the Sky into Fire." The body haunts performance: however paginal, postmodern, or playful. Prelude to birth, precondition of it, death remains intractable. And whatever is said must return to the unsayable, here "the inexplicable mass of rock" from Kafka's "Prometheus." But there is also a Postext: a song to Prometheus—who "is our performer," who "performs Space and Time"—and to humankind as his performance, as the magic of the Elements, as "the changing form of Desire."

[1] Samuel Beckett, "Dante. . .Bruno. Vico. . Joyce," *James Joyce/Finnegans Wake: A Symposium* (New York: New Directions, 1972), p. 14. Originally published in 1929 as *Our Exagmination Round His Factification for Incamination of Work in Progress*.

[2] Geoffrey Hartman, "Crossing Over: Literary Commentary As Literature," *Comparative Literature*, xxviii (1976), 268.

[3] Philippe Sollers, quoted in Jonathan Culler, *Structuralist Poetics: Structuralism, Linguistics, and the Study of Literature* (Ithaca: Cornell University Press, 1975), p. 131. The translation is Culler's.

[4] Roland Barthes, *S/Z*, trans. by Richard Miller (New York: Hill and Wang, 1974), p. 10. Originally published in 1970.

[5] Roland Barthes, *The Pleasure of the Text*, trans. by Richard Miller (New York: Hill and Wang, 1975), p. 36. Originally published in 1973.

[6] Georges Poulet, "Phenomenology of Reading," reprinted in Gregory T. Polletta, ed., *Issues in Contemporary Literary Criticism* (Boston: Little, Brown and Company, 1973), p. 104.

[7] *The Pleasure of the Text*, p. 16.

[8] Wolfgang Iser, *The Implied Reader: Patterns of Communication in Prose Fiction from Bunyan to Beckett* (Baltimore: Johns Hopkins University Press, 1974). See "The Reading Process: A Phenomenological Approach," pp. 274-294 *passim*.

[9] *S/Z*, p. 21.

[10] Julia Kristeva, quoted in *Structuralist Poetics*, p. 139. The translation is Culler's.

[11] William V. Spanos, "Heidegger, Kierkegaard, and the Hermeneutic Circle: Towards a Postmodern Theory of Interpretation as Dis-closure," *boundary 2*, IV (1976), 456.

[12] *Ibid.*, p. 477.

[13] *Ibid.*, p. 462.

[14] Joseph N. Riddel, "From Heidegger to Derrida to Chance: Doubling and (Poetic) Language," *boundary 2*, IV (1976), 589.

[15] Ihab Hassan, *Paracriticisms: Seven Speculations of the Times* (Urbana: University of Illinois Press, 1975), p. xiii.

[16] *S/Z*, p. 5.

[17] *Ibid.*, p. 4.

[18] *The Pleasure of the Text*, pp. 66-67.

[19] *S/Z*, p. 45.

[20] *The Pleasure of the Text*, pp. 9, 10.

[21] Michael Wood, "Deconstructing Derrida," *The New York Review of Books*, 3 March 1977, p. 30.

[22] Rosmarie Waldrop, "Edmond Jabès and the Impossible Circle," *Sub-stance*, No. 5-6 (Winter/Spring 1973), p. 183.

[23] *Paracriticisms*, p. 25.

[24] Raymond Federman, "Imagination as Plagiarism [an unfinished paper. . .]," *New Literary History*, VII (1976), 574.

[25] Edward W. Said, "Contemporary Fiction and Criticism," *TriQuarterly*, No. 33 (Spring 1975), pp. 244-45.

[26] Michel Benamou, "Postface: In Praise of Marginality," in M. Benamou and J. Rothenberg, eds., *Ethnopoetics: A First International Symposium* (Alcheringa/Boston University, 1976), p. 138.

[27] Beckett, *op. cit.*, p. 22.

[28] Waldrop, *op. cit.*, pp. 185, 186, 189.

[29] *Ibid.*, p. 186.

[30] And see, especially, "A re-Vision of Literature," *New Literary History*, VIII (1976-77), 127-44.

[31] *Paracriticisms*, p. xiv.

[32] *Ibid.*, p. 25.

[33] Richard Poirier, *The Performing Self: Compositions and Decompositions in the Languages of Contemporary Life* (New York: Oxford University Press, 1971), p. 87.

CONTRIBUTORS

MICHEL BENAMOU is Director of the Center for 20th Century Studies and Professor of French and Comparative Literature at the University of Wisconsin-Milwaukee. Among his many publications are *Wallace Stevens and the Symbolist Imagination* (1972), *L'oeuvre-monde de Wallace Stevens* (1975) and, as co-editor, *Ethnopoetics: A First International Symposium* (1976). He has recently contributed to *Minority Language and Literature* (1977) and *The Two Faces of Ionesco* (1977).

CHERYL BERNSTEIN, a free-lance writer and critic, has recently completed the soon-to-be-published work *Félicien Rops: The Tragedy of Misconception*.

HERBERT BLAU, currently Professor of English at the University of Maryland -Baltimore County, and on a Guggenheim Fellowship, is the founder and artistic director of KRAKEN, former Co-Director of the Repertory Theatre of Lincoln Center, and former Co-Founder and Co-Director of the Actor's Workshop of San Francisco. He is the author of numerous articles and *The Impossible Theatre: A Manifesto* (1964).

CHARLES CARAMELLO is Publications Coordinator at the Center for 20th Century Studies and a doctoral candidate in the Department of English at the University of Wisconsin-Milwaukee, He has reviewed books on contemporary fiction in such journals as *Modern Fiction Studies* and *Studies in the Novel*.

DANIEL CHARLES, who teaches aesthetics at the University of Paris VIII (Vincennes) and at the University of Paris IV (Sorbonne), has written numerous articles on contemporary music, including "Cage et Duchamp," in *L'Arc* and "John Cage ou la voix symbole du temps" in *L'autre scène*. He has recently published *Pour les oiseaux* (1976), a collection of conversations with John Cage.

RÉGIS DURAND is Maître de Conférences at the University of Lille III and Director of the Centre d'Etudes et de Recherches Nord-Américaines et Canadiennes. He has written many articles on drama, the novel, and contemporary critical theories, and has edited *Myth and Ideology in American Culture* (1976).

RAYMOND FEDERMAN, Professor of English at the State University of New York-Buffalo, is a critic and bilingual poet and novelist. His works include *Journey to Chaos: Samuel Beckett's Early Fiction* (1965), *Samuel Beckett and His Critics* (1970), *Double or Nothing* (1971), *Amer Eldorado* (1974), *Take It of Leave It* (1976), and, as editor, *Surfiction? Fiction Now and Tomorrow* (1975).

IHAB HASSAN is Vilas Research Professor of English and Comparative Literature at the University of Wisconsin-Milwaukee. His numerous publications include *Radical Innocence: Studies in the Contemporary American Novel* (1961), *The Literature of Silence: Henry Miller and Samuel Beckett* (1967), *The Dismemberment of Orpheus: Toward a Postmodern Literature* (1971), *Paracriticisms: Seven Speculations of the Times* (1975), and, as editor, *Liberations: New Essays on the Humanities in Revolution* (1971).

EDMOND JABÈS was awarded the Prix des Critiques in 1970. His works include *Paul Eluard* (1953), *Je bâtis ma demeure* (1959), *Le livre des ressemblances* (1976), and the seven-volume *Le livre des questions: Le livre des questions* (1963), *Le livre de Yukel* (1964), *Le retour au livre* (1965), *Yaël* (1967), *Elya* (1969), *Aely* (1972), *El, ou le dernier livre* (1974). Parts I, II, and III of *The Book of Questions*, in Rosmarie Waldrop's translation, have been published by Wesleyan University Press in 1976 and 1977.

JEAN-FRANÇOIS LYOTARD, Professor of Philosophy at the University of Paris VIII (Vincennes), is a leading French philosopher whose work is beginning to influence the English-speaking world. He has authored *La Phénoménologie* (1954), *Discours, Figure* (1971), *Des Dispositifs pulsionnels* (1973), *Dérive à partir de Marx et Freud* (1973), *Economie Libidinale* (1974), and a book on Marcel Duchamp (1977).

RICHARD E. PALMER is Professor of Philosophy and Comparative Literature at MacMurray College, Jacksonville, Illinois. He has written many articles on phenomenology, hermeneutics, and postmodernity, and the book *Hermeneutics: Interpretation Theory in Schleiermacher, Dilthey, Heidegger, and Gadamer* (1969).

JEROME ROTHENBERG, who coined the term ethnopoetics, was a Senior Fellow at the Center for Twentieth Century Studies in 1974-75. His translations and collections of his own poetry include *New Young German Poets* (1959), *Poland/1931* (1969), *Poems for the Game of Silence* (1971), and the on-going *Seneca Journal* (1973). In addition, he has edited the anthologies *Technicians of the Sacred* (1968), *Shaking the Pumpkin* (1972), *America a Prophecy* (1973), *Revolution of the Word* (1974), and *A Big Jewish Book* (1977).

CAMPBELL TATHAM, Associate Professor of English at the University of Wisconsin-Milwaukee, was a Senior Fellow at the Center for 20th Century Studies during 1976-77. He has published articles and "critifictional performances" in such journals as *Contemporary Literature, Diacritics, Chicago Review* and *boundary 2*.

VICTOR TURNER, who served as Chairman of the Committee on Social Thought at the University of Chicago, is currently Professor of Anthropology at the University of Virginia. His recent works include *The Drums of Affliction* (1968), *The Ritual Process: Structure and Anti-Structure* (1969), *Dramas, Fields, and Metaphors* (1974), *Revelation and Divination in Ndembu Ritual* (1975), and *Image and Pilgrimage in Christian Culture* (1977).

INDEX

Indexed by Paul S. Ogren